Peter Charley began his career as a reporter on the *Sydney Morning Herald* and the *Sydney Sun* newspapers. He later worked as an on-air news and current affairs reporter and producer at the Seven Network in Australia before moving to New York, where he worked as associate producer at *Sixty Minutes* and as a reporter for National Public Radio. He was appointed show producer of the weekly, current affairs program *The Reporters*, before working as executive producer of the ABC's flagship news program *Lateline* then SBS's international current affairs program *Dateline*. In 2014, Peter took up the role of executive producer of Al Jazeera's North American investigative unit based in Washington DC.

A BAFTA finalist, he is the recipient of countless Australian and international awards for his journalism, including seven New York Festivals gold medals and two Walkleys. For his documentary *How to Sell a Massacre*, he received the Kennedy Award for Outstanding Investigative Reporting, the Walkley Scoop of the Year Award and his seventh New York Festivals gold medal.

T0049977

How to $ell a Massacre

PETER CHARLEY

ABC
BOOKS

The ABC 'Wave' device is a trademark of the
Australian Broadcasting Corporation and is used
under licence by HarperCollins*Publishers* Australia.

HarperCollins*Publishers*
Australia • Brazil • Canada • France • Germany • Holland • Hungary
India • Italy • Japan • Mexico • New Zealand • Poland • Spain • Sweden
Switzerland • United Kingdom • United States of America

First published in Australia in 2020
by HarperCollins*Publishers* Australia Pty Limited
Level 13, 201 Elizabeth Street, Sydney NSW 2000
ABN 36 009 913 517
harpercollins.com.au

A catalogue record for this book is available from the National Library of Australia.

ISBN 978 0 7333 4108 3 (paperback)
ISBN 978 1 4607 1282 5 (ebook)

Cover design by Michelle Zaiter, HarperCollins Design Studio
Cover images by istockphoto.com and shutterstock.com
Typeset in Bembo Std by Kirby Jones
Printed and bound in Australia by McPherson's Printing Group
The papers used by HarperCollins in the manufacture of this book are a natural, recyclable
product made from wood grown in sustainable plantation forests. The fibre source and
manufacturing processes meet recognised international environmental standards, and carry
certification.

To Clare and Tom

Preface

In more than a decade working as a US-based journalist, I've witnessed a staggering level of gun violence in America. In fact, the number of people killed by guns in the US since 1963 – the year President John F. Kennedy was shot to death – is now estimated to be more than double the number of US soldiers who died in the First World War, the Second World War, the Korean War, the Vietnam War, the Afghanistan War and the Iraq war combined.

How has this crisis developed and why has it been allowed to continue?

In 2016, I launched an investigation for Al Jazeera in an effort to find out. I wanted to understand how the US gun lobby continues to enjoy the support of Congress, the White House and millions of Americans as gun violence ravages their nation.

The three-year investigation involved the recording of more than five hundred hours of undercover video, and it led my team back to Australia – my home country – and to the political party, Pauline Hanson's One Nation.

This book gives a detailed, behind-the-scenes account of the investigation and the making of the two-part documentary *How to Sell a Massacre* that emerged from it. I have included key scenes from unreleased, covertly recorded video, and I reveal previously undisclosed conversations between Al Jazeera's undercover operatives, the National Rifle Association of America, and the One Nation delegates as they travelled to the US in September 2018, in search of funding and support from the American gun lobby.

Though Al Jazeera played no part in the production or publication of this book, the network allowed me full access to footage recorded for the investigation, and to transcripts of all discussions captured for the assignment. Quotes in this book are taken directly from those recordings and transcripts, and from contemporaneous notes I had made as I oversaw the project.

Chapter 1

Cameraman Colin McIntyre sat hunched over a lamp in his hotel room in Louisville, Kentucky, squinting through the holes of a loose shirt button.

'Can you see the lens?'

Rodger Muller leaned down and peered at the button.

'The lens?'

Colin carefully pushed a needle and thread through the holes of the button, into the shirt, and drew a strand of dark cotton high into the air.

'The camera lens. It's in the button. You can't see it?'

He worked the thread back and forth as he stitched the tiny button camera onto the shirt that Rodger would wear the following day.

'Because if *you* can't see it, *they* won't see it.'

He handed the shirt to Rodger, who slipped it on and walked to the wardrobe mirror.

'Bloody amazing,' he said, leaning into his reflection. He twisted to see whether the hotel room light might pick up the pinhead-sized lens concealed within the button. 'No one would ever know.'

Colin tossed his sewing kit into his Pelican camera case and snapped the lid shut.

'That's the whole idea, mate.'

The hidden camera was one of three that Rodger would wear on the first day of the National Rifle Association's May 2016 annual meeting, which would begin just after dawn.

Colin had also sewn a lens into Rodger's sports coat, and he had concealed another in a mobile phone Rodger would carry as he wandered through the 500,000-square-foot firearms display that the NRA had set up in Louisville's vast Exposition Center.

I had hired Rodger at the beginning of that year as part of an elaborate effort to infiltrate America's gun lobby. The mission I had given him was simple enough, but it had the potential to cause Rodger enormous complications at home: he was to adopt a new persona – that of a gun-loving Aussie who wanted a softening of Australia's strict gun control laws.

At the NRA's Louisville convention, he was to spread the message that he'd formed the group Gun Rights Australia specifically to lobby for the reform of firearms laws Down Under. He was to engage with the NRA's senior leadership, and to wear concealed cameras to secretly film conversations inside the group.

Apart from my bosses and a small team from Al Jazeera's Investigative Unit that I had assembled for this assignment, nobody knew that Rodger's pro-gun persona was a ruse – not even his closest friends and family.

He slipped off his shirt and draped it over a coat hanger. The concealed cameras were ready. And in a few hours, Rodger Muller would begin his new life as a gun fanatic.

* * *

'No guns, no knives, no umbrellas, folks!'

No *umbrellas*?

The security teams were taking no chances as they herded people into the convention centre the next morning to hear speeches from NRA leaders Wayne LaPierre and Chris Cox at the official opening of the event. Among the many dignitaries who would also speak was US presidential candidate Donald Trump.

In front of a standing-room-only audience, LaPierre walked onto the stage, resplendent in a blue suit and blue silk tie, and stood before the iconic image of US marines straining to hoist the American flag in the Battle of Iwo Jima. For the next seventeen minutes, the NRA's chief executive would fan the fires that keep his organisation's five million members angry and engaged.

'We know a Hillary Clinton White House would be ground zero for a massive attack on our freedom,' he warned.

'A haven for all the Hollywood elites to plot the destruction of our Second Amendment.

'The elites have huddled in rooms in Washington and New York, San Francisco and Hollywood, and cooked the nomination for Hillary.

'On Wall Street, they'll pay you $250,000 a pop to talk in those rooms. Well, maybe not you or me. But if you're

Hillary Rodham Clinton you can make a fortune talking in those rooms. And she did.'

The mob below him let out a roar. Rodger Muller, standing among them, shouted, 'Hear, hear,' held his hands above his head and applauded.

'The truth is that if, God forbid, a terrorist should enter this room,' LaPierre continued, 'he would learn firsthand that the best way for law-abiding Americans to defend their lives – the surest way to stop a bad guy with a gun – is a good guy with a gun!', repeating an NRA catchphrase that he introduced after the massacre of twenty children and six adults at Sandy Hook Elementary School in Connecticut four years earlier.

Not even a good guy with an umbrella would have stood a chance against the nightmare LaPierre had invoked today. But the unarmed crowd didn't seem to care about such details.

Again, they shouted their approval, energised by LaPierre's contempt for the loathsome, overpaid, gun-hating, hand-wringing socialists, led by Hillary Clinton and her out-of-touch associates – 'the elites'.

Worst of all, they were told, Hillary wanted to take Americans' guns away – just as Australia's government had done to its own people – a frequent NRA reference point for how bad things can get when governments get involved with gun control.

'If she could, Hillary would ban every gun, destroy every magazine, run an entire national security industry into the ground and put your name on a government registration list,' he told the crowd.

'They think Americans all over the heartland are stupid. Do they think we can't see their tone, their inflection, their agenda?'

That LaPierre is paid an estimated one million US dollars a year didn't seem to bother the masses cheering him on. Nor did the $3,767,345 one-off supplemental retirement payout he'd received from the NRA the previous year, nor reports that he had spent $274,695.03 on Italian suits between 2004 and 2017.[1]

Something in LaPierre's showmanship, something in his pinched-face rage – his *own* tone, his *own* inflection – gave the rank and file a way to overlook their leader's significant wealth and elitist tendencies, and to believe he was just like them: a battler from 'the heartland', rankling at the Clintonesque notion that the NRA is an organisation of simpletons, offended by the excessive payments made to Hillary for her speeches, and weathering the sneers of Washington's smug and arrogant overlords.

LaPierre moved closer to the microphone for his savage summing-up.

'In all of history, there has always been a time and a place where patriots rise up against the decree of the elites and shout, "*No more* ... get your hands off my freedom!"'

It was classic us-versus-them: LaPierre had laid out the NRA's fight for survival against dark forces massing at the gate, who wanted more than anything to strip the good guys of the firearms that keep them safe.

And he had made it clear over and over again: guns equal freedom. If Hillary Clinton was elected, their guns would be taken away and America's cherished liberty would be lost.

The brave men such as those depicted behind LaPierre – the marines who'd defended America's freedom at Iwo Jima – would have fought, and died, for nothing.

Rodger was jostled as the crowd surged, cheering their champion of freedom, their protector, the man in the Zegna suit who truly understood them.

LaPierre stepped away from the podium, making way for his deputy, Chris Cox, head of the NRA's Institute for Legislative Action or the NRA-ILA – the association's lobbying arm.

Rodger cast a furtive glance down to his shirt. The button was holding, the camera still rolling. He let out a roar and applauded again as Cox stepped up to the microphone.

* * *

If guns are a religion in America, the NRA's annual conference is its megachurch. In addition to the spectacle of Wayne LaPierre slavering at the microphone, the gathering involves a massive display of pistols, rifles, shotguns, holsters, gun safes, camouflage outfits, ammunition, shooting games, gun scopes, crossbows, tactical gear, and assorted other weaponry and NRA paraphernalia, assembled by more than 750 exhibitors in a warehouse spanning about three hectares.

The *American Rifleman* magazine described the 2016 Louisville convention's gun display as a 'Gateway to Fun', with the 'Wall of Guns' listed as one of the most popular attractions: a display of more than seventy makes and models of firearms. For twenty US dollars, visitors can buy a raffle ticket to choose any weapon they like from the exhibit –

with a winner drawn from every hundred tickets purchased. According to the magazine, 'For attendees in the market for a new firearm, there's no better venue than the Exhibit Hall to get hands-on with all the top brands before making a decision.'[2]

It's a gunmetal love fest: a chance to fondle, stroke and caress weapons of all sizes in what was then perhaps the biggest-ever public assembly of guns for sale.

Rodger strolled the aisles, stopping here and there to pick up a gun or chat to NRA officials. He peered through the scope of a sniper rifle and lingered at a stall advertising a sixteen-round shotgun – the NRA's 'Gun of the Week'. A video ran on a loop behind the salesman, showing a man in a ragged camouflage outfit pumping round after round into a mannequin dressed in Arab garb.

Beside Rodger, two men with beards and buzzcuts lugged duffle bags filled with rifles and pistols. Their eyes were gleaming. One said to the other, 'Let's put 'em in the truck and go back and buy some more!'

To Rodger's left, an NRA official reached across his desk and tugged at a length of rope, clanging a bell that hung above him. It was to celebrate the signing-on of a new member to the organisation. The bell was met with cheers as old-timers welcomed an addition to the flock. The bell rang again. And again. And again – as newcomers queued to join up.

Outside of the main exhibition hall, a series of lectures were being held, offering advice on how to survive in the hostile political environment so starkly spelled out by Wayne LaPierre. Lectures included 'The War on Guns: Arming Yourself Against the False Claims That Will Be Made

Against Guns During the Election', 'Current and Emerging Threats: How it Affects You', 'Bad Reputation – Do These Guns Deserve a Bad Rap?' and 'Refuse to be a Victim'.

Many of the convention attendees would soon become Rodger's new best friends. Here and at the NRA's Atlanta convention the following year, he would befriend hunters, gun makers, lobbyists, volunteers and dozens of NRA officials. He would learn how those entranced by the world of guns thought, where they lived and worked, how they spoke, what they loved and what they feared. And he would copy their behaviour as he tweaked the rhetoric of Gun Rights Australia to position it as an organisation that NRA's leaders could trust.

With its motto 'Unite. Protect. Reform.', GRA would become *Australia's* NRA, posing as a group pushing for easier access to guns, for *freedom* – just like America – and for political recognition that Australia's gun-control laws were too severe and needed revision.

Word quickly spread through the Louisville convention that an attendee from Australia was angling for a review of the nation's gun laws. The gun legislation in Australia had long infuriated the NRA, which saw it as a dangerous harbinger of potential restrictions in the US.

Rodger was invited to appear on NRATV, an NRA-funded, online video channel pushing an aggressive pro-gun, anti–mainstream media agenda.[3] Cam Edwards, the host of the channel's *Cam and Company*, a daily talk show, stepped away from his flood-lit set to greet Rodger on the convention-room floor. They were joined by an NRATV camera operator who positioned Cam and Rodger in front of a sign saying, 'I'm not going to let some clowns tell me what guns I can have', before fitting his camera onto a tripod and signalling to them that he was rolling.

Cam said, 'I'm very pleased to have with us Rodger Muller, who is here all the way from ...'

'... Sydney, Australia,' Rodger answered.

'My goodness gracious! ... Do they have anything like this in Australia?'

'Absolutely not, we've got the odd gun meet, swap meet, but nothing like this ...'

'So, you're the founder and president of Gun Rights Australia, right?'

'Yes, we're an organisation trying to build awareness of guns in Australia and to de-demonise legal gun owners and to just get a rational debate happening, you know. So that's what we're trying to do.'

I stood with a small group that had gathered to watch the interview take place as Rodger, his pro-gun persona now in full gallop, drove home the message he knew the NRA was dying to hear.

'Twenty years ago, the government arguably illegally put legislation through without consultation with the rest of the country twelve days after the Port Arthur mass murder,' he said.

'And that was unfair to the Australian people, I think. And since then, if you want to talk about guns, you're a hate-talker. And that's wrong.'

Rodger was referring to laws brought in by Prime Minister John Howard following the 1996 massacre of thirty-five people mainly in and around the Tasmanian historic site of Port Arthur. The incident led to the nationwide banning of assault weapons, along with the buy-back and destruction of more than 650,000 firearms – something the NRA has described as 'a huge over-reaction'.[4]

'I appreciate you fighting there in Australia,' Cam said. 'And, look, self-defence is a human right. We've got our right to keep and bear arms enshrined in our constitution, but you don't need a constitution to be able to defend yourself.'

Rodger nodded. 'It's common sense.'

At the end of the chat, Rodger handed Cam a 'Gun Rights Australia' cap. Cam smiled and tucked it under his arm.

'Thanks very much! You know about me and hats, then.'

'Everyone knows about you and hats,' Rodger chuckled.

He turned, caught my eye, and winked.

***

Chris Cox, head of the NRA's lobbying arm, stepped onto the stage dressed in a blue suit and purple tie, his gimlet eyes blinking into the spotlights.

His firebrand boss had laid the groundwork – now it was Cox's turn to ramp up the attack on Hillary Clinton, listing the horrors she had in store for America if she made it to the White House.

'Hundreds of thousands of people will lose their firearms and lose their jobs,' he thundered.

'As bad as that sounds, it's just the beginning. It ends with no right to own a gun in your own home anywhere in America. Anywhere, period.

'She wants us to live in a place where only law enforcement has guns and everything is free. Free meals. Free health care. Free education. Well, Hillary, that place does exist and you might just get to live there. It's called prison!'

Cheers erupted from the floor.

And what if Hillary managed to introduce gun confiscations such as those enacted in Australia? Cox had this warning: 'So, what happens to those of us that say, "The hell with that, I just won't turn [my guns] in"? They have a message for us, too. "Think about it now or you can get twelve months to think about nothing else." Prison rape. That's not exactly subtle, but it's the truth. When Hillary talks about remodelling America's gun policies after Australia, that's the very raw, very real future she's dreaming about.'

The LaPierre–Cox double act had the audience horrified. No guns *anywhere*? And the raw, real prospect of *prison rape*?

The dire messages had unsettled the crowd, but they knew there was a treat to come: the business-savvy star of reality TV show *The Apprentice*, the suave billionaire from New York City, would soon be on stage. With his voice rising in excitement, Cox called Donald J. Trump to the microphone with a stunning announcement from the gun lobby.

'We have to unite and we have to unite right now,' Cox said. 'So, on behalf of the thousands of patriots in this room … I'm officially announcing the NRA's endorsement of *Donald Trump for president*!'

Trump entered stage right. For nearly two and a half minutes, he lingered, applauding the audience as they applauded him, soaking up their adoration and pointing into the cheering mob as if to acknowledge someone special over here, someone important over there, someone precious down the back. He was *connecting* with them. He was loving them, and they were loving him right back.

To the strains of country music singer Lee Greenwood's 'God Bless the USA', Trump strode to LaPierre and Cox, shook their hands and slapped them each on the shoulder before turning for a photograph, flanked by them, holding his thumbs up, his capped teeth glowing an otherworldly white as he locked his face into a grin for the NRA's photo-op of the year.

The three amigos were bonded in a very public way not so much by mutual adoration as by a hatred for the political alternative. And by the narrative driving fear into the room: the distortions and exaggerations, the raw emotions – often conjured regardless of the facts – that made up so much of the Trump–NRA us-versus-them story. After all, the crowd had just learned that if Hillary Clinton were to be elected, she would take everyone's guns away – and anyone who resisted would be raped in prison.

'Thank you, thank you,' Trump said, craning from left to right as he scanned the autocue screens.

'You are great American patriots. I just said to Wayne and I just said to Chris, I will not let you down.' He slowed his delivery for emphasis as he repeated his promise. 'Remember that: I … will … not … let … you … down!'

In case the earlier attacks on Hillary Clinton weren't enough to convince NRA members that Trump's opponent was a heartless imposter, he took it up a notch.

'Hillary Clinton will release violent criminals from jail,' he said.

'[She] is telling everyone, and every woman living in a dangerous community, that she doesn't have the right to defend herself. So, you have a woman living in a community, a rough community, a bad community: "Sorry, you can't defend yourself."'

'I tell you what, my poll numbers with women are starting to go up ... I will say my poll numbers with men are through the roof. But I like women more than men. Come on, women, let's go! Come on! And most people know that about me. Most people know.'

The audience ate it up.

Riffing on LaPierre's I-might-be-stinking-rich-but-I'm-just-like-you theme, Trump touted credentials he believed might endear him to the dungaree-clad farmers and factory workers below. Not many people know it but he carries a gun, he said. And his sons do too.

'They have so many rifles and so many guns, sometimes even I get a little concerned and say that's a lot!'

Like all performers, though, Trump saved his best for last. He is, he declared, gifted with the Midas touch. He couldn't help but to win. And he had to warn Americans to prepare for an overdose of success.

'We're going to win at everything. And some of you are friends, and you're going to call. You're going to say, "Mr President, please, we can't take it anymore. We can't win any more like this. Mr President, you're driving us crazy. You're winning too much. Please, Mr President, not so much!" And we're going to keep winning because we're going to make America great again. Thank you. We *love* you. Thank you. Thank you, everybody. Thank you, Kentucky. Thank you, everybody. Thank you!'

* * *

'Need battery change,' Rodger texted.

Cameramen Colin McIntyre and Craig Pennington had been waiting for the message. We all knew that, sooner or later, the camera battery would need to be replaced. At the hotel room the night before, we had agreed on a plan: once Rodger saw the battery was running low, he would identify a bathroom in the conference centre and settle himself in one of the toilet booths. He would then text details of his location, and one of the cameramen would enter the booth next to his. A fresh battery would be handed to him under the dividing wall.

Colin walked into the bathroom. A few minutes later, he emerged.

'Done.'

He tossed the spent battery into his backpack.

A couple of minutes later, Rodger walked out and moved back into the exhibition hall. He sidled up to a man selling Glocks.

'G'day. I'm from Australia.'

Chapter 2

It's hard to miss the National Rifle Association of America's national headquarters while driving west out of Washington, DC. The building – set just off Interstate 66 – looms over Waples Mill Road in Fairfax, Virginia, thirty minutes' drive from the capital. The building is an imposing V-shape, with mirrored blue windows and the letters 'NRA' – in pillar-box red – beaming from the apex. Two multistorey office blocks stretch outwards from the logo – like open arms, beckoning people to enter.

In October 2015, I was driving past the NRA HQ – en route from Washington to Dulles International Airport – when I heard on my car radio that there had been another mass shooting in an American school. Eight students and a teacher had been killed in Oregon, and nine others were wounded. The shooter had then killed himself. I glanced across at the NRA building and wondered what on earth people working there were saying about this latest mass shooting. How did they reconcile this news with the association's efforts to portray guns as a symbol of freedom?

Definitions of a 'mass shooting' vary in the United States, but the FBI and the Gun Violence Archive – a non-profit research group which catalogues shootings in America – both define such shootings as events in which four or more people are killed or wounded in the same incident.

Already in 2015, there had been seven mass shootings in America, leaving forty-six people dead and thirty-two wounded. The Oregon massacre pushed the death toll to fifty-five.

The NRA was awkward, at best, in addressing these issues – often directing anger towards the media when questions were asked about how the organisation representing gun owners felt about guns being used against innocent civilians.

When twenty-six people, including twenty children aged between six and seven, had been shot dead at Sandy Hook Elementary School in Newtown, Connecticut, three years earlier, LaPierre had stayed silent for a week as the country reeled from the horror. The slaughter of innocent children seemed to be a game changer. If anything had the power to bring in gun control, to stop the NRA from wielding its vast membership to punish or reward members of America's Congress, it surely had to be this.

When he finally spoke, LaPierre raged against the media that had reported the shooting. At a packed press conference on 21 December 2012, at Washington, DC's Willard InterContinental Hotel, LaPierre, dressed in black, spoke haltingly at first – offering the NRA's 'earnest prayers' to the families of those shot dead at Sandy Hook. He then launched a scorching attack on the press.

'In a race to the bottom, media conglomerates compete with one another to shock, violate and offend every standard of civilised society by bringing an ever-more toxic mix of reckless behaviour and criminal cruelty into our homes – every minute of every day of every month of every year,' he said. 'Too many in our national media, their corporate owners, and their stockholders, act as silent enablers, if not complicit co-conspirators.

'Rather than face their own moral failings, the media demonise lawful gun owners, amplify their cries for more laws, and fill the national debate with misinformation and dishonest thinking that only delay meaningful action and all but guarantee that the next atrocity is only a news cycle away.'[5]

LaPierre appeared to be arguing that there was something even more egregious than the murder of six- and seven-year-olds in what should have been the safety of their school – and that was the media that dared to bring the 'ever-more toxic mix of reckless behaviour and criminal cruelty into our homes'. In LaPierre's world, reporting on the crime was worse than the crime itself.

But changes could be made straight away, he said, that would prevent another incident like this from occurring.

'I call on Congress today to act immediately to appropriate whatever is necessary to put armed police officers in every school – and to do it now, to make sure that blanket safety is in place when our children return to school in January.'

In other words, put guns *directly* into all American schools to ensure that there were no more gun deaths in schools.

In the end, the NRA's dominance of the US Congress – achieved through its ruthless excoriation of anti-gun lawmakers over the past several decades – meant that, even after the Sandy Hook massacre, calls from the House of Representatives for an expansion of background checks on people buying guns, and a law banning assault weapons (such as the one used by the Sandy Hook killer) were both defeated by the Senate in April 2013.[6] And that was with memories still fresh from the January 2011 mass shooting in which a member of Congress – Gabby Giffords – had been shot in the head while meeting with constituents on a street corner in Arizona. Six people had died in that attack, including a nine-year-old girl.

Though mass shooting events like that deeply troubled America, gun violence there would continue to rise. In 2014, a year after the Senate struck down the assault weapon ban, the Gun Violence Archive reported twenty-seven mass shooting deaths in the US. There would be seventy-five more the following year, rising to one hundred and eleven in 2016 and one hundred and sixty the year after that.

I wondered whether LaPierre would also blame the media for being 'complicit' in the school shooting in Oregon I was now hearing about on my car radio. Or would he and his executive team simply decline to say anything about this latest attack, hoping that the news cycle LaPierre had referenced would sweep it all away?

And what about his executive team? Were debates taking place in the building that pointed to dissent over the NRA's responses – or lack of them – to mass shootings that were now taking place in America at a rate of roughly one a day?

When the NRA was formed in 1871 by two American Civil War veterans – one of them a former *New York Times* reporter – it was focused primarily on firearm safety and helping hunters shoot more accurately after a review of the Union Army's combat performance had found that some soldiers fired a thousand rounds for every bullet that hit a Confederate.

At one point, the group even lobbied for gun control, working with Congress and the White House to help introduce the *National Firearms Act of 1934* and the *Gun Control Act of 1938*.

The dynamics of the NRA shifted radically in 1977 when a hardline faction staged a coup at that year's national convention, ousting moderates and refocusing the association on an aggressive opposition to gun control.

The organisation shifted from offering help to hunters to fiercely defending the Second Amendment of the US Constitution: a guarantee that all US citizens have the right to 'keep and bear arms'.

The group was particularly active in working to oust members of Congress who supported a 1993 bill requiring federal background checks for gun purchases – action seen as the beginning of an alignment between the NRA and the Republican Party.[7]

In 1998, the NRA appointed as its titular president a thespian perhaps most famous for his roles as a saviour and a fighter: Moses and Ben-Hur. Academy Award winner Charlton Heston became the public face of the association, popularising what became one of its most enduring battle cries: 'I'll give you my gun when you pry it from my cold, dead hands.'[8]

In that speech, delivered to help defeat Democratic presidential candidate Al Gore in 2000, Heston played on themes that would come to define the organisation's take-no-prisoners philosophy. 'When freedom shivers in the shadow of true peril, it's always the patriots who first hear the call,' he said. 'When loss of liberty is looming, as it is now, the siren sounds first in the hearts of freedom's vanguard … they know that sacred stuff resides in that wooden stock and blued steel – something that gives the most common man the most uncommon of freedoms.

'When ordinary hands can possess such an extraordinary instrument, that symbolises the full measure of human dignity and liberty. That's why those five words issue an irresistible call to us all.'

Someone walked to the podium and handed Heston a rifle.

Clutching the gun, he forged on. 'So, as we set out this year to defeat the divisive forces that would take freedom away, I want to say those fighting words for everyone within the sound of my voice to hear and to heed and especially for you, Mr Gore …'

Hoisting the gun in the air, he raised his voice.

'… *from my cold, dead hands!*'

Wayne LaPierre built on Heston's bellicose – if slightly absurd – rants, supercharging the NRA's battle against anyone, or anything, that stood to dampen US gun sales. Having earlier served on the boards of the American Conservative Union and the National Fish and Wildlife Foundation, and holding a master's degree in government and politics, LaPierre fashioned the NRA's battle plan into two key strategies: the organisation would work to convince Americans that they needed to carry guns for self-protection, and it would work to persuade NRA members to distrust the mainstream media.

The scorched-earth methods by which he developed those arguments would soon demand the attention of congresspeople throughout the US, even when empirical evidence proved that a number of the NRA's claims were untrue.

Former NRA lobbyist Richard Feldman explained to me one of the tactics he used when trying to strong-arm senators.

'I went to see a couple of senators that we had supported in the past, and I remember very distinctly playing real hardball with them,' he said during a meeting in Biloxi, Mississippi, in 2018.

'I handed the senator two letters. I said, "Look, you have to do what's in your interests and I understand that. But, naturally, I'm going to have to let our 1500 or 2500 members that live in your senatorial district know what you decided to do when we needed you."

'So, there are two letters, and one letter essentially says, "Dear fellow NRA member, when we came to see your senator, he was more concerned about what the *New York Times* had to say than what you believe in back in the district."

'The other letter said the opposite: "Dear fellow NRA member, when we came to meet with your senator, he was far more concerned about your interests and your rights than what the editorial board of the *New York Times* had to say." Now that's hardball. That's how you play the game.'

With such pressure being brought to bear on US lawmakers, the NRA hammered the idea that guns, alone, would offer safety to the inhabitants of an inherently unsafe nation.

The second of LaPierre's strategies – the vilification of the media – has led to a bruising confrontation with reporters and academics in America as the battle to define 'truth' has played out across social and political lines. In a classic attack-the-messenger manoeuvre, LaPierre jabbed back at his critics with renewed claims that news outlets are responsible, in part, for inspiring the very mass shootings they report on. Referring to the gunman who killed thirty-three people at Virginia Tech in 2007, LaPierre said in a blog post that year, 'There's not a doubt in my mind that the press coverage of this individual gave comfort and validation to others with the same twisted evil in their hearts.'[9]

LaPierre's campaign to vilify and discredit the media was backed by a series of blistering advertising campaigns produced by the Oklahoma-based ad agency Ackerman McQueen, the creators and producers of NRATV. The two-pronged media assault would gather momentum as news of still more mass shootings began to dominate national headlines.

I decided to find a way inside the NRA to hear directly from those who worked there. I wanted to know how they formulated their messages, what they *really* thought about mass shootings, and how they kept members onside when horrific details of massacres dominated the news. But I knew I wouldn't find the truth of the NRA's inner workings if I entered it as a journalist – as one of LaPierre's 'silent enablers' to gun violence. I needed to sidestep the doublespeak in order to ensure that the organisation would talk freely and honestly. And the only way to do that, I believed, was to get somebody into the building whom they believed they could trust.

As NRA HQ disappeared behind me, I formed a plan: I would create an Australian organisation that mirrored the association's rhetoric. I would appoint an Aussie as its 'founder and president', and I would find ways for that person to climb as high as possible up the NRA's hierarchy.

That I was prepared to do this – to set a trap to find the truth – was a sign of how immensely powerful the gun lobby had become in the US. 'I want to build a Trojan Horse,' I told my boss, Clayton Swisher, in a phone call that evening. 'I want to create a "grassroots", pro-gun organisation in Australia with the sole purpose of leading the NRA into believing they can speak openly to us. I've chosen Australia because that's the country the NRA keeps bashing for its gun control legislation.'

It was also a place I knew many Americans viewed with fondness. I thought that, in the eyes of the gun lobby, a white guy from Down Under would probably be one of the least-threatening visitors to the US imaginable – a perfect undercover operative.

In 1996 the NRA launched a sustained attack on Australia's post–Port Arthur gun control legislation, publishing articles and posting videos that claim the laws are a draconian government overreach and that they've done nothing to arrest gun violence in Australia. Republican Senator Ted Cruz – who received more than forty thousand US dollars in donations from gun rights groups in 2015 and 2016 – has also weighed in, asserting that the rate of sexual assault and rape in Australia has increased specifically because women there no longer have access to guns for self-protection.[10]

But an analysis by the *Washington Post*, citing Australia's Bureau of Statistics, found that 'there was no obvious jump or decrease' in the rate of reported sexual assaults in Australia following the gun buy-backs there.[11] In fact, studies have found a significant reduction in homicides and suicides in Australia following the introduction of legislation banning automatic and semiautomatic firearms.[12] Harvard University's School of Public Health determined that the average homicide rate in Australia per one hundred thousand people dropped more than 40 per cent in the seven years following the introduction of Australia's gun control laws.[13] In 2015, when I was speaking with Clayton Swisher about infiltrating the NRA, America's gun homicide rate sat at 4.04 deaths per one hundred thousand people; in Australia, the gun homicide rate that same year was just 0.12 deaths per one hundred thousand people.[14]

'If they think there's someone there who can claim that he supports the NRA's view that Australia's anti-gun legislation needs to be reviewed, the NRA might just welcome them in,' I said to Swisher. 'And, if they do, we'll use hidden cameras to record everything they say and put it in a documentary about the inner workings of the US gun lobby.'

Swisher, a straight-talking ex–US marine, had hired me the previous year to lead Al Jazeera's North American Investigative Unit.

When I had been summoned to the company's Doha, Qatar, headquarters for the job interview, Swisher and his deputy, the former BBC executive producer and correspondent Phil Rees, had made it clear that we were hunting the biggest stories in the world. 'Elephants', they called them – the largest game on the planet. 'Come to me with a good idea, and I'll back you all the way,' Swisher had said. 'But don't bring me small stuff.'

I knew my NRA idea was more than small stuff – but I wasn't convinced that Swisher would take to such an audacious and elaborate sting.

He paused before he responded to my pitch. 'You pull this off, and it'll be more than just an elephant – it'll be a herd,' he said. 'Go for it.'

Project Freedom, as we would later call it, had been green-lit.

Chapter 3

I'd already had experience with hidden cameras and was keen to explore new ways of using the technology as a means of peeling back the curtain to reveal what some wanted to remain hidden. At Channel Seven in Australia I'd once concealed miniature cameras in a shirt while investigating a religious cult. In 1988 one of my colleagues – working with me in New York City on a Fox television program, *The Reporters* – had hidden a camera in a cowboy hat to record a crisis meeting of airline executives in the days following the bombing of Pan Am flight 103 over Lockerbie in Scotland. I'd also used miniature camera footage to expose conditions in detention centres on the island of Nauru during my time as executive producer of the SBS current affairs program *Dateline*.

Al Jazeera's investigative team had recently deployed an undercover operative to South Africa to infiltrate the criminal syndicates trafficking rhino horn. Our concealed cameras captured a connection between the traffickers and senior members of the South African government. The reporter also travelled to Guangzhou, China, where his hidden cameras recorded vision of a man offering him an entire, freshly severed rhino horn, which he produced from a plastic bag in the front seat of his car.

We had used the same methods to work our way into the world of the illegal sale of surveillance equipment. Our undercover reporter had filmed covertly as the manufacturers offered military-grade spyware – capable of listening in on mobile phone conversations, reading and altering private text messages, and hacking into personal email accounts – for sale in contravention of strict international laws forbidding the trade of such items to non-government or non-military customers.

This was all a long way from the notepad-and-pen reporting I'd grown up with in the 1970s as a newspaper journalist in Sydney. But so was the political environment journalists were now working in. Journalism had been overtaken by allegations that the media were now peddling fake news – a term that emerged in 2016 when a slew of false 'news' reports, generated from Macedonia, were posted on Facebook.[15] Donald Trump was quick to embrace the term, and would soon also use the language of autocrats and dictators to accuse journalists trying to find the truth of becoming the 'enemy of the people'.[16] As I'd made my way from newspapers to television in Australia and, later, in the United States, I'd become increasingly aware that as society's view of journalism changed, the means by which we gathered stories needed to change too.

In a world of ever-more sophisticated corporate spin, it was clear to me that, in the right circumstances and with sufficient prima facie evidence of wrongdoing, hidden cameras had their place as a tool for us in uncovering criminality and exposing corruption. They were also a means to explore the behind-the-scenes world that powerful lobby groups – such as the NRA – wanted to keep from public scrutiny.

Undercover stings such as the one I had proposed weren't new in America. In 1887, journalist Nellie Bly feigned madness to infiltrate New York's notorious Blackwell's Island insane asylum to gather material for a series of newspaper reports on abuses taking place there; her articles shocked authorities and led to reforms. Journalist Upton Sinclair Jr worked undercover in Chicago's stockyards in 1904 to bring to light appalling practices within the city's meatpacking industry; his exposé led to the introduction of the *Pure Food and Drug Act* and the *Federal Meat Inspection Act*, among other reforms. And the *Chicago Sun-Times'* 1977 purchase of a bar to allow undercover reporters, posing as bar staff, to observe shakedowns by city officials ended up exposing entrenched criminal behaviour – again, leading to a series of significant reforms.

Our infiltration of the NRA would borrow from the audacity of those and other undercover stings, taking us further than anything we'd done before. Our team would inveigle their way into the NRA, using up to nine hidden cameras at a time. Though at first we had no intention of the project lasting more than several months, the cover story would remain in place for three years as more and more revelations came to light.

* * *

Wanted: Australian man prepared to pose as a gun enthusiast pushing to reverse Australia's cherished gun laws while wearing hidden cameras to a US lobby group with five million zealous members – all armed. Assignment may take years. No experience necessary.

Are you *kidding*?! It's one thing to imagine how an investigation like this might come together – it's another thing to make it happen. How would people react when I approached them to lead a fake pro-gun group in Australia, where strict gun control laws are considered to be one of the nation's crowning achievements?

It felt like madness when I ran through the complexities of selling the idea to potential undercover operatives. But the hardest thing would be to ensure that if I managed to persuade someone to do this, they'd have to guarantee to me that they would tell nobody – *nobody* – that their sudden interest in guns was part of an undercover assignment for Al Jazeera. They would have to maintain a double life, keeping the truth from even their families and closest friends. One whisper to the wrong person, and the whole thing would be lost. It's not an exaggeration to say that lives could be put in danger.

From my office in Washington, I started phoning contacts I'd accumulated over my many years in journalism. The conversations went something like this:

'Hey, I was wondering whether you'd be interested in me putting you on the payroll while you build a public profile as somebody who thinks Australia's gun laws are too strict?'

Crickets.

Not a single taker. And that was before I got to the scary bit: 'Oh, and you'll have to cosy up to high-level NRA execs while secretly recording sensitive conversations with them. Then we'll reveal to them it was all a ruse and put what they said on television around the world, most likely making them extremely angry.'

I'd gone through former colleagues, ex-cops, military contacts – straight, white men who I thought would fit into the NRA's conservative, mostly white culture and who I hoped would have the swagger to pull something like this off.

All of them said no.

When it seemed I'd never find the right person, I thought of an old friend.

Rodger Muller and I had first met in 2001 when I was working as executive producer of the ABC's *Lateline* – a position I would hold for seven and a half years. At the time we were both living in the suburb of Alexandria in Sydney's inner west and had gotten to know each other through mutual friends there.

Rodger was born in Paddington women's hospital in Sydney's eastern suburbs on 18 August 1969, and he grew up in a housing commission flat on Bilga Crescent, Malabar, right next to Long Bay Prison.

His Norwegian-born mother sent him to a kindergarten in Darlinghurst where he remembered being 'the only Australian-born kid in the school'.

'My neighbours and mates were Aborigines and my schoolmates were Greeks, Spanish, Chinese kids, blacks. That's what I thought Australia was. A big mix of all kinds of kids from all over the place. Migrants everywhere.'

Rodger struggled at school with dyslexia, and his parents, who worked in Sydney's rag trade, saved enough to enrol him at the city's exclusive Scots College, hoping a private education might improve his ability to read and write. He told me, 'They were working out of a garment factory in Darlinghurst – right next to what was then Kinselas funeral home, now the famous nightclub – so, it was a bit of a stretch for them to send me to Scots.'

Life was tough at his new school at first. Rodger found it difficult to adjust to a highly ordered environment. But a few years in, he settled into the school's routine – developing a reputation as a prankster, the kid with an innate ability to put an edgy crowd at ease in the playground.

'I reckon Scots is where I learned how to get along with all sorts of people, how to walk straight into a bunch of strangers and find a way to make friends,' he said.

'And if someone didn't like me, I knew there was always a way to change their mind.' He added, 'That's something I don't think I've ever forgotten. And it's served me well – all over the world.'

At Scots, Rodger entered a world of wealth and privilege. And he very much liked what he saw.

He bonded with the children of successful lawyers, accountants, doctors and businesspeople. He embraced sport, joined the rowing team, and took to yachting at the weekend on Sydney's Rose Bay. He developed a passion for cricket and rugby, throwing himself into bone-crunching conflicts on private-school football fields. His face still bears the scars of brutal clashes from those days.

'If someone's running at you, you just smash right through 'em,' he told me. It was a philosophy he referred to often.

'That's served me well over the years, as well.'

Rodger's academic skills improved as he moved into senior school. When he graduated, he chose to study podiatry while earning pocket money as a barman at the White Horse Hotel in Surry Hills.

His podiatry studies lasted two years before he dropped out.

'Corns and bunions just weren't doing it for me,' he said.

'I was looking for something that gave me more of a thrill.'

Before he withdrew from podiatry studies, Rodger had come up with an idea for how to make money – without touching anyone's feet. His eureka moment had struck him after a friend complained to him about the exorbitant cost of the uniforms he had to purchase for his work as a chef.

Rodger had spent his life watching his parents make clothing, so he figured he could do it too. He developed RAM Chef's Uniforms, custom-made and less expensive than those in the shops – and he delivered the freshly stitched garments on his pushbike, direct to his customers.

'I did very well with that little idea,' he said.

'So, when I pulled out of uni, I already had plenty of money to keep me going.'

Cashed up and with his business booming, he began to travel. He took skiing trips to Europe and the United States, and he explored the beaches and port towns of the Caribbean and Central America.

On one trip to Cuba, he had another eureka moment. In the teeming streets of Havana, he purchased a box of Cohiba Espléndidos cigars and slipped them into his luggage.

Maybe there'll be interest in these in Australia, he thought.

Through his cigar business, Rodger made more money and powerful friends, including former Prime Minister Bob Hawke to whom Rodger would sometimes hand-deliver boxes of cigars – occasionally joining Hawke for dinner at his beach-side house after the drop-off.

Rodger and I met up most mornings at Bitton Gourmet, our local coffee shop, as we prepared for work. His showmanship – his tendency to play to a crowd – was always on full display. Though he could afford a luxury car, he'd recently bought an old soft-top army jeep, painted in full camouflage, which he would drive to the café with the top down even in a heavy downpour – he'd shield himself from the rain with an umbrella.

His experiences in life had taught him that opportunities existed everywhere; he simply needed to identify them, then use his charm and wit – and maybe some theatrics – to turn them to his advantage.

When, in October 2015, I called Rodger from my Washington office, he answered on the first ring. 'G'day, Pete.'

When I made the offer that so many had rejected, the response was typical of the man who thrived on living on the edge.

'Love to, mate! You've caught me just at the right time. I'm between businesses just now, so I've got a bit of time to spare.'

* * *

My tough-as-nails introduction to journalism at the *Sydney Morning Herald* and the Sydney *Sun* newspapers in the mid-1970s had helped prepare me, in many ways, for the drama we were about to experience.

Throughout my career, I'd been attacked by thugs and drunks; I'd been pushed around by riot police and street protesters; I'd been threatened and abused by people who saw the media as a threat, a dog, a menace.

I'd been called a ghoul, a leech, a bottom feeder, a monster, a low-life, a pig.

Old-timers at the paper had told me that being called names would only make me stronger.

If it didn't, the rough-hands at *The Sun* had a suggestion: take a spoonful of concrete and harden up.

After time as 'police roundsman' – covering the seedy world of Sydney's crime and violence – I was assigned to general news and seated at a desk that had once been occupied by the reporter turned Hollywood actor Peter Finch.

He'd famously gone on to play American newscaster Howard Beale in the 1976 movie *Network*. The character announces to his viewers that because he's about to be axed by network executives, he has decided to blow his brains out live on air.

He implores viewers to open their windows and shout into America's streets: 'I'm as mad as hell and I'm not going to take this anymore!'

The spectacle of Beale's unhinged behaviour revives his

flagging ratings as city after city hears the cries of people following his call.

From Finch's old desk, I couldn't help but note the parallels between the satire of *Network* and *The Sun*'s often lurid front-page polemics. The paper's howling headlines were designed to stoke outrage, playing to the readers' notion that there are two societies: the often cruel and unfair one to which most of them belonged, and another one occupied by the wealthy and the famous – those who seemed, incomprehensibly, to influence the destiny of the former.

This was a paper that traded on emotion: repulsion and anger on page one, lust on page three, and the warm blanket of dogs, nags, footy and cricket down the back.

* * *

Forty years after my time on Sydney's newspapers, I moved with my family to Washington, DC, to take charge of Al Jazeera's North American Investigative Unit.

Clayton Swisher had started the unit in 2013, a couple of years after making global headlines with the publication of a tranche of confidential negotiating records on the Arab–Israeli conflict, the so-called 'Palestine Papers'.

Clayton had gone on to produce and report the 2012 Al Jazeera documentary *What Killed Arafat?*, an investigation that found traces of radioactive polonium in the personal effects of the late Palestinian leader – a suggestion that Arafat had been poisoned.

Clayton had not only recruited Phil Rees as his deputy and story structure guru, but he'd also brought in a host of high-ranking British, American and Australian producers, reporters and camera operators to form what became a powerful and influential unit headquartered in Doha, with bureaux in London and Washington.

We were given licence to pursue complex, long-term investigations – Clayton's 'elephants' – and provided with the cash and resources we needed to bring those stories to air.

Spend what you need, just don't be profligate, we were told.

Phil, who would later take over as director of investigations, described the unit's remit as fearlessly speaking truth to power. An essential part of that process, he said, was to dig into the work of some of the biggest lobby groups around the world … groups like the NRA.

Our unit understood that lobby groups try to manipulate democracy, to influence political outcomes, by managing voters' understanding of the truth.

It was our job to point out the extent of that manipulation and the means by which they were attempting to achieve it.

Clayton's demand for us to aim at giant targets called for total secrecy about what the unit was examining.

My unit in Washington, DC, was housed in a bunker within Al Jazeera's downtown headquarters. The offices were windowless to prevent anyone – even journalists from Al Jazeera's news division – from peering into our workspace.

We simply couldn't risk anyone spotting a confidential document on someone's desk, or overhearing discussions among my team about the progress – or targets – of our investigations.

Getting into the bunker was complicated. Staff had to use an electronic key to pass through two barriers, both manned by guards, and then enter a special code to open a door to a room that led to my office, which was accessed by using one of only two keys ever made for its lock.

Inside my office was a combination safe, its access codes known only by me. Inside that safe were highly confidential records containing details of the progress of our investigative assignments.

We were using these documents to try to separate truth from fiction.

'I think the problem that we've got is that there's a battle for verifiable truth, now,' Phil Rees told Al Jazeera Balkans in 2019. 'It's as if there's no consensus over it.'

He said he thought the world of journalism had recently split into two distinctive strands.

'One is one that reveals things, new truths, and shines a light into the dark areas.

'The other is the kind of news that's based on fear. It scares people. It reinforces their prejudices. And I think the politics of fear ... was deliberately formulated by certain vested interest groups that have now seen the fruition of it.

'This is why long-form investigative documentaries are necessary, because you've got to present the evidence. And that evidence cannot be questioned. It has to be copper-bottomed. It has to be solid. Because what you have now is people saying, "I have an alternative truth."'

In my years as executive producer of *Lateline*, I often felt the weight of lobby groups trying to attach dominance to those 'alternative truths'.

These groups were keenly aware of the power of a program's nightly broadcasts to set the following day's news agenda, and they worked hard, often in caustic, late-night calls, to persuade *Lateline* to present reality the way *they* saw it – even if that represented a distortion or suppression of the truth.

At the ABC, at least, I never felt pressured by news and current affairs management to shape our nightly program in order to accommodate the wishes of an outside vested interest.

Independence was king.

But I knew already that, sometimes, speaking the truth can come at a price.

In 1986, while covering civil unrest as a freelance journalist in Santiago, Chile, I'd been warned that President Augusto Pinochet's henchmen were listening in on news reports I was filing via my hotel telephone.

'They're monitoring your calls,' a contact from the Chilean Telephone Company told me. 'Be careful. They don't like the way you're interpreting events here.'

Days later, I was set upon as I was leaving my hotel. Pinochet's thugs smashed my body with batons, breaking ribs down my right side.

After some time convalescing in Santiago, I made my way to the coast and caught a ride south on a supply ship as it traversed the country's fjords, depositing me eventually in Tierra del Fuego.

I had avoided further run-ins with Pinochet's henchmen, but the message they'd given me was clear.

Tell *our* version of the truth.

Or you will be punished.

* * *

What if our cover is blown? I thought.

What if Rodger can't bear living a double life anymore?

What if we record material inside the NRA but it ends up revealing nothing of substance and we've exposed Rodger to ridicule – even hostility – in Australia by asking him to pose as a gun enthusiast?

If that happens, how do we deconstruct what we've built?

'This is going to be a bit like climbing a tree – there's a chance you'll get way up then end up on a branch with nowhere to go and no way to get down,' I told Rodger when Clayton Swisher and I visited him to sign him up for the project. 'And that could be very awkward. *Very* awkward, indeed.'

'I get that,' Rodger replied.

Clayton was more to the point.

'You realise this is a potentially very dangerous assignment?'

'Yeah, I get that too,' Rodger said.

We were sitting outdoors at a coffee shop at The Rocks in Sydney in January 2016. With us was an Australian journalist, Claudianna Blanco, whom I'd hired to work with me when I was executive producer of *Dateline* some years earlier. She had shown all the right qualities to join my top-secret team: she was highly intelligent, amicable, agile and loyal. Born in Venezuela and educated in America and Japan, she was multilingual to the extent that she had earned a Japanese-language master's degree in documentary filmmaking from Nihon University. She also possessed the ability to read the mood of a crowd – a vital skill in this undercover assignment. She would be Rodger's 'communications director': running his gun rights website, scripting his video appearances, and liaising directly with the NRA to line up meetings for him in the US.

This was our get-to-know-you session.

'I need to run through some questions,' Clayton said to Rodger. 'Don't be offended, please.'

Rodger nodded.

'Do you take drugs?' Clayton asked.

'Nope.'

'Drink?'

'Yep.'

'Much?'

'Depends on how thirsty I am. I mean, a man's not a camel.'

Rodger looked at me with a half-smile, as if to ask, *It's okay to say that sort of thing to the boss, right?*

'Do you have a criminal record?' Swisher continued.

'Got busted for drink driving once. That's all. Paid a fine and lost my licence for a couple of months. I was an idiot.'

'Nothing else?'

'Nothing.'

'What's your view on gun violence in America?'

'Seems like an issue. I mean, so many people are being killed there. But I haven't really studied it closely.'

'Because you're going to be asked to get friendly with people who may well believe that gun violence *isn't* an issue there. At least, not an issue that's been created by the NRA.'

'I kinda figured that might be the case.'

'So, just to be clear,' Clayton said, 'you're comfortable working with us on this assignment? Because once you're in, you're in for good.'

Rodger didn't hesitate. 'Totally.'

Clayton turned to Claudianna.

'Same with you?'

'I'm in,' she answered.

Chapter 4

'**W**e're going to give you gun safety training,' I said to Rodger.

It was early February 2016, and I wanted to be sure that he was able to look the part and manage a weapon without hurting himself.

I already understood guns and was well aware of the damage they can do. Knowledge of how to use a rifle had been a rite of passage for boys in 1960s country Australia, and having a gun in our house in Deniliquin, New South Wales, felt like part of everyday life. Dad kept his rifle on top of a bedroom cupboard, the bullets rolling loose in his bedside drawer. Safety lessons were delivered without fuss, and I saw guns as neither evil nor threatening.

In my teens I used rifles and shotguns on my friends' farms to hunt rabbits, kangaroos, snakes and foxes: animals considered vermin or a danger to crops and livestock.

It wasn't until I started work as a journalist that I saw the damage guns can do when they get into the wrong hands.

Over more than forty years I covered murders, gun fights, suicides, mass shootings and more.

In 1980, I was the first reporter on the scene after Turkey's consul general and his bodyguard were shot dead outside the consulate in Sydney. The two men lay on the street in front of me, their blood streaming onto the bitumen.

I spent a stomach-churning Saturday night in the Baragwanath hospital in Soweto, South Africa, as gunshot victims were rushed in – one after the other after the other – until the emergency-room floors were slick with gore.

I was in El Salvador during its bloody civil war, in Nicaragua during its revolution. I saw the grisly aftermath of the Guatemalan genocide. I worked in violent East Timor and reported from the frontline trenches in Cambodia's fight against the Khmer Rouge.

I helped carry a man to an ambulance after he shot himself in the head in the bedroom of his Sydney home – the bullet entering his right temple and exiting his left. He gasped for breath as medics gave him morphine – remarkably, he was still alive. But not for long.

I had seen blood and brains and skull fragments spattered across living-room carpets, bathroom walls, office ceilings, the inside of cars.

Now, I wanted to be sure that Rodger not only knew how to handle a gun without hurting himself or someone else, but that he also *looked* like he knew how to handle one. If he was to play the role of a pro-gun advocate, he had to be totally at ease with firearms, so we flew him to Washington and enrolled him in a series of courses. He would learn how to load and shoot a gun, how to clean and maintain a gun, how to conceal a gun in his clothing and how to secure a gun in his home.

The courses confronted him with America's gun culture. When the tutor in one session asked those present to 'bring out your guns', Rodger was astonished to see dozens of handguns produced from handbags, pockets, briefcases, purses, backpacks and shoulder holsters. The hidden world of firearms was laid bare.

* * *

'What are we going to call this thing?' I asked the undercover team in a phone call from Washington. In February 2016, Rodger's lobby group still had no name.

A few titles were suggested and rejected before Claudianna offered the name 'Gun Rights Australia'. The lobby group that would take Al Jazeera into the heart of the National Rifle Association of America had been born.

Operating under the pseudonym 'Diana Armatta', Claudianna started writing, filming and editing video clips of Rodger championing the need for 'a sensible discussion' on guns, posting each of his messages on the Gun Rights Australia website which went live in April 2016.

Drawing in part on the NRA notion of victimisation in a world of out-of-control political correctness, Claudianna built Rodger's profile as an Australian who saw his country's laws as too restrictive, out of touch with modern-day Australia's sensibilities. Week after week, Claudianna crafted a layered history of Rodger as a plain-talking, likeable Aussie with a genuine, alternative point of view. That he

was, in real life, building a dog food business – Man's Best –
seemed to give Rodger's Gun Rights Australia persona even
more credibility – along with the flexibility to travel for the
Investigative Unit when required.

Each of Claudianna's scripts was sent to me in Washington
for approval via an end-to-end encryption app. Once I'd
signed off on her writing, she would travel with Rodger to
locations within Australia to videotape the messages.

In one of his videos, he says, 'Hi guys, Rodger Muller,
GRA. Well, I've come to Canberra to get a sense of what's
happening with guns in Australia.

'We need to have law-abiding firearms owners have a
simple system for their licensing and the ability to protect
themselves from these home-grown madmen and new
arrivals. We don't want our rights as gun owners diluted, as
law-abiding citizens, and let the criminals run riot.'

Another script took the side of returned servicemen –
and their sentimental attachment to weapons of war.

'I've got a story to tell you that was shared with us by one
of our members,' he said.

'Her father was an Australian digger from the Second
World War. Among his things was his .303 rifle.

'Now, she rang the police to see if she could have it
decommissioned and kept as a family heirloom.

'All they could do was basically rush the house, take the
weapon and have it destroyed.'

Rodger also put himself forward as a man unafraid to
take the lead in pushing for a review of Australia's gun laws.

'I'll be talking with politicians, academics, key
stakeholders to really make a difference and formulating

what's happening in Australia and where we go moving forward.'

Over time, Rodger became so 'in character' that such words came to him quickly and easily. At a bar in Washington months later, he told me the Al Jazeera assignment had caused him to think seriously about 'the other side' of the gun debate.

'You know,' he said, 'not *all* of this pro-gun talk is rubbish.'

It took me a moment to digest his comment.

'Don't go down that rabbit hole,' I said.

He took a sip of his beer and nodded slowly as he peered out at the passing crowd.

* * *

Rodger also needed training in how to record concealed-camera vision, so, in March 2016, I flew with him to London where a specialist technician supplied miniscule cameras to Al Jazeera's Investigative Unit, using a 3-D printer to custom-build the devices.

Our specialist trained Rodger in how to operate the cameras, and how best to position himself to capture the most engaging images.

Sit with your back to the light, Rodger was told, in order to illuminate your subject's face. Avoid backlighting with people you're recording, a problem that may result in subjects disappearing into shadow. Stand close enough to record conversations, especially in a noisy, crowded room. Make sure the camera isn't pointing upwards – a common problem in sit-down meetings if the person wearing the device leans too far back in a chair. Take wide shots and tight shots. Move your body slowly from left to right in order to record a scene-setting pan that might provide imagery for a voice-over. Place a second camera to capture your subject from a different angle. And a third to film you both.

Rodger learned how to change batteries and SD cards and how to thread tiny cables into his clothing. He was schooled in how to operate cameras built into mobile phones that could record broadcast-quality vision while lying flat on a desk or a restaurant table. He learned how to conceal a camera in his trademark Akubra, and how to operate another, stitched into the lining of his briefcase.

The specialist sent me and Rodger into Borough Market in London's Southwark to test his skills in a crowd, and we visited pubs and cafés nearby to expose him to a range of locations that resembled venues in which he would most likely need to record images when he began his work in America.

Rodger learned quickly and impressed his teacher, who assessed his work via a video monitor back at the office.

'Not bad, not bad at all. That vision's useable. That could go to air right now.'

'I can do better,' Rodger said.

We ventured again into London's bustling streets while my undercover reporter-in-training honed the art of subterfuge, sharpening the video skills that he would soon carry through the front door of the NRA's national headquarters.

* * *

Three months later, on 12 June 2016, a gunman pledging allegiance to the Islamic State shot dead forty-nine people inside Pulse, a popular gay nightclub in Orlando, Florida. Donald Trump seized the opportunity to rail against immigration and to demonise American Muslims. In comments shortly after the massacre, he made no reference to Americans' ability to access firearms – instead, he called on President Barack Obama to resign for refusing to use the term 'radical Islam'. On 13 June, Trump tweeted: 'Appreciate the congrats for being right on radical Islamic terrorism, I don't want congrats, I want toughness & vigilance. We must be smart!'[17] The NRA's key good-guy-with-a-gun argument would emerge days later when Trump lamented at a campaign rally that there hadn't been 'guns on the other side' during the shooting. The Pulse gunman had, in fact, exchanged gunfire with an off-duty police officer who was on security duty at the nightclub when the attack took place.

Countless politicians have ignored the facts to shape a convenient narrative, of course. Many have invented 'facts' to sway voters with emotion. The 2001 Children Overboard scandal – in which the government of Prime Minister John Howard falsely claimed that asylum seekers coming to Australia on boats had threatened to throw their children into the sea in a bid to secure refuge – is a relatively recent example of this tactic being used for political advantage in Australia. But in 2016, America had moved into territory where even the pretence of smoke and mirrors was no longer considered necessary to cover brazen distortions of reality. Donald Trump was proving to be quite comfortable in being at odds with the truth, and his star-struck base didn't seem to mind that at all.

The *New York Times* and the *Washington Post* grappled with how to report on a presidential campaign that they described, somewhat coyly, as 'unorthodox'.

In fact, the tone of Trump's campaign-trail language, including his accusations that media organisations were producing fake news, would serve to fundamentally reshape the behaviour of the US media. It placed many journalists in a dilemma over how to accurately describe how Trump and his associates were behaving.

'The political lie has existed since the dawn of politics ... yet something changed in 2016,' a researcher for the Reuters Institute said in an examination of Trump's rhetoric. 'Mr Trump presented falsehood upon falsehood throughout his campaign. While US journalists tried to hold him accountable, the falsehoods, or lies, had few consequences.'[18]

The Guardian was more pointed in its observations of how Trump lied as he sought to define the US as a dystopian horror show. 'In Trump's world, crime is always rising (the national rate fell for decades),' an article in the paper declared.[19] 'African Americans are "living in hell" (they are not). Migrants are flooding in (more Mexicans are leaving than arriving), and they bring violence (there is no evidence that they do) ... But amid all this desolation Trump gains three things. He fuels doubt and fear, leaving people vulnerable; he denigrates his opposition en masse, blaming the world on them; and he raises himself up above the non-existent wreckage.'

The would-be president's message that America is a bleak, broken nation seemed to enliven his political base – and the real-life horrors that played out during the campaign generated opportunities for Trump to expand his anti-immigration message.

My team now wondered: how should Gun Rights Australia fashion its message in this 'post-truth' political landscape? What information should we post on our website at a time when a would-be US leader was signalling that adherence to the truth no longer really mattered? What should we be saying we believed in – what should we say we supported – when news was no longer expected to be a representation of verifiable facts?

I'd originally planned to portray Rodger Muller as a man who would back his pro-gun comments with evidence, an advocate who might present academic assessments of gun violence or statistics supporting a review of legislation. Now I wondered whether, instead, he should be someone who would simply stir emotion. Someone who wanted to generate anger. And, like the man pushing to be president, someone who would embrace the power of fear.

Chapter 5

The militiamen stood on the edge of the Cleveland Public Square, staring into a swarming crowd of protesters. It was 18 July 2016, the beginning of the four-day Republican National Convention – a gathering in which the Republican Party would select its nominees for president and vice-president for the coming election. The militiamen wore khaki tactical gear, and stitched onto their bullet-proof vests were patches bearing the words 'West Ohio Minutemen' with a red-and-white image of an eagle clutching a shield, surrounded by a circle of thirteen stars: the number of states in the Confederacy. Each of the men was armed with an AR-15 assault rifle – the weapon used by the Tasmanian mass shooter Martin Bryant in his 1996 rampage at Port Arthur.

'What brings you here today?' I asked one of the militiamen.

'We're here to keep order,' he answered.

'To help the police?'

'If it comes to that.'

The stone-faced militia resembled soldiers, but they were not part of their country's military.

They pledged to maintain order, but they were not police.

Whatever training they may have received had taken place with no official oversight. Whether their interpretation of order conformed with that of state-trained law-enforcement officials was anybody's guess.

Each wore an earpiece through which information was being channelled, presumably, by someone, somewhere, who would determine where and how this group might be deployed.

If and when they might use their guns.

And against whom.

If it weren't for their potential to wreak havoc, the ragtag group would have looked almost comical among the crowd that had flocked to Cleveland, some to protest and others to celebrate the Republican National Convention, which was being held in the city's Quicken Loans Arena just a few blocks away.

I pushed into the crowd of several hundred people.

Protesters pressed against the steps of the Soldiers' and Sailors' Monument at the eastern corner of the square, holding anti-Republican, anti-gay, anti-black, anti-socialist, and anti-abortion signs.

A group railed against the disproportionate number of African Americans who'd been shot dead by white police. In all, 1091 blacks would be killed by police in the US that year.[20]

Under the monument's statue of the Goddess of Freedom – commemorating those from the region who died in the mid-1800s Civil War on the anti-slavery Unionist side against the Confederacy – chants of 'Black lives matter!' were countered by '*All* lives matter!'

Police circled the crowd, forming barriers with their bicycles, barely managing to hold one group from another.

I could see pistols, shotguns and assault rifles in the hands of several people in the square – all legal under Ohio's 'open carry' statutes, which permit gun owners anywhere in the state to carry firearms openly in streets such as those in Cleveland, now heaving with protesters.[21]

A security guard I had engaged to move my team to safety if shooting broke out touched my elbow and pointed to police sniper nests, visible through open office windows and on rooftops around the square.

This was the First Amendment holding hands with the Second Amendment in a chaotic dance.

I stepped deeper into the mob as more police poured in, pushing more bicycles together. The West Ohio Minutemen moved from the perimeter of the square to a set of steps nearby where they stood in a row, hands on guns, staring down into the crowd.

* * *

'Imagine a young mother at home with her baby when a violent predator kicks the door in.'

The NRA's Chris Cox was addressing a full house the following day at the Republican National Convention.

'He's a three-time loser who was released from prison early because some politician wanted to show their *compassion*.'[22]

Cox spat the word 'compassion' as if it were deserving of the nation's contempt.

His unspoken message was clear: *they* give compassion, *we* don't.

They are weak, *we* are strong.

'What's she going to do?' Cox continued.

'She'll dial 911 and pray. The police will do their best to get there quickly. But their average response time is eleven minutes. So, the question is: should she be able to defend herself with a firearm in her own home?'

It was a theme familiar to NRA members: Women are *vulnerable*.

Predators are real.

And those who deny women access to guns are *contemptible*.

'Friends, that question is on the ballot in November,' Cox said.

'The right to protect your life is the most precious right you have.

'The five million men and women of the NRA will fight without apology for your right to protect your life. But we are on the cusp of losing this great American freedom. And with it, this great nation. The only way we save it … the *only* way we save it … is by electing Donald Trump the next president of the United States. Thank you, God bless you.'

* * *

On the third day of the Republican National Convention, I stood on the floor of the arena with a small group of

56

journalists during a break in proceedings. We had heard from officials that 'someone important' was in the room.

We were directed towards the stage.

After a few minutes, Donald Trump strode into view. He walked to the edge of the stage and peered down at us.

'I love the media,' he said. 'You're so *honest*.'

Then he turned and left.

* * *

When Trump stepped back onto the stage at the arena to accept the party's nomination the following evening, he said, 'We will be a country of generosity and warmth.

'But we will also be a country of law and order.'

He spoke of 'violence in our streets and chaos in our communities'.

'Many have witnessed this violence personally, some have even been its victims. Homicides last year increased by 17 per cent in America's fifty largest cities. That's the largest increase in twenty-five years. In our nation's capital, killings have risen by 50 per cent. They are up nearly 60 per cent in nearby Baltimore.'[23]

NRA talking points were tumbling from the stage: America was going to the dogs. Violence and danger were everywhere.

'Beginning on January twentieth, 2017, safety will be restored,' Trump said.

'We will honour the American people with the truth and nothing else. [To] the forgotten men and women of our country ... people who work hard but no longer have a voice ...

'*I am your voice!*'

* * *

Six weeks later, on 31 August 2016, the official Republican Party presidential nominee stepped onto the stage at Phoenix, Arizona, and stood before a long row of US flags.

The awe-struck audience chanted, 'Trump, Trump, Trump!'

Many in the crowd were NRA members who had already seen Trump in person: when the gun lobby had endorsed him as a presidential candidate at their Louisville, Kentucky, convention in May.

Brimming with confidence, Trump quickly turned to a subject he knew would stir the crowd to anger. 'Countless Americans who have died in recent years would be alive today if not for the open border policies of this administration.'

The crowd took its cue, erupting into boos against what Trump called 'the Obama–Clinton open border policy'.[24]

'This includes incredible Americans like 21-year-old Sarah Root. The man who killed her arrived at the border, entered federal custody and then was released into the US ... Sarah had graduated from college with a 4.0, top student in her class one day before her death. Also, among the victims of the Obama–Clinton open border policy was Grant Ronnebeck ... ninety-year-old Earl Olander ... Kate Steinle, gunned down in the sanctuary city of San Francisco by an illegal immigrant. In California, a 64-year-old air force veteran, a great woman … was sexually assaulted and beaten to death with a hammer. The truth is, our immigration system is worse than anybody ever realised. But the facts aren't known because the media won't report on them. The out-of-touch media elites think the biggest problem facing America … is global warming!'

The message struck a chord: America is under threat because of murderous immigrants freely crossing the Mexican border – less than half a day's drive south from Phoenix – and the media are so inept that they can't even see the danger.

A report by the nonpartisan group FactCheck, though, found no evidence to support that claim. FactCheck cited a study by the libertarian Cato Institute that examined 2015 police data from the US/Mexican border state of Texas and concluded that the homicide arrest rate for native-born Americans was 'about 46 percent higher than the illegal immigrant homicide arrest rate'. And it referred to the journal *Criminology*, which examined criminal trends from 1990 to 2014 and found that 'increased concentrations of undocumented immigrants are associated with statistically significant decreases in violent crime'.[25]

But the facts did not appear to be important to the crowds applauding Trump in Phoenix that night. The fear of foreigners and the love of guns had intersected.

'We will build a great wall along the southern border,' Trump continued.

The audience shouted back. 'Build the wall! Build the wall! *Build the wall!*'

'And Mexico will pay for the wall.'

Applause thundered through the stadium. The crowd was feeding on an energy unlike anything they'd felt before: *This guy is amazing!*

'One hundred per cent,' Trump added. 'They don't know it yet, but they're going to pay for the wall.'

The crowd reacted: *This guy is more than amazing! He's got the balls to make Mexico pay for the wall … to pay for all the pain they've caused us. Trump's going to save America!*

'To me, this is unbelievable,' Trump continued. 'We have no idea who these people are, where they're from. I always say "Trojan Horse". Watch what's going to happen, folks. It's not going to be pretty.'

'Build the wall!' the crowd chanted. 'Build the wall! *Build the wall!*'

Trump stood at the microphone and pushed his chin out, tilting his head back a little, soaking it all up, basking in the adoration, as the shouts from below built to a crescendo.

Chapter 6

Glen Caroline, the director of the NRA's Grassroots Division, leaned back in his chair, chewed a stick of gum, and blew a large pink bubble.

Rodger watched as it ballooned from Caroline's mouth, popped and slumped against his bottom lip. His tongue swept the gum back into his mouth. He worked it against his teeth.

'Politicians are motivated by two things,' he said. 'What can you do to help me, and what can you do to hurt me?'

He chewed and blew again.

It was 15 September 2016, and Rodger had secured his first sit-down meeting with an executive from the NRA in the association's national headquarters. Though he had secretly recorded on-the-fly chats with gun lobby representatives at the bustling NRA convention in Kentucky months earlier, gaining official NRA approval to enter their fortress HQ was a big deal – and an important step forward for our investigation.

The pitch to Caroline had been framed as a call for guidance from the masters of political power play.

'We're just like you. But we're working in hostile, anti-gun Australia,' Rodger had said.

'We'd like to know how you've managed to galvanise political support for firearms in America against sometimes daunting opposition – like that awful incident at the Sandy Hook school.'

I was hoping Rodger might coax Caroline to reveal the way he and others at the NRA work to frustrate America's formidable and increasingly vocal anti-gun lobby. Did the NRA use any dirty tricks? Could they let us in on their methodology?

The Gun Rights Australia website had been active for more than five months, and already Rodger was gaining a profile in Australia as a voice in favour of gun law reform. He had pointed Caroline to the site, which featured several video clips of Rodger fondling guns and chatting to NRATV and others at the Louisville convention.

Rodger had also used a brief encounter there with the NRA's chief lobbyist, Chris Cox, as a calling card to help pull off this get-together – and as a way to open other doors in the future.

'I was chatting with Chris at the convention,' he would tell people in the gun lobby. He would go on to say, 'I caught up with Glen the other day. Lovely bloke.'

Each meeting not only opened new doors but also deepened Rodger's cover story as a man with top-level connections.

To Caroline, Rodger seemed genuine, and his arguments for gun law reform in Australia made sense. Caroline was only too happy to give a fellow traveller – and someone who knew Chris Cox – thirty minutes of his time.

'Grassroots is really about mobilising our supporters for political action,' he said to Rodger, explaining the purpose of his NRA division.

He suggested that a way to 'move the needle' on gun reform in Australia would be to focus on what he called the 'correction' of politicians who opposed more firearms there – pick your targets based on a realistic assessment of how successful you'll be in changing their minds, he said.

Then give them the 'help or hurt' speech.

'So, what you have to do is find where you can actually make an appreciable difference. Where can you replace an anti-gun lawmaker with a pro-gun lawmaker? If you don't have a chance of winning, you're just spinning your wheels.'

The help-them-or-hurt-them strategy reminded me of pressure tactics I'd seen in South America years earlier. Narco-traffickers seeking assistance from local *campesinos* had given the farmers a simple choice: *¿Quieres que te paguen en plata o plomo?* Do you want to be paid in silver or lead?

Help us and we'll make you wealthy. Stand in our way and we'll kill you.

Your choice.

'We're a single-issue group,' Caroline said. 'Everybody rows in the same direction.'

Rodger had placed his mobile phone on the table, its tiny lens – specially designed to film through the end of the device while the phone lies flat – aimed at Caroline's face. He leaned forward and adjusted the angle slightly.

My team had spent the previous day scoping out the premises to make sure there were no metal detectors or security wands used to scan people entering the building.

Searches like that would have presented us with enormous complications in moving Rodger inside while he was rigged with cameras in his shirt, jacket and phone.

We'd found that by sidestepping the front desk and moving directly to the NRA's public-access cafeteria, guards at the entrance could be avoided altogether.

As patrons filed past with lunch trays, Rodger's one-on-one encounter with a key NRA operative was already touching on the association's strategies for how to manage – or frighten – anti-gun politicians.

If you're serious about changing Australia's gun legislation, Caroline advised, it's best for you to start small and work upwards.

'Find pieces of legislation, even if it's at the localised level, not just the national level, where you can make an impact,' he said.

'You're starting something new, you're going to make mistakes. It's better to make mistakes on a small level and learn from them as you expand than to make big mistakes where you can't put the toothpaste back in the tube.'

He blew another bubble and took a sip of soda.

'So, strategically, those are some of the first things I would do if I were in your shoes.'

* * *

I'd been waiting for Rodger in a car parked a few blocks from NRA HQ. When he texted that the meeting was over, I drove to a side street to pick him up.

'How'd you go?'

'Good, I think. But, fuck, I'm glad it's over.'

The assignment had been stressful, but Rodger had found a thrill in the experience too. He climbed into my car and patted a slick of sweat from his forehead.

'Cameras work okay?' I asked.

He reached into his shirt.

'Feels kind of warm.'

'Warm is good. Means it's working.'

We drove east, back to Washington, DC. In the safety of the Investigative Unit's high-security office, one of my producers removed the SD cards and began to download the data. A monitor was set up in my office.

Rodger and I sat in silence, waiting for the images he'd recorded to flicker onto the screen.

Craig Pennington, a six-foot-seven cameraman from Launceston, Tasmania, and one of my team's concealed-camera specialists, viewed the video with us.

'Not a bad first effort inside the HQ,' Craig said.

'But you've got to sit up straight to square that camera up to the subject. Don't ever slump back in the chair.'

Rodger had heard this advice before – at his camera course in London – and he was angry with himself for not delivering a perfect product.

'That's never going to happen again,' he said.

'You can count on that.'

* * *

On a crisp evening four weeks later, an NRA volunteer stepped into the middle of a conference room at a hotel in Toledo, Ohio, closed her eyes and bowed her head in prayer.

'Dear Lord, thank you so much for this wonderful day,' she said.

'Thank you for helping us as we make these phone calls, God. And these people that we call, help them to be receptive to what we say, and if they haven't made a decision, that they will make a decision on Trump's side.'

She was standing in front of a dozen NRA members who'd gathered at the hotel to hold a phone drive, set up by Glen Caroline's Grassroots Division to persuade Ohioans to vote for Donald Trump.

Or, more to the point, to make sure Hillary Clinton didn't get in.

'We're your best little things, just use us,' the woman continued.

'We thank you, we give you all the glory and the praise in Jesus' most precious name. Thank you.'

The crowd murmured amens.

The leader of the group raised his voice to announce that a special guest had come to visit them tonight, sent with the blessings of Glen Caroline himself.

'Rodger Muller here is from Gun Rights Australia, if you haven't met him already. He's here observing us, hoping to take what he sees back to Australia to get those guns back. I appreciate having him here.'

'G'day,' Rodger said, smiling.

He turned his body slowly from left to right to make sure the camera concealed in his sports coat captured video of everyone present.

The people who'd volunteered that night were from townships and farms in America's Midwest. But their weatherworn faces could have been from properties in Australia's Coonabarabran. Or Wangaratta. Or Jimboomba.

Or Deniliquin.

One by one, they came to Rodger to offer their support for what they believed were his heartfelt efforts to review gun control legislation in Australia.

'You going to get your guns back in Australia?' one asked.

'I hope I see in my lifetime you guys swing that around, turn that around,' another said.

One man told Rodger that if he succeeded in making it possible for Australians to access more guns, he'd like to give him a reward for his hard work.

'I'll send you over some rifles,' he said. 'I got extras.'

Beside them, a volunteer picked up the NRA's phone-drive guidelines: a list of phone numbers and suggested talking points for those they were about to call.

He dialled a number from the list.

'Hello, my name's Dave and I'm a volunteer with the NRA. Can I ask you two questions about the upcoming election?' There was a pause as he listened.

'Okay,' he continued. 'The first question is: is a candidate who strongly supports the Second Amendment important to you?' Another pause.

'The second question is: the NRA has endorsed Donald Trump with his promise to do everything in his power to protect our Second Amendment rights. Were you planning on supporting Clinton or Trump?'

The volunteer nodded at the response he received.

'Thank you very much for your time, sir. And this call was paid for by the NRA Political Victory Fund, not authorised by any candidate.'

He hung up, crossed a number off his list, and picked up the phone to call another.

As the Toledo phone drive was drawing to a close, Rodger was approached by a man with advice for how to push through gun reform in Australia.

You have to exploit the vulnerability of women, he said.

And create a climate of fear.

'Women, women. You know, women protecting themselves,' he said.

'See, the angle is: shouldn't she be allowed to protect herself? Why are you trying to take this away from her? If I can somehow put it into that context, I can win the argument. "Why are you taking away her choice to protect herself? Man, what kind of *barbarian* are you?"'

The volunteer put his hands on his hips and leaned back, laughing.

'That's exactly what you want. A young lady, you know, the *victim*. And I think the NRA does a really good job of doing that.'

A woman, listening to the conversation, nodded in agreement while another pushed forward, keen for Rodger to meet her twelve-year-old son. The boy is an NRA volunteer too, she said. And in the past few weeks alone, he's made more than two thousand calls, urging voters to elect Donald Trump.

Rodger leaned down to shake the boy's hand.

'Wow, mate. Amazing. Two thousand calls!'

The boy swelled with pride.

'Other kids volunteer too,' his mother beamed.

The mother and son exemplified the mood that night: their work was part of a proud and critical push to maintain a key 'freedom' in a dangerously uncertain world. Above all, they said, they couldn't risk the election of a candidate who would contemplate an Australian-style model of gun control.

Donald Trump may not be perfect, one of the men in the crowd told Rodger. But at least he'd promised the NRA that he'd never take anyone's guns away.

'[Hillary] said back in October 2015, that the Australian example was certainly worth looking into. And that scares me,' the man said.

'[But] do you think that if Hillary gets in, they're going to take your guns off you?' Rodger asked.

'Nope,' was the reply.

'We have militias throughout the state. We're very well prepared.'

Rodger slipped his hand into the inside pocket of his coat. The recorder was warm against his fingertips.

Chapter 7

What worried the Ohio volunteer group most about Australia's gun laws was the nationwide confiscation of firearms that took place following the Port Arthur mass shooting.

Martin Bryant, a 28-year-old white Australian man, killed the first of his thirty-five murder victims there around noon on Sunday, 28 April 1996.

Bryant had driven from his house in the Tasmanian capital, Hobart, south to the Seascape Guesthouse. There, he bashed and fatally shot Noelene Martin, one of the owners, then gagged her husband, David, stabbed him and shot him in the head.

Bryant continued south to the historic convict settlement of Port Arthur, driving through the site's tollgates at around 1.10 p.m. He parked his yellow Volvo sedan near the Broad Arrow Café and walked into the building, carrying what patrons described as a large sports bag.

He ordered a bowl of fruit, which he ate on the café's outdoor deck.

He then took his lunch tray back into the building, allowing someone to open the door to make it easier for him to enter.

He placed his sports bag on a table, opened it, and reached inside.

* * *

Carolyn Loughton and her fifteen-year-old daughter, Sarah, were also at Port Arthur that day, at the end of a four-day holiday in Tasmania.

'We'd been out on a boat to the Isle of the Dead that morning,' Loughton told me in the loungeroom of her Melbourne home. 'That's where all the convicts were buried from the days when Port Arthur was a brutal penal colony. Sarah said, "Can we have lunch at the café?" and I said to her, "We were there yesterday. We're packed, ready to go back to the mainland." And she said, "Oh, Mum, *please* can we just have something to eat in the café?" So, there we were.'

* * *

From his sports bag, Bryant lifted a Colt AR-15 SP1 Carbine. The rifle was fitted with a thirty-round magazine.

He held the gun to his hip and started shooting.

The first to be hit were Moh Yee Ng and Sou Leng Chung, both visiting from Malaysia. Both were shot in the head.

Bryant then took aim at Mick Sargent, who fell to the ground, wounded.

Kate Elizabeth Scott, Sargent's 21-year-old girlfriend, was then killed by a bullet to the back of the head.

Jason Winter, a New Zealand winemaker, is said to have thrown a tray at Bryant, trying to distract him as he turned towards Winter's wife, Joanne, and their fifteen-month-old son, Mitchell.

Jason Winter was shot dead.

Anthony Nightingale shouted, 'No, no, not here!'

Bryant shot him dead.

Bryant turned to 68-year-old Kevin Vincent Sharp and shot him in the side of the head.

He fired at Walter Bennett, sixty-six. The bullet passed through Bennett's neck and hit Kevin Sharp's brother, Raymond John Sharp, sixty-seven.

All three men died.

* * *

'I'd never heard a gun before,' Loughton said.

'So, my immediate reaction was that it was a car backfiring, and as quickly as I'm thinking of that, I'm seeing plaster coming off the walls. I'm seeing people being shot.

'And then I saw him. And he had this massive, very large military rifle.'

Loughton took a deep breath and sighed.

'And he was coming up behind my daughter.'

She paused.

'She stood up, she stood up with both her arms out. I'd say like Jesus on the cross. And the look on her face was sheer and absolute terror and what she would have been seeing was people behind myself being killed. She was immediately in his line of fire and I saw him and I stood up and lunged at her and pushed her to the floor.'

* * *

Bryant then shot Andrew Mills in the head.

He then shot Tony Kistan in the head.

And he walked towards Carolyn Loughton and her daughter.

'He was, like, next to me,' Loughton told me. 'I could've touched him. And he fired and that blew out my ear drum. I could feel fluid coming out of my eardrum.

'At this point, everybody's either dead or they're on the floor pretending to be dead. No one's running, no one's screaming. But with every shot that's fired – and it's very, very loud in that confined space – there's another life gone.

'And there's another life gone.

'And there's another life gone.

'And you're feeling your own mortality.

'So, he goes up to the other end of the café and he's shooting people hiding behind the counters. And people ran towards the green exit door and … earlier they decided to lock the door because the public were stealing postcards off the postcard rack. And they were piled up because they couldn't get out – and he shot them dead.

'Then he walked past myself and my daughter.

'He shoots me in the back.

'And he shoots my daughter in the back of the head.

'And I could see his feet when he went past me.'

* * *

At Bryant's trial six months later, horrific details emerged of the damage he'd inflicted inside the Broad Arrow Café.

The court heard of 'massive fatal head injuries', which included one victim being 'shot in the right rear of his head behind the ear', and another being 'shot in the left rear of the head'.

A man 'sustained a gunshot injury to the neck near his jaw and the bullet exited at the right back of [his] neck'.

'He fell to the floor … almost suffocating on his own blood.'

Another received 'a gunshot injury to the head which was fatal and towards the left side of his face'.

The court was told of survivors who described 'feelings of utter helplessness and almost a fatalistic acceptance that they were likely to be the next to be shot', and of how – as he was walking from table to table, shooting people at point-blank range – Bryant 'was not saying anything but he appeared to be laughing in an aggressive way rather than in an amused way'.[26]

In the Broad Arrow Café, Bryant had killed twelve people and wounded ten more.

It had taken just fifteen seconds.

But the massacre wasn't over.

Bryant moved to the café's gift shop where he killed another eight people. He walked into the car park where he shot dead and wounded more people, then he returned to his car and drove along Jetty Road, back towards the tollgates.

He saw Nanette Mikac beside the road, running in panic from the car park with her six-year-old daughter, Alannah. Mikac was carrying her other daughter, Madeline, three, in her arms.

When she thought they had run far enough from the car park, Mikac said to Alannah, 'We're safe now, pumpkin.'

A witness later said Alannah, who had been running ahead, seemed to be reassured by her mother's words and moved closer to her.

As Bryant approached the Mikacs, he slowed down and opened his car door. Nanette Mikac started to walk towards him – most likely thinking he was offering to help her escape.

Someone shouted, 'It's him!'

Bryant got out of his car with his gun and ordered Nanette Mikac to her knees.

She pleaded with him, 'Please, don't hurt my babies.'

He shot her in the head.

He then fired at Madeline, hitting her in the shoulder, the chest and abdomen.

She died on the spot.

Alannah ran and hid behind a tree. Bryant chased her around the trunk and shot her dead.

* * *

Bryant would be taken into custody the following day, having returned to the Seascape Guesthouse with a hostage and set the building alight. He killed the hostage, Glenn

Pears, whom he'd abducted from a nearby service station where he'd murdered the man's girlfriend, Zoe Hall.

The final toll: thirty-five dead and twenty-three wounded.

In a videotaped police interview, Bryant seemed at times almost jubilant as detectives informed him of the number of people he'd murdered.

'See, if people didn't do these unfortunate things, you people wouldn't have a job,' he said, smiling at his interrogators.

When he was shown the AR–15 he'd used in the killings, he said, 'That was the one. It's a sweet little gun.'[27]

And when detectives confronted him with graphic photographs of the people he'd shot, he sat forward in his chair, seemingly entranced.

Bryant's lawyer, John Avery, told Channel Seven that his client seemed 'thrilled' by the killings.

'He evidenced to me that it was as thrilling as driving a car at high speed,' he said.

'There was certainly that aspect of thrill-seeking that he appears to have achieved in this horrible day.'[28]

* * *

Australian Prime Minister John Howard had been in office for less than eight weeks when news reached him of the massacre.

He flew to Canberra from Sydney that day and convened an emergency Cabinet meeting on 29 April – the first of several in which the subject of a nationwide ban on guns would be discussed.

On 6 May, Cabinet agreed to a total ban on automatic and semiautomatic firearms, the creation of a nationwide gun registration program, and a system allowing for the government to buy back banned firearms from gun owners. Those guns would then be destroyed.

The plan would be called the National Firearms Agreement, or the NFA.

Before a packed press conference, the prime minister announced the measures.

'I will do everything humanly possible to get an effective tightening of the gun control situation in this country,' he said.

'Most Australians would find it absolutely unacceptable that weapons of this kind are available.'

The gun lobby was furious.

Australia's Firearms Owners Association gathered in Gympie, Queensland, on 16 May 1996, as its vice-president, Ian McNiven, railed against the gun control laws.

'You can send a message all the way down to Canberra to that sawed-off little dickhead, Jackboot Johnny,' he said.

'I know you're a bit angry about this shit.

'The only currency that you can purchase freedom back with is blood!'[29]

Members of Parliament began receiving death threats. A grave was dug on a block next to the home of a Queensland MP, and federal police warned Howard that they'd become aware of a credible plot to assassinate him.

The prime minister was urged to wear a bullet-proof vest at his scheduled appearance at an upcoming pro-gun rally in the Victorian town of Sale. Reluctantly, he agreed to do so – making him the first Australian leader ever to wear body armour in public.

Though no attempt was made to shoot him, Prime Minister Howard was heckled by some in the crowd who gave Nazi salutes and chanted, 'Sieg Heil!'

The following day, the *Daily Telegraph* newspaper carried an editorial declaring that the Sale meeting – and the fact that the prime minister had required body armour to attend it – marked a 'confronting milestone' in Australia's history.

'Just as the Port Arthur massacre brutally convinced us we are not immune from senseless slaughter, the subsequent gun debate has produced another frightening lesson,' the paper said.[30]

John Howard said later that he believed there was another by-product generated by the NFA.

According to Howard, the gun control laws he introduced 'gave impetus' to the rise of a new political force in Australia – a group empowered, he said, by a sense of outrage over an 'insensitive, out-of-touch … Sydney-centric government taking away our weapons'.[31]

This new force would be led by a woman from Queensland.

Her name was Pauline Hanson.

Chapter 8

When Rodger turned up to the party, an albino python was moving towards the check-in queue.

The snake had been basking in North Carolina's late-afternoon sun when it had been disturbed by the hundred or so people who were now walking from a car park, across the front lawn, to the black-tie gathering nearby.

Rodger stepped around the python and moved towards the party's giant marquee.

In front of the entrance, he saw a leopard pacing in a cage. Beside it, a pair of kookaburras were perched on a branch.

'They're a long way from home,' their handler said when she noticed Rodger looking at the birds.

'So am I,' he replied.

The Felliniesque scene – complete with wallabies hopping past champagne-sipping party-goers – was taking place in October 2016, at a vineyard owned by former NASCAR racing driver Richard Childress, an NRA board member.

Childress, one of the wealthiest men in North Carolina, was hosting a fundraiser for the Congressional Sportsmen's

Foundation, a powerful player in Washington, DC's gun lobby circles.

Guests that night included members of Congress, gun makers, lobbyists, businessmen, the NRA's senior executive team – and Donald Trump Jr, one of the presidential candidate's sons.

Rodger took a name badge and pinned it onto his jacket, taking care not to block the line of sight of the camera concealed in his lapel.

He adjusted his glasses. A second camera had been built into the frames.

His mission was to engage with the most important people in attendance – to use his Aussie charm and the story about Gun Rights Australia to make contacts who might lead him deeper into the US gun lobby.

Rodger found his table and turned to shake the hand of the man sitting next to him.

* * *

I'd driven Rodger to the Childress vineyard from a log cabin I had rented a few miles down the road as a base for the evening's activities.

Earlier, cameraman Craig Pennington and I had visited the vineyard to gauge the level of security Rodger would encounter that evening. We could see no signs of potentially problematic metal detectors and no suggestion that metal-seeking wands would be used to search guests as they entered the gathering – something that might have found the hidden cameras that Rodger was carrying.

At sunset, Craig and I dropped Rodger at an empty corner of the car park, making sure nobody saw the three of us together. I watched through the rear-view mirror as Rodger made his way across the front lawn to the party.

He was used to the routine by now: he would activate his concealed cameras, enter our selected location, scan the crowd for the most valuable targets, move towards them and start a conversation.

Typically, he'd begin with something like this: 'G'day, Rodger Muller, Gun Rights Australia ... You know, you blokes are so lucky to have the Second Amendment here in the States. We've got nothing like that at home – just the gun laws that took away semiautomatics after Port Arthur ...'

Many Rodger spoke to would express sympathy that he had to endure something as outrageous as having his guns taken from him by the government.

One east coast–based gun maker told Rodger, 'I saw the video of them chopping up those guns. It was heartbreaking, it was *disgusting.*'

Rodger would play along – sometimes drawing on videotaped NRA speeches or gun lobby PR campaigns that he had studied carefully and learned to recite verbatim.

'Charlton Heston had it right,' he would say, *'cold, dead hands.'*

Sometimes he would add another line or two to show just how much US gun culture he'd absorbed.

'Sacred stuff resides in that wooden stock and blued steel,' he would say, 'something that gives the most common man the most uncommon of freedoms.'

The people he was talking to would invariably nod.

'You got that right, buddy.'

When Rodger's meetings took place in public bars or restaurants, I'd sit or stand as close to him as possible without making it obvious that I was eavesdropping. I'd act like just another guy jostling for a place at a crowded bar, or a man dining with a friend at the next table. By monitoring Rodger's discussions, I was able to guide him if I felt a follow-up question was required, or if he needed to drill deeper into a topic.

When I wanted Rodger to ask something specific, I'd send him a discreet text with the question spelled out.

His phone would ping, and he'd glance at the screen, often with a comment like: 'You reckon the bastards back home would leave me alone long enough to have a quiet beer with a mate now and then.'

Then he'd ask my question.

His persona as a friendly, fun-loving advocate for Aussie gun rights played well into the hands of the US gun lobby. The more meetings he held, the more people he persuaded to talk to him.

***

The Childress vineyard event was taking place just weeks from the US presidential election, and – though the cocktail-sipping guests were doing their best not to show it – alarms were beginning to ring around America over the behaviour of their NRA-endorsed, Second Amendment champion.

Trump's carefully constructed image as a strongman, a protector of the vulnerable, had been knocked sideways with the release just five days earlier – on 8 October 2016 – of a videotape in which Trump was captured on a hot microphone talking about how the power of celebrity can be exploited to prey on women. The video recorded a 2005 conversation between Trump and the presenter of an entertainment news program, *Access Hollywood*, and had been leaked anonymously to the *Washington Post*.[32]

'I did try and fuck her,' Trump said in the recording. 'She was married. And I moved on her very heavily ... I moved on her like a bitch. But I couldn't get there.'

What if the woman Trump had 'moved on very heavily' and had 'tried to fuck' had been carrying a gun?

'When you're a star, they let you do it,' Trump went on to say. 'You can do anything. Grab 'em by the pussy. You can do anything.'

The twenty-five allegations of rape, sexual assault and sexual misconduct against Donald Trump that would begin surfacing before – and continue after – his election was, at the very least, a deep inconvenience to the NRA and the 'women are vulnerable' narrative the organisation had worked so hard to develop.[33] That they did not reference allegations of Trump's predatory behaviour risked them being seen as a group that viewed sexual assault as ... well, serious, yes ... but not quite as serious as the confiscation of firearms.

The guests Rodger was mixing with at the vineyard talked down the presidential aspirant's sex comments, parroting the line from Trump's campaign office that the lewd *Access Hollywood* remarks had simply been 'locker-room talk'.[34] But polls would soon show that most Americans were so troubled by the tape that they were beginning to doubt that Trump had what it took to lead the country. An ABC America News poll press release, issued on 23 October 2016, carried the headline: 'Clinton Vaults to a Double-Digit Lead Boosted by Broad Disapproval of Trump'.[35] 'All told, Clinton leads Trump by 12 percentage points among likely voters, 50 to 38 percent, in the national survey,' the report said. '[This is] her highest support and his lowest to date in ABC News and ABC News/*Washington Post* polls.'

But if the polls showed that Clinton all but had it in the bag, Rodger was hearing a different story at the vineyard gathering. 'Trump's going to win, mate,' he told me later that night.

The enduring confidence in the Republican presidential candidate among those at the party seemed to show that no matter how grievous Trump's missteps, nothing could shake the belief of those who had embraced him as their Second Amendment saviour.

Rodger had seen this, as well, on a recent tour through rural America when I sent him out of the 'insensitive, out-of-touch, city-centric' orbit — as former Australian Prime Minister John Howard might have described it — to immerse him in America's rural gun culture. He had visited gun shows and met with firearms makers. He had mixed with NRA members in bars and county fairs and gun shops. 'Everywhere I go in the sticks, it's all pro-Trump,' he told me after that trip.

Now, while I was reading about Hillary Clinton's pending victory, Rodger told me he was convinced the pollsters and the mainstream media had it all wrong. What he was learning was that there were two Americas. There was the America that the NRA dismissed as 'elitist' – those who were simply unable to see the suffering of struggling farmers and laid-off factory workers; those who didn't understand the world of hunters and gun owners, and of the poor folk with little education who felt abandoned by arrogant Washington 'swamp-dwellers', a term used to deride the fat-cat lobbyists and bureaucrats who live in the nation's capital – a city partially built on a former swamp. And there was the other America: the one that had stood with Rodger on the floor of the NRA's Louisville convention, and those who were now mingling with him at the North Carolina vineyard – gun-lovers rich and poor, entranced by a TV-star-turned-political-wannabe who promised he'd 'never let them down'.

Though Donald Trump claimed to be a billionaire, though he flew in a private jet, though his wife had been photographed pretending to eat diamonds and jewels – like fruit – from a bowl, though he boasted about not paying taxes, and now – with audio to prove it – he had bragged about using his celebrity to pressure women for sex, somehow he had managed to shapeshift into a person America's disenchanted and dispossessed believed could truly feel their pain.

* * *

'This is the kind of gun, I tell you what, your grandkids are going to fight over,' the auctioneer crowed at the vineyard gathering as a young woman held a rifle aloft, weaving around tables to show it off.

'Twelve thousand dollars ... *thirteen* thousand ...' the auctioneer shouted.

'Do I hear more, folks?'

Hands shot up, and bids rang throughout the gathering.

Rodger saw Donald Trump Jr walk past, and he stepped towards him, catching images of the president's son on his coat camera and managing a fleeting discussion with him about hunting in Australia.

'*Sold* for *sixteen* thousand dollars!'

The auctioneer slammed his gavel and moved to the next item for sale.

'So, this is going to be an opportunity for you to have a flight on your own private jet. It's for six people. *Six* people! Let's start at fifteen thousand, folks ... *sixteen* thousand ...'

Through a break in the crowd, Rodger spotted Chris Cox and Wayne LaPierre sitting at a table across the room.

'Seventeen thousand, ladies and gentlemen. Think of the luxury, folks, up there in the sky. A *private jet*. Eighteen ... *nineteen* thousand ...'

Rodger stood and pushed through the crowd.

'Twenty thousand dollars ... Come on, folks ...'

The NRA CEO turned to Rodger just as he reached his table.

* * *

Craig Pennington struck a match and held the flame under kindling in the fireplace of our cabin. Rodger had been gone for three and a half hours, and a chill was settling into the forests around us.

I'd heard from Rodger once that night – a text simply saying, 'Wayne's here.'

I knew Rodger would try his hardest to get to the leader of the NRA, but recording conversations in a loud and crowded room would be a challenge.

Craig had worked hard to position the coat and glasses cameras for the best angles in situations where Rodger was both standing and sitting.

And, as back-up, he'd handed Rodger a phone camera.

But until we had access to everything recorded that night, we would have no idea whether he'd succeeded in capturing useable sound and vision.

Craig blew into the kindling. A flame curled and spread into a layer of twigs.

He leaned back.

'Reckon he's going okay?' he asked.

We both knew the critical importance of this assignment.

'I bloody well hope so.'

The fire took hold, crackling into the splinters of a log. Smoke drifted, ghost-like, up the chimney and streamed into the dark woods.

* * *

Rodger calculated that his encounter with Chris Cox at Louisville was just the excuse he needed to interrupt LaPierre's table.

He circled the table before making his move.

Those seated with LaPierre saw Rodger step first towards Cox with a smile and say the words 'G'day, Chris, Rodger

Muller, Gun Rights Australia!', before he turned to his primary target.

He held out his hand. The NRA's CEO stood to shake it.

Rodger had done it. He'd reached the top.

As he introduced himself to LaPierre, the Childress party's host stepped onstage to make an announcement.

'Ladies and gentlemen, please welcome a special guest, Rodger Muller. He's come all the way from Sydney to be here tonight. And he's fighting to get his guns back Down Under!'

Wayne LaPierre and Chris Cox applauded with the crowd.

'Rodger's from Gun Rights Australia,' the host continued. 'He's one of us.'

The brave Australian fighting his country's gun laws was a hero.

Rodger turned his torso slowly from left to right to video the cheering crowd.

Then he reached inside his coat. His fingers touched the camera.

It was cold.

* * *

'Fuck, fuck, fuck.'

Rodger's text needed no further explanation.

Craig and I sat in silence, staring into the fire, as we waited for Rodger's Uber to bring him back to the cabin.

His coat camera had shut down just twenty minutes into the party.

It had recorded images of him walking through the car park, stepping around the albino python, looking at the leopard in its cage, talking with the woman who kept the kookaburras, entering the party and sitting down.

There were images of the auction, and he'd captured his meeting with Donald Trump Jr.

Then nothing.

Craig checked the camera he'd concealed in Rodger's glasses.

That had failed too.

He checked the camera in Rodger's phone.

Nothing.

* * *

'How did it go?'

Clayton Swisher had called from Doha as I drove us back to Washington, DC, the following morning.

'Um, well, the *good* news is that Rodger finally got to meet LaPierre,' I said.

'The *bad* news is that all three cameras he was carrying failed to video any of it.'

Clayton stayed silent for a moment.

'*Failed* to record?'

'Um, yes. Don't know why. We have a little video at the start of the evening but the bulk of it we missed.'

Silence again.

'It's an absolute bugger,' I added. 'We're all totally pissed off.'

Clayton was a man who didn't like to hear about failure, and my attempt to show that we were unhappy didn't seem to be doing anything to placate him.

'So, you went there, you sent Rodger in, he carried three cameras, and now you've got fuck-all?'

'Um. Yes. Well, not *entirely* fuck-all. We've got a great shot of an albino python on the lawn and the crowd at the start of the event … Oh, and we got Rodger meeting Donald Jr.'

Rodger, sitting in the passenger seat beside me, couldn't hear the specifics, but it was obvious the boss wasn't pleased to hear what I was saying.

I pressed the accelerator a little harder as the monuments of the capital shimmered into view.

Chapter 9

Donald Trump was confirmed as the forty-fifth president of the United States of America on 8 November 2016. The following week, Wayne LaPierre recorded a video for NRA members, declaring them to be the 'special forces' that had swung the election in Trump's favour.

'*You* did this,' he said. 'Don't let anybody else tell you otherwise. *Gun* owners made this election happen!'

Flushed with victory, triumphant military music playing in the video's background, LaPierre took a swipe at the many journalists who'd reported to the very end that Hillary Clinton had been poised to win.

'The same disgraced group of so-called experts, talking heads, pundits and pollsters that got everything wrong before the election are trying to deceive you once again,' he warned.

'The disgraceful media attempted to manipulate your emotions, they tried to suppress your enthusiasm, your speech, your vote. We must face these very real challenges with the strength, courage and purpose you have proven to possess.

'Our time is now!'

***

On 4 December 2016, barely three weeks after the presidential election, 28-year-old Edgar Maddison Welch drove five and a half hours from his home in Salisbury, North Carolina, to the Comet Ping Pong pizza restaurant in Washington, DC's Chevy Chase neighbourhood. Welch was determined to free children he believed were being held captive in the building's basement – victims of a paedophile ring allegedly being run by former presidential candidate Hillary Clinton.

Welch was armed with an AR-15 assault rifle, a Colt .38 calibre handgun and a folding knife. He fired three rounds inside the building before police were called and took him into custody.

The bizarre incident sprang from reports circulating on Facebook and Twitter, and which had gone viral through right-wing platforms including *Infowars* and *Breitbart*, which accused the former first lady of conducting satanic rituals at Comet Ping Pong – a conspiracy theory dubbed 'pizzagate'.[36] In fact, no children were being held captive in the restaurant. There was no paedophile ring. There were no sex slaves. There were no satanic rituals. There wasn't even a basement in the building.

But the gunman's efforts brought together two disturbing and defining strands of American life at that moment: crazy and gullible people with guns, and others, using claims – backed by the President – that the mainstream news is 'fake', to manipulate those crazy and gullible people with guns.

Even months after Welch's attack on the restaurant, Comet Ping Pong's owner, John Alefantis, continued to receive threats online from people who could not accept that the sex-slave story had no basis in fact. Alefantis told *Inc.* that one of the messages said, 'I pray that someone comes in with an assault rifle and kills everyone inside Comet. I want to cut open your guts and watch them spill out on the floor.'[37]

* * *

From the time of Trump's election victory to his inauguration, on 20 January 2017, the president would accuse the mainstream media of spreading 'fake news' at least nineteen times, according to *Factbase*, a website that monitors his use of the term.[38] When the media pushed back, questioning White House claims that crowds attending Trump's inauguration were larger than those at the inauguration of Barack Obama in 2009, Trump's presidential counsellor, Kellyanne Conway, fiercely defended the US leader.

Standing on the White House lawn on 22 January 2017, Conway introduced the term 'alternative facts' to buttress the White House's patently bogus crowd-size claims. Conway's comments seemed a declaration that those in the presidential mansion were happy for *anything* to be couched as 'true' or 'fake' now, even if all evidence showed otherwise – as long as it comported with *their* view of reality, or as long as it supported *their* political agenda.

* * *

After pumping more than thirty million US dollars into the Trump campaign, the NRA finally had their man in the White House.

They had overcome the very real threat of Hillary Clinton.

Their cherished Second Amendment was no longer in danger.

Everyone could relax.

But then something odd started to happen: gun sales, already slowing, took a sharp drop.

A Pew Research survey found that by early 2017, around 30 per cent of Americans owned a gun – down from what a CBS/*New York Times* poll had found to be a high of 53 per cent in 1994.[39]

The drop-off has been labelled the 'Trump Slump' – a fall in sales, according to the National Shooting Sports Foundation, from 15.7 million firearms in 2016 to 14 million in Trump's first year in office.

Part of the problem confronting the NRA was that those opponents used by LaPierre, Cox and others to frighten members into voting against perceived threats had all now been defeated.

In his video to members following Trump's victory, LaPierre turned to other targets, clawing at billionaire gun control advocates George Soros and Michael Bloomberg. *They* were now the enemies of the NRA. *They* were now the ones trying to take everyone's guns away.

'They will continue to enjoy the support of an openly dishonest media that *truly hates* your right to speak, your right to worship and your right to vote,' LaPierre said.

How the media truly hates Americans' right to speak, worship and vote was never made clear by the NRA chief. But it seemed to me that he was on his knees, paddles in hand, trying to jolt life back into the Frankenstein that had collapsed just as it delivered to the NRA its ultimate political prize.

'Clear!'

He needed that monster alive.

'C'mon, buddy, you can do it!

'CLEAR!'

* * *

Though 21 more mass shootings would take place that year, bringing the 2017 toll to 714 dead and wounded – a forty-four per cent fatality increase on the previous year – NRA spokesman Colion Noir, one of LaPierre's foot soldiers, unleashed a wave of video attacks on NRATV as Trump took office. These were aimed at journalists who'd reported on massacres in America and around the world.

Noir's main message was that the media secretly and cravenly yearned for mass killings because such tragedies lifted their ratings.

'No one on this planet benefits more from mass shootings and motivates more people to become mass shooters than our mainstream media,' Noir says in one video.

'Sure, they love to get up in front of the camera and sell the lie that mass shootings are all the NRA's fault and falsely claim that the NRA is a soulless organisation selling guns to killers for profit. But all my years of watching these events play out have led me to one conclusion: the mainstream media love mass shootings.'

Noir stares at the camera in silence for effect.

'I'm going to say it again,' he says.

'The mainstream media *love* mass shootings. If there's one organisation in this country that has a vested interest in the perpetuation of mass tragedy, it is our mainstream media. Their dirty secret is mass shootings have become their *Game of Thrones*, their *House of Cards*, their *Seinfeld* and their *Friends* all wrapped into one. And whenever they get one, they wring out every last episode they can to juice their ratings and push their agenda …'

But worse than the media's 'dirty secret', even worse than their love of mass shootings, their lust for ratings or their 'agenda', Noir says, is the damage journalists do when they publish the names of mass killers.

When that happens, he claims, they have 'just put out a casting call for the next mass shooter'.

Another of LaPierre's frontline fighters against the media was NRATV's Dana Loesch.

Doubling down on Noir's comments, she launched a scathing attack on the United States' most powerful newspaper, the *New York Times*.

'We the people have *had* it,' she says in a video.

'We've had it with your narratives, your propaganda, your fake news. We've had it with your constant protection of your Democrat overlords. Your refusal to acknowledge any truth that upsets the fragile construct that *you* believe is real life. And we've had it with your pretentious, tone-deaf assertion that you are in any way truth or fact-based journalism ... this old, grey hag, this untrustworthy, dishonest rag ... has subsisted on the welfare of mediocrity for one, two, three or more decades. We're going to laser-focus on your so-called "honest pursuit of truth".

'In short, we're *coming* for you!'

Her threat hangs in the air like gun smoke. The I-ain't-gonna-take-no-*shit*-from-*nobody* message is stunning in its sneering vulgarity. But it sent tingles of excitement through the loins of NRATV viewers – men and women alike.

In response to the video, one viewer posted: 'You are SO hot when you get like this, Dana. Dunno what it is about you, but GAH!! Luv u!'

Another wrote: 'Good lord, my mouth is watering. luv ya girl.'

And another: 'Stahhhhhp, Dana!! I'm having inappropriate thoughts about you! So flipping gorgeous.'

Loesch's warrior-princess performance showed the immensely effective role rage could play to animate – and even seduce – the gun lobby's national base.

It pointed out the depth of resentment the NRA felt towards reporters – people like me and Rodger Muller.

And it demonstrated to me just how closely LaPierre's messaging had come to mirror that of the man he had helped to install as president.

While Donald Trump was railing against 'the failing *New York Times*', Loesch attacked the paper as a 'pretentious ... tone-deaf ... old, grey hag'. While Trump was accusing the mainstream media of generating 'fake news', Loesch used that very term. When Trump labelled the media 'the enemy of the people', Noir called for laws to control what journalists could say.

The White House and the NRA were in lock step.

Their approach to dealing with mainstream journalists followed three simple rules:

One: attack the media.

Two: attack the media again.

Three: continue to attack the media.

Through intimidation, incendiary accusations and threats of punishment through the polls, the NRA had constructed a narrative around guns that served to block commonsense legislation at federal, state and local levels.

The organisation's propaganda machine steamed on, unchecked by the new Trump administration, as the firearm lobby pushed for the sale of more and more guns.

Chapter 10

In the sixteen months we'd been working on the project, we had gathered hundreds of hours of video: unguarded conversations with executives, rank-and-file members and associates, and valuable images of life inside the NRA's pro-Trump election drive.

And much more was soon to come.

We arranged for Rodger to attend a second NRA annual convention – this one in Atlanta, Georgia – where even stronger bonds were formed with key lobbyists, gun makers, firearms salesmen and NRA executives. It would be his fourth trip to the United States that year.

Rodger was confident that everybody he had met believed his cover story: he was an independently wealthy Australian businessman with a passion for guns, and he was in America for his new dog food business often enough to foster strong ties with the nation's like-minded pro-gun community.

The NRA appeared to have bought his story that he wanted to learn from them how to work with politicians and how to sway public opinion, so he could do in Australia what they had done so successfully in the United States.

Rodger and I were convinced that nobody suspected he was undercover. No one had any idea that his story was an elaborate construct designed to give Al Jazeera's Investigative Unit unprecedented access to the inner sanctum of the US gun lobby.

With each phone call Rodger made, with each meeting he filmed, his confidence grew that his cover would never be blown.

But then he took an NRA lobbyist to lunch.

And everything changed.

* * *

I checked into a hotel on Atlanta's Peachtree Street around midafternoon on Wednesday, 26 April 2017. I spent the rest of that afternoon and the early evening surveilling the lobby, car park, corridors and public spaces to familiarise myself with routes our potential subjects might take as they moved around the building during our four-day stay.

I had guessed that high-level NRA staffers and associates would choose the same establishment, and soon enough I was proven right. Donald Trump Jr, surrounded by a team of security guards, strode out of the elevators into the lobby, and I spotted Chris Cox walking past the hotel's check-in counter.

Rodger was with our cameraman Colin McIntyre in his room upstairs, stitching hidden cameras into the clothes he would wear at meetings in and around the NRA convention.

I texted Rodger: 'Cox and Trump junior both in lobby.'

He responded with a thumbs-up emoji.

I was hoping that, at this convention, Rodger would reconnect with contacts he'd developed on his previous visits to America. With some, he'd built a special rapport. One prominent firearms manufacturer he'd met several times had even asked Rodger to open a business for him in Australia – an offer he'd declined.

Others were keen to hear the latest on Rodger's fight for 'commonsense' firearms reform Down Under; Australia's firearms confiscations still triggered outrage in America's gun community, and they cheered Rodger on as a battler for a common good.

From Sydney, Claudianna had laid the groundwork for several Atlanta get-togethers, and she had scripted video links for Rodger to record at the convention just as he had in Louisville a year earlier. The videos would be transferred from the US to Sydney for broadcast on the Gun Rights Australia website. This sort of work was already paying off: the GRA website was gaining more and more attention in Australia, with videos and comments from Rodger attracting several thousand views and expressions of support from gun advocates around the country. One Australian political party even courted Rodger as a potential Senate candidate. Rodger turned the party down.

Rodger's cover story was so effective in Australia, in fact, that he was beginning to encounter aggression from strangers who were enraged by his online promotion of a pro-gun culture. One man had even punched Rodger in the face at a party on the NSW south coast, accusing him of making Australia a more dangerous place. Rodger had taken the blow and walked away.

Someone else had spat at him. Again, Rodger took it in his stride, believing that such events simply confirmed that, in his undercover persona as an NRA-friendly gun rights advocate, he was doing all the right things.

Now back in America, Rodger was to make new inquiries on the Investigative Unit's behalf. On this trip, I wanted him to learn as much as he could about the NRA's activities overseas. What sort of influence did the association exert in foreign countries? What methods did it use to export its ideology? Could it possibly be active in Australia?

He was to find out what he could about this while we were in Atlanta. Any leads he picked up were to be followed when we returned to Washington the following week.

This time, though, we couldn't afford *any* technical hitches.

No individuals had been blamed for the Childress vineyard camera failures; sometimes, such tiny cameras just fail to record. But we all knew that from now on, there could be no more video slip-ups.

None.

***

As Rodger was gathering secret images of people and places, I was shot-listing the material: viewing the video and making detailed notes of what had been recorded, where it had been filmed, and precisely what had been said. I had filled several ringbinders with information, and the paper records of our investigation were growing by the day.

It was laborious and time-consuming work, but it was critical to the scripting process that would follow – whenever we determined that we'd gathered enough material for a story.

As I was reviewing the material Rodger had captured, I was also regularly briefing our legal teams – in London, Melbourne and Washington – for guidance on how far we could push things.

In some US states, it was legal to covertly record conversations; in others, recording without the consent of all parties involved could lead to time in prison. Even within the states where secret filming was allowed, there were designated no-go zones for concealed cameras. It was imperative that we complied with all laws.

I was also in regular contact with Clayton Swisher and his deputy, Phil Rees, using codewords to convey sensitive information.

If anyone at the NRA learned about our activities, all hell would break loose, and we would be faced with a choice: rush what we had to air or call the whole thing off.

We had succeeded in creating the Trojan Horse that I'd proposed at the end of 2015. Through it, we had infiltrated the biggest gun lobby organisation on the planet, recording conversations in which the NRA's playbook for pushing a radical pro-gun agenda was being openly discussed.

All this at a time when the NRA was under increasing pressure, with mass shootings stoking public outrage across the United States. Against this backdrop, I wanted Rodger to try to find out more about how the NRA spread its guns-equals-freedom ideology overseas. If he were able to gain information on their tactics, I thought, I'd have new material to help flesh out our understanding of the power and influence of the US gun lobby – moving me closer to the process of structuring an hour-long investigative video report.

With what we had already, we were very close.

But we weren't there quite yet.

* * *

On our second day in Atlanta, Rodger took his seat at the lunch table on a balcony overlooking Peachtree Street and glanced around the room. Colin McIntyre and I were sitting at the table immediately to his right.

In front of us on the table were two cameras, both concealed within iPhones. The phones were positioned perfectly to capture video of Rodger and the empty chair that would soon be occupied by his guest.

I sent Rodger a text.

'All good?'

He texted back.

'Ready.'

He had three cameras with him again: one concealed in his phone camera, one sewn into his shirt, and another hidden in his Akubra, which he'd placed at his left elbow on the table.

He was waiting for Brandi Graham, an NRA federal lobbyist whom he'd met at previous meetings in Washington and who seemed happy to pass on details of how she worked with members of Congress.

When she'd agreed to meet him for lunch, I'd asked him to prod her on the NRA's overseas operations – especially whether she could point him to anyone in the organisation who was working in any way with Russia.

I suggested that he start that conversation with a question about what the NRA thought about recent news reports on Russia's alleged interference in the 2016 US presidential election.

Did the NRA have a position on this?

And, if Graham bought into the chat, I wanted Rodger to move into questions about whether the association was connected with gun rights groups in that country. Were they working to ramp up a pro-gun sentiment there?

Rodger looked around the restaurant and took a sip of his beer.

Graham was already ten minutes late.

* * *

Some details of the NRA's foreign operations were already on the public record.

The mantra that more guns are necessary for self-defence in America was now being sold by the association as a tried-and-true method to keep citizens safe in other countries.

State University of New York's Dr Bob Spitzer said the NRA played a role in Brazilian politics, for example, by helping to defeat gun control legislation that was being debated there.

'The NRA has made a conscious political decision to essentially go international,' Spitzer told me when I met with him in 2018 at his university campus in upstate New York.

'And it's not a surprise at all that they're seeking to assist groups … in weakening gun laws in other nations because that's consistent with the NRA's philosophy that fewer gun laws are better. The NRA is saying Brazilians need to arm themselves to protect themselves from criminals and, of course, crime is a big problem in Brazil right now.

'The NRA is happy to see its agenda advanced and to probably provide money, to provide advice, expertise, because they have a lot of expertise in the lobbying process and political campaigning and fundraising and other things. So, the NRA is all behind the Brazilian example, while being against what they see has happened in Australia.'

* * *

Rodger saw Brandi Graham hurrying towards him through the restaurant, and he stood to greet her.

She was sorry she was late, she said, but there was *so* much happening in Atlanta!

She sat, and they ordered food and wine. The conversation quickly turned to Donald Trump's election victory and Graham's disgust at the pearl-clutching lefties who'd failed to see it coming.

'There are all these mummies' armies just, you know, crying and saying, "What do I tell my daughters now?" I'm like, "Are you *kidding* me?"'

Those who were offended by Trump's 'grab 'em by the pussy' and similar comments on the *Access Hollywood* tape must have been living under a rock, she said.

'I've heard worse sitting in the Elvis pub with my father ... And if your husbands haven't told you it's like this, then you don't know your husbands.'

'Like it's a *joke*,' she went on. 'I saw all these like, "Oh my poor daughter," and who does [Trump] look to the most for advice? His *daughter*!'

'Yeah, Ivanka,' Rodger said, his voice trailing off.

'We've been successful since Trump was appointed,' Graham continued. 'We're trying to do as much as we can through the administration, rolling stuff back.'

She took a sip of wine.

'He got rid of the lead ammo ban, so that's good.'

'That was very quick,' Rodger said.

'Yeah, it was like the first thing,' Graham went on. 'You know, I've got a neighbour who is Muslim. And she's always like, "We're so peaceful." And you're not at all. I'm sorry. Maybe *you* are, but you're not.'

Colin shot a glance at me.

I knew he was thinking, *Wowza ... if only she knew that she was talking to a hidden camera–wearing undercover operative for Al Jazeera ...*

'Shooting is the most therapeutic thing I do,' Graham said. 'Like, forget the spa. Forget whatever. There's something about the calmness. Like if I'm shooting trout, the *calmness* ...'

Rodger nodded.

'And then it goes off – boom!' he said.

'And you go, "Uh-huh, right," and then you relax,' Graham said. 'People don't understand that who've never shot.'

Rodger ran with the sentiment.

'If the government has their way, you won't be able to touch a gun till you're eighteen.'

'Which is crazy,' Graham chimed in. 'Absolutely insane!'

Rodger saw a chance to move to the question of foreign influence.

'What's with [Trump] and Russia?' he asked. 'There seems to be this constant Russia, Russia, Russia.'

'It's the media that's driving that,' Graham answered.

'The media? It's not …'

'… there's nothing, like, nefarious at all,' she said.

Besides, she said, the media couldn't be trusted.

'When the media gets involved, things get nasty.'

Rodger let it rest for a moment.

Further into the lunch, he tried the Russia question again.

'If there's real stuff about Russia and Trump, right, what do you think Chris [Cox] will do?'

Graham hesitated.

'Why did you go back to that?'

'It's all I hear in Australia.'

'Are you kidding me?' Graham said. 'I don't know. We're *over* it. I have no idea.'

'But what would Chris do if it were proven?' Rodger persisted.

'Why do you keep going back to that?' Graham asked again. 'That's, like, complete shit. Nobody talks about it here. It's total crap. It's bullshit!'

Rodger decided to pull away from the subject altogether.

But it was too late. Something about the way he'd phrased his questions, something in the tone of his voice, had made Graham suspicious.

She stared at him across the lunch table and narrowed her eyes.

'What are you *up* to?'

Rodger was taken aback.

'Um, what do you mean?'

'I thought you were Australian,' she said.

'I *am* Australian.'

'You don't *sound* Australian.'

Colin tapped his foot against my ankle under the table.

Shit! What's going on?

'What *do* I sound like?' Rodger said, forcing a smile.

'*I* wouldn't know,' Graham answered. '*You* would know.' It was obvious now that Rodger's NRA lobbyist contact smelled a rat. Though his Aussie accent hadn't changed, she could sense that something about the Gun Rights Australia president didn't add up.

'Why do you ask that?' Rodger said. He shifted in his chair.

'I heard it earlier … you didn't have the same accent. So *that's* weird.'

Graham glared at Rodger.

'That's awfully strange,' she said slowly.

I felt like we were witnessing a twisted version of Sherlock Holmes on the verge of cracking a case.

Our case.

Colin looked at me.

Fuck.

'I'm going to go,' Graham said.

'I'm confused … I'm not quite sure what you mean.' Rodger was desperately trying to keep her at the table.

'Um, excuse me,' Graham said.

She pushed her chair back and stood up to leave.

* * *

Rodger and I had an escape plan.

We'd agreed at the beginning of Project Freedom that if his cover was blown, he was to head straight for the exits, carrying his hidden cameras.

I would then step in to engage with his targets, giving him a chance to get away.

If things weren't totally out of control by then, I planned to hand people my business card and explain Al Jazeera's undercover assignment, possibly passing them the contact details of our Washington-based lawyers.

If there was a risk of violence, I'd do my best to get to safety along with any accompanying crew members.

With Graham now on her feet, I looked over at Rodger.

Was it time for him to leave?

Or could he salvage this?

'Well, you don't have an *American* accent,' Rodger said, looking up at her from his chair.

Graham stopped.

'I *don't*? What kind of accent *do* I have?'

'I don't know …'

'All of a sudden you *changed*,' Graham said, 'your accent *changed*. It was kind of weird.'

'Why are you doing that? Why are you saying that?' Rodger tried to smile.

'It was weird,' Graham said again.

'Nah, you're being silly,' Rodger said.

Graham looked down at her chair.

Rodger smiled again and gestured for her to sit.

He was pulling it back.

Graham paused for a moment.

'Alright, I'll let it go.'

She sat back down.

***

The first real crisis of the assignment had passed.

Rodger was shaken, but he'd managed to stabilise the situation. And once he and Graham had settled back down to finish their lunch, she explained to him why she'd been spooked.

'I'm sorry. Just got a little paranoid for a little bit because that happens to us all the time.'

'*What* happens?' Rodger asked.

'I'm suspicious. I'm sorry … There's people who just want to take us out … I really have to be careful.'

'You had a little crazy moment,' Rodger said.

'I *did* have a crazy moment,' Graham replied, 'because shit happens to us a lot. It does, it happens to us regularly. We get crazy every day. We have a lot of crazy.'

'Crazies in your wheelhouse?' Rodger asked.

'We get a lot of crazy.'

The lobbyist would apologise another fifteen times to Rodger before they ended their lunch in Atlanta.

'It's okay,' he said to her. 'It's all good.'

Graham's paranoia would re-emerge at another lunch with Rodger, months later, her comments leaving my investigative team astonished and disturbed. But for now, at least, Rodger was safe.

* * *

On a muggy midmorning in late June 2017, I drove north along Washington's 14th Street and turned right onto Corcoran, looking for a parking spot close to my home nearby.

My phone rang.

The screen said 'Swisher'.

I pulled over to take his call.

'Hey, Peter, I have Phil Rees with me,' Clayton said.

That wasn't good. Whenever Clayton called with Phil in attendance, it was because a crisis of some kind required all three of us to talk together.

'I'll get straight to the point,' Clayton said. 'I've just reviewed the costings for Freedom. I'm shocked at what we're spending.'

'Um, okay,' I said.

'Like, this is way too much. *Way* too much!'

Phil chimed in.

'Hey, Peter, why don't we just ease off this for a while? You know, just let the costs drop a bit.'

'You want me to *stop*?'

'Well, cut the costs. Cut it back.'

'But that means we'll lose momentum. We're moving forward, now. Rodger's got contacts, we're getting great stuff here.'

There was silence from Doha.

'Hello?' I asked.

'Um, we want you to call Rodger and tell him we'll be using him less often. We're just spending too much flying him to America all the time,' Clayton said.

'Less *often*?' I asked.

'Yes. Less often. We can't sustain this spending. It's been a year and a half now.'

Clayton let that sink in for a moment, then gave a final order.

'Call Rodger today.'

He paused.

'And cut back his fees.'

Chapter 11

Our Trojan Horse was inside the gates; we had developed powerful contacts at a time when the NRA and the White House were working hand in hand. Rodger had met Wayne LaPierre and his deputy, Chris Cox, and he was working hard to do so again. The idea of scaling back the project at this point was a blow to everyone working on it.

'Hey, Rodger. You sitting down?'

I imagined how I might break the news of Clayton's call.

You've been doing a brilliant job. It's just amazing that you actually got to meet Wayne (shame about the bloody cameras), and I thought you handled Brandi's weirdness really, really well. Um, we're now going to cut your pay.

No, that wouldn't work.

Remember how I once told you we could access whatever funds we need to complete an investigation? Well, guess what?

Nope.

I dialled Rodger's number.

'Mate, we're putting the project on ice for a little while. Think of it as "suspended animation".'

'*What?!*'

'And when your contract comes up for renewal, we'll be paying you less.'

* * *

'Now standing in one corner of a boxing ring with a .22 calibre Colt automatic pistol, shooting a bullet weighing only 40 grains and with a striking energy of 51-foot pounds at 25 feet from the muzzle ...' Ernest Hemingway wrote in a piece published in *Hemingway on Hunting*.

'I have killed many horses with it, cripples and for bear baits, with a single shot, and what will kill a horse will kill a man. ... Yet this same pistol bullet fired at point blank range will not dent a grizzly's skull, and to shoot a grizzly with a .22 calibre pistol would simply be one way of committing suicide.'

Is this where I am now?

Am I the guy with the gun that can kill a man but not a grizzly?

Am I underequipped here?

Rodger had accepted the pay cut, and Claudianna Blanco had recalibrated her approaches to the NRA based on the order to 'ease off this for a while'.

But they were disheartened.

And the four members of the Washington Investigative Unit working with them on this project were disheartened, too. I told Rodger and Claudianna to keep posting material on the Gun Rights Australia website. If there was any hint to the NRA that the Australian group was flagging, Rodger's contacts might no longer consider him a significant force

in Australia – and everything we'd worked for would be at risk.

I was determined, I told them, to make sure we finished this project.

If I were to take down a grizzly, I needed a bigger gun.

I trawled the international papers, searching for references to the NRA.

* * *

Twelve weeks later, on 25 September 2017, Stephen Paddock arrived at Las Vegas' Mandalay Bay hotel and booked into adjoining suites 32-134 and 32-135.

Over several days, Paddock stocked the rooms with suitcases containing more than twenty guns along with bags of polymer-tipped hollow-point bullets and specially made, armour-piercing ammunition.

The guns Paddock took to the hotel were part of an arsenal of at least sixty-seven firearms that he is known to have purchased, including a number of Smith & Wesson 9mm semiautomatic pistols, a Glock 9mm semiautomatic pistol, several Mossberg twelve-gauge pump-action and semiautomatic shotguns, multiple AR-15 rifles fitted with bipods and scopes, two Arsenal Saiga 12 AK-47 style semiautomatic twelve-gauge shotguns, two Beretta 9mm semiautomatic pistols, an FN 5.7mm semiautomatic pistol, and a Remington Arms 870 Tactical twelve-gauge pump-action shotgun.

In his hotel room, he is reported to have had fourteen AR-15 rifles, eight AR-10 rifles, a .308 calibre bolt-action rifle and a Smith & Wesson revolver.[40]

Within view of Paddock's hotel-room window, twenty-two thousand people were gathering for the final night of the annual Route 91 Harvest country music festival in the outdoor Las Vegas Village lot, a 6.1-hectare space located about four hundred metres away from the Mandalay Bay.

Paddock stuffed paper tissue into his ears and attached a snorkel mouthpiece to a length of tubing, with a fan blowing air into a funnel at the other end – a device he had presumably constructed to help him breathe as he used a hammer to smash a hole in his hotel-room window and began, at 10.05 p.m. on 1 October, to shoot into the crowd below.

Within ten minutes, Paddock had killed 58 people and wounded 413 others, several critically.

As concertgoers scrambled for safety, many who were not hit by bullets or shrapnel suffered cuts, bruises, sprains and broken bones – taking the total number of injured to 869.

Video from the music festival shows people running in panic as police scream, 'Get down, get *down*!'

Gunfire crackles from the hotel.

A man shouts, '*Help* me! I'm *hit*!' as a woman nearby sits in silence, staring into the rushing crowds, while blood pools around her.

The concert ground is littered with cups, shoes, bottles, handbags, mobile phones, hats.

Lifeless bodies lie where they have fallen as Paddock strafes the panicked masses again and again and again.

Helicopters hover overhead, their searchlights raking the streets and nearby hotels in a frantic search for the killer.

Inside his room, with guns propped in a bathtub, scattered on couches, beds, floors, pillows and tables, Paddock fired more than 1100 rounds into the concert grounds.

Nearly ten minutes into the shooting, police identified the source of gunfire and dispatched a SWAT team to break down Paddock's door.

As they were approaching, he put the barrel of a Smith & Wesson handgun into his mouth and pulled the trigger.

The SWAT team found Paddock dead on the floor surrounded by a carpet of spent bullet shells, as the warm evening air rushed through the broken window and sent curtains billowing into the room.

He had just carried out the deadliest mass shooting by an individual in the history of the United States.

* * *

'We're with you one hundred per cent,' President Trump told a group of survivors of the massacre at a meeting at the Las Vegas University Medical Center three days after the shooting.

'He was a very demented person,' Trump said to journalists after the meeting.[41]

'I said, "If you're ever in Washington, come on over to the Oval Office,"' Trump said, referring to his discussion with survivors of the massacre. 'And they're all saying, "We want to do it." And, believe me, I'll be there for them. But the message that I have is that we have a great country, and we are there for you, and they're there for us.'

A journalist asked Trump about America's spiralling gun violence.

'We're not going to talk about that today,' the president answered.

* * *

I'd searched the internet, newspapers, and television and radio broadcasts around the world, looking for signs that the NRA was trying to export its philosophy to new territory abroad. I wanted to know whether they were actively involved in manipulating politics beyond the United States – using the lobby's help-them-or-hurt-them philosophy to seed new customer bases as gun violence consumed the US.

Then, on 17 November 2017, I found an article in a Queensland newspaper.

The *Sunshine Coast Daily*, based in Maroochydore and with a weekly circulation of 11,865, ran the headline: 'Gun Lobby Funding One Nation Candidates'.

The article said, 'Gun advocates affiliated with the American National Rifle Association are helping fund One Nation's return to Queensland politics and another shooters' body is paying for full-page ads urging voters to "flick" the major parties.'[42]

Could it be that the NRA had identified Pauline Hanson's One Nation Party as a political ally in Australia?

Were they using the party to gain a foothold in the place they despised for its gun control policies?

I called Rodger and asked him to find a way to access Hanson's party.

Chapter 12

Hanson was first elected to Parliament in 1996 – the same year the Liberal government introduced Australia's tough gun control laws. She entered the House of Representatives as an independent candidate, having earlier been disendorsed by the Liberal Party for divisive comments she'd made about Australia's Indigenous community.

In her maiden speech to the House, on 10 September 1996, Hanson railed against 'reverse racism' – which, she said, had emerged from over-the-top 'political correctness' in Australia.

Wearing a dark, military-style dress with gold buttons, her hair teased into a frozen flame, she spoke with both a confidence and a halting uncertainty – as if her anger had conjured much to say, but some of the words had stumbled on her tongue.

'I come here not as a polished politician but as a woman who has had her fair share of life's knocks,' she said.

'I am fed up to the back teeth with the inequalities that are being promoted by the government and paid for by the taxpayer under the assumption that Aboriginals are the most disadvantaged people in Australia.'[43]

The feisty single mother was calling it the way she saw it, unafraid to speak out about what she said she believed many Australians were secretly thinking.

Rivals in Canberra scrambled for ways to slow her political momentum, while much of the media adopted a type of sneering groupthink to portray her as a racist and a bigot.

When she was asked by a *60 Minutes* reporter whether she was xenophobic, Hanson stared blankly at the interviewer for a moment before saying, 'Please explain?'

The phrase stuck as a rallying call for Hanson's detractors; proof positive, they thought, that the newly elected MP was an ignorant buffoon, the laughing stock of Parliament.

But, like the voters who would later rally around Donald Trump, many in Australia's rural areas were offended by the ridicule of a woman they saw as someone who truly understood them. Hanson supporters identified with the 'fair share of life's knocks' that she'd referred to in her maiden speech. The fact that she'd left school at fifteen and had worked in a fish and chip shop was something that showed the MP to be more 'real' than the sniggering university-educated toffs who were so quick to write her off.

Pauline Hanson may not have been capable of penning a thesis on ethical non-cognitivism, she may not be able to solve the Riemann hypothesis, but she understood her constituents, she had the courage to speak her mind, and she didn't suffer fools.

Many voters believed that was good enough for them.

* * *

But while One Nation was a force to be reckoned with, a series of fierce internal struggles soon threatened to destabilise the party as Hanson clashed with staffers.

Liberal MP Tony Abbott helped fund anti-Hanson forces that alleged she and one of One Nation's co-founders had made false claims in an application for electoral funding.

In August 2003, a Queensland court found Hanson guilty of electoral fraud.

She was sentenced to three years in prison.

'Rubbish, I'm not guilty,' she said when the jury delivered its verdict.[44]

Hanson was so outraged by the prospect of entering jail that when she was asked to give her name to prison officials, she refused to answer.

A photograph of the disgraced MP from that day shows her standing before a bare brick wall, holding a mugshot ID card with the words:

BWCC. 21.08.03.
HANSON Pauline
27.05.54 C70079

After eleven weeks in custody, Hanson was released when her sentence was overturned on appeal.

Her reputation as a battler was never stronger. Her supporters saw her as the victim of a system that couldn't accept her popularity and would do anything it could to bring her down. To them, she was a truth teller in a world where political-correctness-gone-mad had turned good guys into bad guys, and right into wrong.

'I blame [former Australian prime ministers] Tony Abbott [and] John Howard for my imprisonment and no one will ever change my opinion on that,' Hanson later said.[45]

* * *

When Hanson rejoined One Nation in 2013 and took on the leadership again in 2014, she invited a young man into her inner circle who would go on to help her gain a seat in Parliament for a second time – now in the Senate.

The addition to her team was James Ashby, a trim, clean-cut Queenslander with a colourful background in media. His work as a radio presenter in Newcastle had ended abruptly in 2002 when he pleaded guilty to abusing a drivetime host from a rival station.

The *Daily Telegraph* reported that when the rival station's host told Ashby his call was being recorded, Ashby said, 'Yeah, go for it you fucking psychopath. Next time I see you riding on your fucking bike I'll hit you, you idiot, all over the sloppy road, you dumb prick. Fuck it, if I was your mother, I would have drowned you at birth.'

Ashby was fined $2060 and given a three-year good behaviour bond.

He claimed the call was 'a practical joke'.[46]

Later, as PR manager of a Queensland strawberry farm, 'Mr Ashby said that poison had been discovered in the property's water supply', the *Brisbane Times* reported in 2011.[47] Ashby was back in the headlines the following year when he alleged that he'd been sexually harassed by a federal MP, Peter Slipper, the speaker of the House of Representatives.

The sensational claims made their way to a Federal Court, where they were dismissed as 'an abuse of process' that had taken place 'for the predominant purpose of causing significant public, reputational and political damage to Mr Slipper'.[48]

Soon enough, Hanson's news-making recruit would create scandalous headlines involving One Nation too.

But James Ashby would prove to be someone Hanson would not wish to let go – no matter how damaging the news he generated.

* * *

In 2016 Hanson was elected to the Senate, leading her gun-friendly One Nation Party back into political relevance after she'd spent nearly twenty years in the wilderness.

Hanson's maiden speech to the Senate echoed the controversy of her first address to Parliament twenty years earlier, but she'd since identified new threats to Australia.

'Now, we are in danger of being swamped by Muslims,' she told the Senate in September 2016.

She said that if Muslim immigrants weren't prepared to fully embrace Australia's culture and way of life, they should 'go back to where [they] came from'.

'If it would be any help, I will take you to the airport and wave you goodbye.'[49]

She called for an immediate prohibition of Muslim immigration into Australia, and a ban on the burqa – comments that so offended senators from the Greens Party that they walked out of the chamber en masse, declaring later that they 'did not want to give any kind of legitimacy to her racist views'.[50]

In August of the following year, Hanson would cause a sensation in Australia by wearing a burqa into the Senate chamber – a further protest by her against the full-body Muslim dress.

The burqa stunt was Ashby's idea. The incident made people go 'ballistic', he would later say. 'Every senator, every senator went fucking wild, and it was mad. We proved something to the whole world ... we smashed it! It was a big day!'

Applauding the actions of Ashby and Hanson was another man who would play a critical role within One Nation.

Steve Dickson, formerly of the Liberal National Party, had joined Hanson's party in January 2017 as head of operations in Queensland, while throwing his hat into the ring as a Senate candidate.

Dickson brought to One Nation the valuable experience of having once worked as a minister in Queensland's state government.

He was also fond of guns.

Very fond of guns.

Dickson harboured a deep bitterness towards the federal government for taking away his firearms as part of the Port Arthur-inspired buy-back program, the National Firearms Agreement.

Years after he surrendered his weapons, Dickson would tell people that the memory of that moment still made him weep.

* * *

In September 2017, a month after the burqa incident, Hanson was videoed with Dickson shooting at targets at a firing range – with a cheery comment to camera that pumping hot lead out of a Glock was a *really fun* thing to do.

'Well, I've had the best day I've had for about twenty years,' Hanson says in the video.

'It's like *Dirty Harry*.'

She strides down the range, places a hand on her hip, and points to bullet holes in a cardboard target.

'Don't mess with me,' she says.

'Just make my day!'[51]

In the same video, One Nation's Queensland leader Steve Dickson stands rock-jawed, arms held in front of him, gripping a handgun. His hands jolt at the firearm's recoil as he squeezes off round after round.

From the moment that video was released, there could be no misunderstanding that One Nation was a pro-gun party.

Dickson used his video to help launch One Nation's 21-point firearms policy: a document headlined 'One Nation Will Stop Making Criminals out of Gun Owners', which sought to recast shooters as 'good guys' who'd been unfairly tainted by gun-phobic extremists.[52]

With Pauline Hanson squinting into the Queensland sun beside him, Dickson made the case for a streamlining of overly complex gun control laws, while arguing that police in Queensland should be able to practise with their service weapons at registered pistol clubs, and promising that One Nation would advocate for cops to tax-deduct ammunition.

'Sounds sensible, commonsense,' Hanson said.

* * *

Over the next several months, Rodger and Claudianna looked for ways to connect with One Nation's James Ashby. They knew that in order to avoid suspicion, the meeting had to appear to be 'organic'. Rodger joined One Nation's NSW branch, and looked through party correspondence for upcoming events where Ashby might be present. Then he spotted a meeting that was scheduled to take place in the western suburbs of Sydney. He finally had his opportunity.

Chapter 13

America's open sore was oozing again.

It was Saint Valentine's Day 2018, and there had been another school shooting. Another AR-15 had been used. Seventeen more US students were dead.

The incident had taken place at Marjory Stoneman Douglas High School in Florida's affluent Parkland – a town of some thirty-three thousand people just north of Fort Lauderdale and south of West Palm Beach.

The *New York Times* declared the massacre to be the 239th school shooting in America since the Sandy Hook atrocity.[54]

The killer, nineteen-year-old Nikolas Cruz, had been the subject of at least two tip-offs to the FBI and multiple 911 phone calls to police, including one prompted by an online message in which he said that he wanted to 'shoot up the school' and another in which he had written, 'I'm going to be a professional school shooter.'[55]

Cruz had also been reported to police for pressing a gun to the heads of his mother and his brother, for hitting his mother with a hose and for throwing her against a wall, for hurling a rock at another boy, for shooting a chicken with a BB gun, and for swallowing gasoline and cutting himself in an apparent effort to commit suicide.

The Broward County Sheriff said that one report from Cruz's peer counsellor noted that he was 'in possession of items concerning hate-related communications/symbols' and that he had expressed interest in acquiring a gun.[56]

Cruz had once been a student at Marjory Stoneman Douglas High School, but he had been expelled for what the school called 'disciplinary reasons'.

In spite of all these red flags, the clearly unstable teenager was able to walk into Sunrise Tactical Supply, a gun shop in Coral Springs, Florida, and purchase a Smith & Wesson M&P 15.223 – an AR-15-type assault rifle.[57] The gun shop had given Cruz a background check to determine whether he had a criminal history and whether a US court had ever found him to be 'mentally defective'.

Cruz passed the check.

'He was ticking none of those boxes,' said Peter Forcelli, from the Bureau of Alcohol, Tobacco, Firearms and Explosives in South Florida.

The rifle Cruz bought at Sunrise Tactical Supply would be used by him to carry out the massacre at his former high school.

* * *

An exhausted America once again began its bleak post-massacre ritual of mourning the murder of innocent children.

One blood-drenched event seemed to blur into another. And another into another into another.

I'd seen the nation go through this sick and tragic performance many times before, and I was beginning to feel a sense of resignation towards gun violence among my American friends and colleagues.

These mass shootings are hideous, yes. They're absolutely unacceptable, yes! But what can you do? America has the Second Amendment, after all ...

Killing after killing – including an event three months before the Parkland massacre in which a gunman shot dead 26 people and injured 20 others in a Texas church – could not seem to shake the NRA's core argument that guns made America a safer place. Though Trump had assured survivors of the Las Vegas mass shooting that, 'we have a great country, and we are there for you', it was obvious that firearms violence in America was getting worse. In fact, America's Pew Research Center had found a 14 per cent increase in firearms-related deaths in the US in 2017 from five years earlier. The Center reported that 44 per cent of Americans said they 'personally knew someone who had been shot, either accidentally or internationally' and that gun owners were more likely than non-gun owners to know someone who has been shot: 51 per cent versus 40 per cent.

Now, with news that yet another school shooting had taken place, America was being exposed once more to images of panic-stricken students streaming from their classrooms, photographs of shocked and grieving parents, and of flowers and condolence cards and mourners huddling by schoolyard fences.

New calls for gun control were met with accusations from the gun lobby that the media had again acted inappropriately in their reporting of the school killings.

'As usual, the opportunists wasted not one second to exploit tragedy for political gain,' the NRA's Wayne LaPierre told the Conservative Political Action Conference in National Harbor, Maryland, on 22 February 2018.

He condemned 'the break-back speed of calls for more gun control laws, and the breathless national media eager to smear the NRA'.

'They hate the NRA, they hate the Second Amendment,' he said. 'Their goal is to ... eradicate *all* individual freedoms.'[58] The Parkland massacre might have been swept away by another story – a Hollywood scandal, a freak weather event, an angry tweet from the president – as the news cycle churned.

But the survivors of *this* school shooting did not want news of their ordeal to slip away.

They formed protest groups and started a public push for a serious review of firearms legislation. There was an urgency and an anger to their message, and soon the students' rallies were leading US news broadcasts.

'[We wanted] to get on the news, to make sure people would not forget about this, and make them realise that this would not be just another mass shooting,' Parkland student David Hogg told MSNBC on 24 February 2018.

'This is the story of children being massacred as a result of NRA-backed politicians.'

Hogg derided the NRA's good-guy-with-a-gun-versus-bad-guy-with-a-gun mantra, and he called for reforms to the Second Amendment.

'We need limitations on the Second Amendment, just as we have limitations on the First,' he said.

'In the same way that you can't yell "fire" in a crowded theatre, you shouldn't be allowed to own an AR-15 if you're mentally ill. Think about it – you create a positive feedback loop where the more violence you create, the more guns you sell because people get afraid.

'And the more guns you sell, the more violence is created, that's really what's growing here. It's the amount of gun sales in this country, and that's what the NRA is trying to serve.'[59]

After the Sandy Hook massacre in 2012, Wayne LaPierre had argued for the 'hardening' of schools – calling for armed guards to protect students.

But there *was* an armed guard at Marjory Stoneman Douglas High School. Instead of challenging Nikolas Cruz, he stayed outside the school, waiting for help to arrive.

The good guy with a gun *hadn't* stopped the bad guy with a gun. And in a blustering defence of this good guy/ bad guy concept, the NRA – and its champion, Donald Trump – wrote the armed guard off as a 'coward'.

Trump even claimed that if *he'd* been tasked with protecting the Parkland students, he wouldn't have hesitated to enter the school in order to confront the gunman.

'I really believe I'd run in there, even if I didn't have a weapon,' he said at a 26 February 2018, White House meeting.[60]

As David Hogg and others from the high school organised a rally in Washington, which they called March for Our Lives, the NRA unleashed its myrmidons, hammering the schoolchildren who'd just witnessed their classmates being shot to death.

NRA spokesman Colion Noir, who had earlier proclaimed on NRATV that the mainstream media 'love mass killings', recorded a new video. In it, he taunts the shooting survivors for generating primetime coverage of their experience.

'They're running season five of their gun control reality show, featuring the freshest cast of characters yet in their modern-day march on Washington – except this time for less freedom.'

He adds that if the armed guard at Parkland had killed Nikolas Cruz, 'your classmates would still be alive and no one would know your names, because the media would have completely and utterly ignored your story'.

'These kids ought to be marching against their own hypocritical belief structures,' he says.

'They hate machines that cause death, and yet, hold on, no! You ain't never gonna take their cars away!'

What did he just say?

I tried to imagine the NRA meeting in which Noir's video message had been workshopped: 'These Parkland kids are really getting some serious airtime, we have to shut this down. So, how many were killed this time? Seventeen, huh? Some of the survivors drive cars, right? Okay, everyone, I've got it! We're going to call them *hypocrites*!'

* * *

Seven days after the Parkland school massacre, Donald Trump sat on a chair in the centre of a circle of visitors in the White House's State Dining Room to preside over a 'listening session' on the issue of gun violence.[61] Perched oddly on his chair, as if he might have been sitting on a lavatory, Trump assured the gathering that he was working to put an end, at last, to mass shootings in America.

'It's not going to be talk like it has been in the past,' Trump had said at the beginning of the session. 'It's been going on too long; too many instances. And we're going to get it done.'

A student named Justin Gruber took the microphone. 'I was born into a world where I never got to experience safety and peace. There needs to be a significant change in this country because this has to never happen again. There needs to be a change ... people need to feel safe.'

Gruber's father spoke next. 'It's not left and right, it's not political, it's a *human* issue,' he said. 'People are *dying*. And we have to stop this ... we cannot have our children die. This is just heartbreaking. Please.'

On a piece of White House stationery, Trump had written notes with a black Sharpie. Numbered one to five, the final note prompted him to say, 'I hear you.'

'Thank you,' Trump said, as the Grubers sat down.

Another man stood to talk. 'We're here because my daughter has no voice,' he said. 'She was murdered last week ... shot nine times ... We, as a country, failed our children. Nine/eleven happened once, and they fixed everything. How many schools, how many children have to get shot? All these school shootings, it doesn't make sense. *Fix it!* It should have been one school shooting and we should have fixed it. And I'm *pissed*. Because my daughter, I'm not going to see her again. She's not here. *She's not here.*'

The following week, on 28 February 2018, Trump held a meeting with politicians on school safety in which, in a discussion about whether to extend age limits for the purchase of firearms in the United States, he pointed to Republican Senator Pat Toomey and, chuckling, said, '*You're afraid of the NRA.*'[62]

'No, no, no, I think you underestimate the power of the gun lobby,' another at the meeting said to Trump.

'They *do* have great power, I agree with that,' the president answered. 'They have great power over *you* people. They have less power over me.' He smiled.

Just a week later, after a reported discussion with the NRA's Wayne LaPierre, Trump appeared to back off his push for a change to age restrictions.

'Yes, once again, Mr Trump's brave words prove to be meaningless as the White House unveils exactly what Trump wants to do about guns,' the *Washington Post* wrote in an editorial board opinion piece.[63] 'The plan, if you can call it that, is centered on a promise ... to help provide firearms training to school employees, a controversial idea long favored by the National Rifle Association but opposed by most teachers and school officials. Not the universal background checks that are needed, no ban on weapons of war, not even an increase in the legal age to buy certain weapons, something Mr Trump had said made sense but seems to have abandoned in the face of NRA opposition.'

* * *

Psychologist Dr Dorothy Espelage leaned forward in silence as she watched Noir's anti-Parkland video.

I'd travelled to Florida State University in October 2018 to ask her to analyse the message he'd given to America.

Dr Espelage, a professor of education and a world-renowned expert in bullying, hit pause and looked up from the screen.

'It just really kind of breaks my heart that we have to live this way,' she said.

'Attacking high school students for being advocates – isn't our country built on this? Freedom of speech and advocacy?

'And don't we want young people to take on these campaigns and be involved? I mean, this is what we *want* our students to do!'

She played the rest of Noir's video and looked up at me again.

'He kind of reminds me of people that deny Sandy Hook, he reminds me of people that deny the Holocaust.'

That the NRA, through Colion Noir, was attacking the Parkland survivors was 'sad and desperate', she said.

And it was feeding America's growing sense of vulnerability.

'The American Psychological Association just did a survey of stress in America among people aged between fifteen and twenty-four, and they found the number-one stress is fear of a mass shooting,' Dr Espelage said.

'We live in a state of fear and hatred and discrimination. Fearing one another ... fearing anybody that's different from us. And, to be honest ... *I'm* constantly waiting for that shooter to come out.

'When I lecture in a big hall and someone comes in late, I'm constantly thinking, *Is that going to be the shooter?*'

* * *

The Parkland students' march on Washington, which took place on 24 March 2018, drew crowds of several hundred thousand, including students from schools across America.

One by one, speakers from Parkland and other US schools took turns at the microphone to talk of the moments they realised a gunman was among them, hunting them, as they cowered under desks, in darkened rooms, in cupboards and corridors, desperately texting police, parents and friends for help.

Among the speakers was Emma Gonzalez, a nineteen-year-old student from Marjory Stoneman Douglas High School. She stepped to the podium with a shaved head, wearing torn jeans and a khaki jacket covered in badges and patches.

'In a little over six minutes, seventeen of our friends were taken from us,' Gonzalez said.

'Fifteen more were injured, and everyone, absolutely *everyone* in the Douglas community was forever altered. Everyone who was there understands. Everyone who's been touched by the cold grip of gun violence understands. For those who still can't comprehend, because they refuse to, I'll tell you where it went: six feet into the ground, six feet deep.'

Fighting tears, Gonzalez went on.

'Six minutes and twenty seconds with an AR-15, and my friend Carmen would never complain to me about piano practice.

'Aaron Feis would never call Kyra "Miss Sunshine".

'Alex Schachter would never walk into school with his brother Ryan.

'Scott Beigel would never joke around with Cameron at camp.

'Helena Ramsay would never hang around after school with Max.

'Gina Montalto would never wave to her friend Liam at lunch.

'Joaquin Oliver would never play basketball with Sam or Dylan.

'Alaina Petty would never.

'Cara Loughran would never.

'Chris Hixon would never.

'Luke Hoyer would never.

'Martin Duque Anguiano would never.

'Peter Wang would never.

'Alyssa Alhadeff would never.

'Jamie Guttenberg would never.

'Meadow Pollack would never ...'

Gonzalez stopped and stared into the crowd, then closed her eyes. Tears trickled down her cheeks.

She stayed that way, gripping the podium in silence, for more than four minutes while the crowd broke into a chant.

'Never again ... never again ... never again!'

***

Wayne LaPierre, chief executive and executive vice president of the National Rifle Association of America. *(Gage Skidmore/Wikimedia Commons)*

Charlton Heston, former president of the National Rifle Association of America, holds a rifle as he tells his audience that they can have his gun when they pry it 'from my cold dead hands.' *(Candice Towell/Getty Images)*

Rodger Muller at the National Rifle Association headquarters in Fairfax, Virginia, during one of his first excursions undercover in 2016. *(Al Jazeera)*

Rodger Muller greets National Rifle Association chief lobbyist, Chris Cox, at the NRA annual convention in Louisville, Kentucky, on 20 May 2016. *(Al Jazeera)*

Pauline Hanson wears a burqa in the Senate chamber on 17 August 2017 — the stunt was the idea of her chief of staff, James Ashby. *(Lukas Coch/AAP)*

Inside Al Jazeera's Investigative Unit 'bunker' in Washington, DC, Peter Charley reviews transcripts of covertly-recorded conversations between Rodger Muller, the NRA and One Nation. *(Al Jazeera)*

A man browses a display of AR–15 variant rifles at a gun shop in Utah, United States. A semi-automatic civilian variant of the military M16, the AR–15 has gained a dark reputation as the mass shooters' weapon of choice. *(George Frey/Getty Images)*

'March For Our Lives' student protestors in Los Angeles hold portraits of students killed in the mass shooting at Florida's Marjory Stoneman Douglas High School in February 2018. *(Mark Ralston/Getty Images)*

Rodger Muller's first encounter with James Ashby at a One Nation gathering in Penrith, NSW, on 5 May 2018. *(Al Jazeera)*

Undercover vision of Claudianna Blanco greeting Steve Dickson as he arrives in Washington, DC, on 3 September 2018. *(Al Jazeera)*

Rodger Muller and James Ashby pose next to a stuffed lion at the Congressional Sportsmen's Foundation annual meeting in Washington, DC, on 5 September 2018. *(Al Jazeera)*

Undercover vision of Steve Dickson, Rodger Muller and James Ashby, taken from inside the car used to drive the One Nation visitors around Washington, DC in September 2018. *(Al Jazeera)*

Claudianna Blanco, Rodger Muller and James Ashby talk with a guest at the Congressional Sportsmen's Foundation annual meeting in Washington, DC, on 5 September 2018. *(Al Jazeera)*

Rodger Muller poses for a photograph with Senator Pauline Hanson in Penrith, NSW, on 5 May 2018. *(Al Jazeera)*

Steve Dickson and James Ashby hold a media conference in Brisbane on 26 March 2019, to condemn the release of Al Jazeera's documentary *How to Sell a Massacre*. *(Dave Hunt/AAP)*

Senator Pauline Hanson breaks down in tears during a 30 April 2019 interview on Channel Nine's *A Current Affair* after the resignation of Steve Dickson from the One Nation party. *(Nine)*

Gonzalez's speech galvanised America's gun control community and drew offers of support for the Parkland students from across the US. New York–based advertising executive and filmmaker Michael Skolnik was so moved by what he heard, he offered his services for free to help the student protesters to spread their anti-gun message.

'I didn't know who [Emma Gonzalez] was, never heard of her before,' he said to me as we sat together in a room in Dumbo, Brooklyn, overlooking New York's East River. A storm was howling into the city, driving snow onto the streets below us.

Skolnik said he heard Gonzalez speaking at the rally while listening to news of the event that day on his car radio in New York City. 'And I felt like I was listening to [Martin Luther] King on the steps of the Lincoln Memorial. I felt like I was listening to Lincoln's Gettysburg Address. I was listening, you know, to the sixties debate between Kennedy and Nixon. I felt this was a moment in American history that might actually do something remarkable.'

The NRA, meanwhile, had taken to Facebook where it tried to blunt the force of the students' potent gathering in the capital.

'Today's protests aren't spontaneous,' the NRA said.

'Gun-hating billionaires and Hollywood elites are manipulating and exploiting children as part of their plan to DESTROY the Second Amendment and strip us of our right to defend ourselves and our loved ones.'

The same group that promoted the sale of functioning miniature rifles with candy-pink trimmings – to appeal to young girls – was now decrying the manipulation and exploitation of children.

While accusing Parkland's shooting survivors of being hypocrites.

'So, you want to attack a teenager who went through a *school shooting*?' Skolnik said, his voice rising. 'That's who your *enemy* is, now? A school-shooting survivor? It's pathetic! It's *pathetic*!' He stopped and took a deep breath.

'I mean, if you take the position that the movement is not *organic*, then the [Parkland] shooting didn't happen,' Skolnik went on. 'And if you're saying it didn't happen, then it's *fake*.'

'The fact that Wayne LaPierre can sleep at night is bewildering to me,' he said. 'This is a corporate lobbyist. In the same way that the tobacco industry told you you're not going to get cancer if you smoke my cigarettes ... they *lied* to you, and we know they lied to you. We *know* tobacco causes cancer. And what we're going to find out very soon is that an AR-15 is the weapon of choice for a mass shooter. And that weapon should not be on the streets of this country.'

The blizzard swirled outside, blurring the Manhattan skyline, as Skolnik's voice swelled with rage. 'Here's the hypocrisy of the NRA: do they advocate for the ownership of *tanks*? Do they advocate for the ownership of *RPGs*? Do they advocate for the ownership of *bazookas*? No, they *don't*, because they know those things kill! So why can someone own an AR-15? *Think* about it. You can't legally own a tank in America. You can't legally own a nuclear weapon. *Why?* Why do we have restrictions on those, but not restrictions on an AR-15?'

Skolnik shook his head.

'They've had *enough!*' he said, wearily, referring to all gun violence survivors. 'They've *had enough* – and they're going to tell you to your face, Wayne LaPierre, that you're pedalling *bullshit!* And if that's painful, look in the mirror and ask yourself if it's *truthful*. Because oftentimes, truthfulness is the *most* painful.'

Behind him, New York's skyline disappeared into a blanket of white.

Chapter 14

Rodger Muller walked into the Penrith Panthers club, on the western edge of Sydney, and made his way to One Nation's Annual General Meeting inside. He was finally at the event he had identified as giving him a chance to meet Pauline Hanson's chief of staff, James Ashby. It was 5 May 2018, and the gathering was taking place in a room decorated with balloons and streamers, and with a coloured disco light strobing onto the walls and ceiling. Overlooking a stage at the end of the room was a plasma TV screen, playing images of an Australian flag rippling in the breeze.

Beside the screen, clutching a microphone, stood Pauline Hanson. 'I'm like a bloody old dog,' she told the gathering, describing her tenacity in the cage-fight world of Australian politics. 'You don't forget.'

A couple of dozen people, sitting at a cluster of black cloth–shrouded tables on the floor below let out a patter of applause.

Rodger spotted James Ashby on a chair at the edge of the room. Rodger scanned the crowd, hoping Steve Dickson might also be there. But Dickson wasn't in attendance that day. If Ashby was listening to Hanson's speech, he hardly showed it; he stared at the screen of his smart phone as she spoke, lifting his head only occasionally to scan the room, as if looking for dissenters.

'I know how to do critical strategy and how to be diplomatic these days,' Hanson told the crowd, with a wry grin. She was working a sympathetic audience. Blue-collar and proud of it, 'the Riff' – as locals call Penrith – is a place where a sense of hardship and alienation had once bonded its people to the policies of the Labor Party, but which was now showing signs of being open to political change.

As if Hanson could smell opportunity, her message to the crowd was clear: One Nation understands you. Vote for us, stand by us, and we will stand by you too.

Those listening could sense an honesty, a *sincerity*, in the One Nation leader.

Pauline Hanson wasn't looking down on them the way others sometimes did, an audience member told Rodger. She seemed to fit right in here in the working-class west.

Another member of the audience stood to make a comment. 'There's a problem in America with the leftists hijacking American society,' he said. 'They're doing the same thing here, and I blame the *universities* for it!'

Hanson agreed, suggesting that cherished public holidays were now at risk. 'I'm sure if we took a vote out to them, Labour Day would go before Anzac Day and Australia Day goes. Australians have been so apathetic for that long – she'll be right, mate.'

More applause.

'And we have the "tall poppy syndrome" in this country as well,' she went on. 'You cut anyone down who puts their head up. Or you're frightened to say anything because you're called "racist".'

She took the opportunity to declare her admiration for the new leader of America. 'We were very pleased to see the election of Donald Trump,' she said. 'My office was outside on the front of Parliament House, toasting his election even before the last three seats were declared because we believed he was going to win it!'

When the senator finished, James Ashby moved to the back of the room. Rodger stood and walked towards him.

This was Rodger's first public meeting since I'd cut his salary and placed Project Freedom into 'suspended animation' eleven months earlier. I had told him that if we could establish that the NRA was finding its way into Australian politics – through One Nation or any other political party – we would have a whole new investigative strand to explore.

If not, we would continue trying to reconnect Rodger to Wayne LaPierre and others in the US gun lobby, then look for evidence of international influence through those channels.

'G'day, Rodger Muller, Gun Rights Australia,' he said as he approached James Ashby. He shook Ashby's hand. 'Got a minute for a chat?'

* * *

The two men walked to a quiet corner of the room and got straight to business. Rodger declared he was passionately pro-gun and keen to push for the reform of legislation that discriminated against law-abiding gun owners in Australia.

Ashby listened with interest.

Rodger said he'd travelled several times to the United States, and that he'd made high-level friends at the NRA, the Congressional Sportsmen's Foundation and other gun lobby organisations there.

He paused to gauge Ashby's reaction.

At the mention of the NRA, Ashby told Rodger, 'They're powerful people, I should really go to America to meet them.'

He asked if Rodger could help set up meetings for him.

'We should plan a trip lasting a week,' Ashby said, adding that he wanted to make the trip to meet Rodger's contacts 'soon'.

My question about whether the NRA had made contacts with One Nation was answered immediately: clearly, no connection existed at that time. But Ashby's eagerness to connect with the organisation – and his suggestion that he travel to America to meet them – was revealing. Even with One Nation presenting itself as gun-friendly, it struck me as odd for the party to seek a relationship with a gun lobby in the US tainted by a seemingly never-ending series of mass shootings. (The US Gun Violence Archive would register another twenty-eight mass shootings in America in May 2018 alone.)

Ashby reached for his phone and gave Steve Dickson's number to Rodger. Could Rodger make contact with Dickson, he asked, to keep this conversation going?

But Dickson got in first: his call to Rodger came through around 8.30 a.m. the next day.

'James told me all about you,' Dickson said. 'Can we get together?'

* * *

Ashby texted Rodger later that day to make sure he and Dickson had connected.

Rodger responded 'yes'.

Further phone calls between Dickson and Rodger followed, which led to the two arranging to meet for lunch a few weeks later at Dickson's Sunshine Coast house. While he was there, Rodger would film a segment for the Gun Rights Australia website which was, at that time, attracting hundreds of visitors weekly. The subject? One Nation's new firearms policy.

Dickson was only too happy to help.

It seemed like a classic win–win. Rodger would get new gun-related material for his website from Dickson, and Dickson would get publicity for his new gun policy from Rodger.

Dickson was eyeing a third win from the relationship: he believed that if he played his cards right, he could pick up valuable contact information from Rodger on the cashed-up political donors in America who'd helped put Trump into the White House.

What could possibly go wrong?

* * *

Steve Dickson had held the position of Minister for National Parks, Recreation, Sport and Racing in the Queensland government during his tenure with the Liberal National Party under premier Campbell Newman.

He'd also served as a member of the Parliamentary Crime and Misconduct Commission, an independent government entity designed to reduce major crime and to combat misconduct in the state's public sector.

In January 2017, declaring that Queensland's two major political parties in the state had 'lost their way' and needed to 'grow a backbone', Dickson had defected from the Liberal National Party to One Nation, his move angering members of the party he'd abandoned. 'This is all about Steve Dickson and Pauline Hanson playing the types of political games that Queenslanders are sick of,' LNP leader Tim Nicholls said. 'They didn't vote for Dickson to change horses midway through a political term.'[64]

Dickson claimed his move was largely motivated by a lack of enthusiasm for his calls for an amnesty for people using medicinal cannabis. 'The only politician in this country that came and offered me any help is standing beside me – Senator Pauline Hanson,' Dickson said the day he announced his switch to One Nation. 'I am a proud Queenslander, but at the moment I am not proud because we are letting children suffer.'

The LNP struck back, accusing Dickson of 'using the suffering of poor families and kids' to justify his defection to Hanson's party.

While Pauline Hanson claimed she had nothing to do with tempting the former minister to join One Nation, she said a man like Dickson gave her party renewed strength as she moved to give the major parties 'hell'. 'They won't know what happened to them,' she said.

* * *

Rodger entered Steve Dickson's Sunshine Coast house on 9 June 2018 with his 'communications director' Claudianna Blanco, using her undercover name 'Diana Armatta', and a freelance cameraman he introduced as Neil.

Rodger said Neil was a local wedding videographer who picked up a little extra cash here and there with jobs in the neighbourhood – including the interview he was about to shoot for the GRA website.

In fact, Neil was working undercover for me too. His real name was Adrian Billing, and for the past eleven years he'd been a video editor for Al Jazeera in Doha. As Adrian had recently relocated to Brisbane, he was perfectly positioned to join Project Freedom to help with our hidden-camera operations in Australia. He was also collating and managing video data in preparation for the investigative documentary that he would eventually end up editing.

But as a relative newcomer to working under a false name, he almost blew the operation within minutes of entering Dickson's house. 'Steve, this is Neil,' Rodger said, gesturing to the man lugging camera gear through the door.

Adrian went to shake Dickson's hand. 'Hi, my name's Adrian,' he said.

Dickson looked confused. 'He's a *cameraman*, mate,' Rodger said, winking at Dickson. 'These blokes don't know whether they're Arthur or Martha.'

Dickson smiled as if to acknowledge the weirdness of the moment, while Adrian busied himself finding somewhere to place the tripod.

Rodger had saved the moment. But then he made a slip of his own. Though Claudianna – known as 'Claude' to her friends – was using 'Diana Armatta' as her undercover name, Rodger called, 'Hey, Claude!' within Dickson's earshot.

Again, Dickson looked bewildered. Rodger, Claudianna and Adrian could imagine Dickson thinking, *Wasn't she just introduced to me as 'Diana'?*

For the second time that morning, Rodger tap-danced his way out of trouble. He turned to Claudianna. 'Diana, *Claude* called me today … you know, Claude from the NRA? Remind me later to tell you what he said.'

Deep breaths, everyone …

The team worked in tense silence as they completed the set-up for the interview.

* * *

Rodger's on-camera questions to Dickson gave the One Nation politician all the time he needed to tout the party's new firearms policy. And Dickson's comments opened the door to the idea of One Nation moving Australia's firearms laws closer to those in America. Dickson told Rodger that he wanted to find 'practical, sensible' ways to close the gap between gun laws in both countries to allow 'more [Australians] to actually get involved in shooting'.

At the end of the officially on-camera talk, Rodger shook Dickson's hand and thanked him for his time.

'Champion!' Dickson replied. 'Thank you for yours.' One Nation's Queensland leader seemed pleased to have had a chance to deliver a message via an emerging pro-gun platform in Australia, but his real agenda with Rodger would only emerge when the cameras were turned off.

Or when *he* thought they were.

After the interview, the two men retired to a local pub. Over beers, with Rodger's concealed cameras rolling, Dickson laid out some thoughts on how the founder and president of Gun Rights Australia might help One Nation gain a political advantage in Australia's upcoming elections.

If Rodger could help persuade the National Rifle Association to spend money promoting One Nation online, the party could avoid being seen receiving financial contributions from what many Australian voters viewed as a malign foreign entity.

'If we could get a million fucking US dollars towards social media, I don't even *need* the money, I just need the grunt,' Dickson said. 'If we get the grunt of that social media supporting us, I don't need to *touch* the money.'

He suggested that he'd just need to supply the NRA with One Nation promotional material as online content – and let the US gun lobby take care of matters from there. 'They're a third party, punching this shit in,' he said. 'We're giving them the stuff, and they're punching it in. I don't need any more than that.' He smiled at Rodger. 'There's the trick.'

As if to reassure Rodger, Dickson spelled out the credentials he believed he possessed that would help a plan like this come off. 'I'm very fortunate that it's *experience* ...

I've been a minister in government. I'm really fortunate because I was on a committee within Parliament called the Parliamentary Crime and Misconduct Committee. It's bad shit. I'm never going to jail, eh? It won't happen. Because I walk the knife.'

Chapter 15

The pub talk with Dickson made it clear that One Nation viewed Gun Rights Australia as a conduit to a whole new field of political influence.

Soon, Dickson would reveal more detail of the party's vision for a bond with the NRA – with more detail on money they were hoping to extract from the association.

Rodger was invited to One Nation's Queensland headquarters in Brisbane for another talk. With cameras hidden in his coat and Akubra, he entered the skyscraper at the edge of the Brisbane River on the morning of 27 August 2018, and took the lift to the thirty-sixth floor.

As he stepped out of the elevator, James Ashby was waiting to greet him. 'Hi, good to see you.'

Inside One Nation's office, Rodger was met by an excited Steve Dickson, keen to make it clear just how much he wanted to connect to the NRA. And how much he wanted the NRA to *like* him for doing so. 'I don't want to go over there and piss them off because that's not the reason we're going there,' he said. 'We're going there to work with them, and we can talk their language about how we want women to be able to defend themselves in this country. At the moment, we've got governments in place who'll let in fuckers from every country in the world that might kill us!'

Dickson looked at Rodger for a moment before asking for guidance on how best to manage his communication with the NRA. 'What language? Do they like straight up and down stuff?' he asked.

'Absolutely, they're straight up and down people,' Rodger said.

'I can give 'em that with tomato sauce,' Dickson replied, looking somewhat relieved.

With Ashby sitting to his side, watching and listening, Dickson turned to the issue of political donations from America. At first, he wanted Rodger to confirm that the US energy giant Koch Industries had given hundreds of millions of dollars to Donald Trump's campaign for the presidency.

'Eight hundred million dollars in the last election campaign in the United States, mate, is that true?' he asked, leaning forward in his chair a little.

'The Koch brothers put in $886 million into the Republican Party in 2016,' Rodger answered.

'Fuck!' Dickson said.

On the possibility of One Nation securing money from the NRA, Dickson made his views perfectly clear. 'Brutally honest, we are making this trip over there because of yourself and also, mate, we want to get funding,' he said. 'I mean, that is really the nuts and bolts, because we can change everything in this country if we can make that happen'

He leaned forward again, staring intensely at Rodger. 'This is the thing I want to get through your head. If they threw ten million dollars at us, we could fucking win a heap of seats, plus a shitload of seats in the Senate.'

But Dickson acknowledged that the trip carried political risk. 'I mean, we're very close to a federal election, and the last thing we want is the Greens and Labor and everybody dragging us over the coals and going, "Look, [Hanson] wants to kill people in schools in Australia." That's what they'll say.'

And then Dickson made a staggering proposal that, if realised, seemed certain to shake the foundations of Australian politics: he suggested that the NRA establish a political branch in Australia.

'There's no reason why they can't do something over here to set up some sort of foundation that they could do something in Australia,' he said. 'Buy a fucking massive big property and do the same thing [as duck hunters in the US], bring people over from the United States on fucking shooting safaris. I think we need to explain to them this is about politics, this is about changing, getting a political wing in Australia, and actually working hand in glove with the United States in a way that the United States thinks. Because I want to be in bed with the United States and I say that unashamedly, and I don't think Pauline's too much different.'

Though Hanson had openly expressed support for Donald Trump, I wondered whether Steve Dickson's comments about her also 'wanting to be in bed' with America truly represented her views. To confirm that, we'd need to reach Hanson herself. But Rodger knew that would take time.

Dickson went on. 'We *love* America. I said this to James this morning. I said, "I feel so passionate about America, sometimes I want to *be* an American." They believe in their *country*. What fallback countries in the world does the United States really have that are like us?'

His question may have been rhetorical, but Rodger answered anyway.

'Well, England and Australia are the two greatest allies, aren't they?'

At the mention of England, Dickson pulled a face as if repulsed by the word. 'But the weather conditions here are a whole lot better than fucking England,' he said. 'And England's been taken over by Muslims, so I reckon we've got to rate number one.'

He then asked for Rodger to arrange for him to visit America's presidential mansion. 'I wouldn't mind getting to have a look around the White House.'

Ashby said Australia's ambassador to the US might help, but Dickson jumped in with another suggestion. 'Congressmen could be a better idea because they're in there, they *live* in there.'

'*Do* they?' Rodger asked.

'They can fucking do whatever they like, mate.' Dickson proclaimed. 'Otherwise you wait in a queue for four hours just to see if you're lucky enough to get in.'

'We're not going to do *that*,' Rodger said.

'*I* don't want to, that's why I'm putting the heat on you now. If you can line that up for us, that would be good.' Dickson leaned back in his chair, delivering a finality to what he'd just said.

Rodger sat for a moment, digesting Dickson's words. It seemed the One Nation politician held the views that America would be prepared to downgrade the UK as a strategic ally based on England's climate and number of Muslim immigrants, that members of the US Congress reside in the White House, and that Rodger was in a position to help secure ten million US dollars for One Nation from the NRA, while working with them to set up an NRA 'political wing' in Australia.

Rodger reached into his coat and touched the camera. Yep, it was rolling.

Dickson steamed on, turning to the lessons he'd learned as a government minister, and the way he now understood how easy it was to change legislation. 'Once I found out about regulation ...'

He was talking about Queensland government provisions that allowed for alterations to laws that aren't subjected to parliamentary scrutiny.

'How easy it was?' Rodger asked.

'Get out of my way, mate!' Dickson said, smiling. 'I didn't know you could do it! And once you find out, mate, it's like finding the genie's lamp!'

'Kid in the candy store?' Rodger suggested.

'Yeah,' Dickson replied, 'you can do *anything*. I was changing shit all the time, it was great!'

Rodger raised the idea of One Nation rewriting politically sensitive firearms laws in Australia. Though everyone in the room understood the potential for a softening of gun laws causing an outcry in Australia, Rodger offered a suggestion for how such changes might be approached. 'If you're packaging it up with some other *good* laws that people will support ...'

Ashby finished the sentence for him. '... You bury it.'

Before Rodger left, Dickson delivered him a final word of encouragement. 'Mate, you make this shit happen, mate, and I'll open any fucking door you need open if we're in a position to do so.'

As Rodger walked back to the lifts, he glanced down at the Brisbane River. It glistened in the sun as it snaked its way through the city. He thought of the old tourism ad that once drew hordes to the state from the country's cooler south.

'Queensland.

'Beautiful one day.

'Perfect the next.'

As undercover stings go, the one he'd just accomplished couldn't have been better.

He stepped out of the building into the heat and phoned me. 'Stand by for a visit from Ashby and Dickson.'

I called my Washington team together and told them to prepare our hidden cameras.

* * *

It was now obvious that Project Freedom was no longer just an investigation into the activities of the NRA. An Australian political party was actively seeking funds from the US gun lobby to influence its chances of success in an upcoming federal election. And my undercover team was right in the middle of it.

Twice now, Rodger had recorded Dickson mentioning money as a motivator for connecting with the US gun lobby: the 'million dollars' he had suggested the NRA spend promoting One Nation online, and the 'ten million dollars' he calculated could win his party seats in Parliament's upper and lower houses.

Multiple additional references to money would follow. Soon, Dickson would attach his request for cash to a sentiment that the American gun lobby very much wanted to hear: that he was open to softening the gun laws that the NRA had so vehemently criticised.

The connection was unmistakable. Political donations to One Nation could lead to the party gaining power in Parliament – possibly even landing Dickson a seat in the Senate. If that were to happen, the party would be in a position to change the laws that Dickson had declared were so harsh they'd brought tears to his eyes.

With a US visit now coming into focus, both Ashby and Dickson encouraged Rodger to line up meetings for them in America with contacts he'd developed in the two years he'd been working undercover there.

For Roger, it was a simple matter of picking up the phone and calling his gun lobby 'friends'. He had maintained contact with NRA executives, lobbyists, gun makers and many others he'd met at functions, gun shows and shooting parties. Many in US gun lobby circles now saw him as an ally, reassured by his regular visits to the US and impressed that he was prepared to risk scorn at home by advocating for gun reform in Australia. Even the NRA's second in command, Chris Cox, knew Rodger well enough to slap his shoulder to say hello at a skeet-shooting event in Maryland the previous year.

Rodger's calls to his contacts carried an enticing message: a firearm-friendly Australian political party was planning a visit to America to meet gun lobby heavyweights. Would anyone care to talk with them?

Soon, Rodger struck gold. One of his contacts, America's powerful Congressional Sportsmen's Foundation, told Rodger it would supply him with four tickets to its twenty-ninth annual banquet and auction in Washington, DC, slated to take place at the Capitol Hill Hyatt Regency on Wednesday, 5 September 2018.

Rodger had already attended a CSF event: the carnival-like gathering at the Childress vineyard in Virginia the previous year. It was there that both of his hidden cameras failed, preventing him from capturing vision of his meeting with Wayne LaPierre. This time around, there would be no such slip-ups.

The Congressional Sportsmen's Foundation, a highly influential gun lobby group which receives donations from the NRA,[65] was the perfect organisation through which Dickson and Ashby could make contact with members of US Congress along with key gun lobbyists and firearms manufacturers from around America, many of whom would be in attendance. Not only that, Rodger had also arranged for Ashby to address the function. The CSF told him that it was so keen to learn about One Nation's new vision for Australia's gun laws that it was prepared to offer Ashby a five-minute speaking spot at the event. The solid gold opportunity had just been sprinkled with diamonds.

Ashby accepted the invitation and started drafting a speech.

Rodger set up additional meetings with NRA executives he had befriended – including the Grassroots Division's director Glen Caroline, who had helped Rodger attend the Trump phone drive in Toledo, Ohio, in the lead-up to the US presidential election.

And Rodger had arranged for Dickson and Ashby to spend time with Brandi Graham, the woman who'd gone 'a little crazy' over lunch in Atlanta, accusing Rodger of faking his Australian accent.

With the Australia-meets-America mission now looking solid, and with the scent of gun lobby cash in the air, Ashby and Dickson purchased their airfares to Washington.

Chapter 16

Rodger and Claudianna flew ahead and were waiting at Washington, DC's Ronald Reagan National Airport when Dickson and Ashby arrived on the afternoon of 3 September 2018. It was Rodger's sixth visit to America for the undercover assignment. His family had again accepted his word that he was travelling to expand his dog food business abroad.

For this crucial part of the investigation, Claudianna would also secretly record video of the One Nation visit, her first time working in this capacity. Posing as 'Diana Armatta', Rodger's 'communications director', she would accompany him, Ashby and Dickson around the city with cameras concealed in her dress and handbag, another in a water bottle and a fourth in her phone. When I asked whether she was prepared to take this extra step into subterfuge, she thought for a moment before answering, 'if you need me to do it, I'm onboard'.

Rodger was glad to have the back-up. While filming undercover by himself had become second nature, he was well aware that there could be no mistakes, no missed opportunities, no failing cameras while One Nation mingled in this coming week with some of the most powerful gun lobbyists in the world. Claudianna's extra cameras would not only ensure that nothing was missed, but they would also give the investigation vision, for the first time, of Rodger as he interacted with the gun lobbyists and the One Nation visitors. Since they started working together at the beginning of 2016, Rodger and Claudianna had become very good friends. Rodger was pleased to have his trusted comrade now operating hidden cameras with him.

'We've got a very busy week coming up,' Rodger told Ashby and Dickson as they wheeled their bags out of the airport.

'*Good!*' Dickson said. 'Busy is good.' At the age of fifty-six he had never been to America before, and he was brimming with excitement as he loaded his bags into the back of Rodger's rented Chevy Tahoe SUV.

Rodger had earlier said he was happy to make his car and driver available to the One Nation visitors whenever they wanted to move around Washington during their seven-day stay. They'd happily accepted his offer.

The driver of the car was introduced to them simply as 'Colin'.

'I hire the same chauffeur every time I'm here,' Rodger said. 'Seems to know his way around the joint.'

In fact, the driver – dressed in a dark suit and tie – was Colin McIntyre, the Investigative Unit cameraman who had demonstrated such skill stitching hidden cameras into Rodger's and Claudianna's clothing.

In preparation for Ashby and Dickson's visit, Colin had spent the past day rigging the SUV with concealed cameras. Over the next week, as many as nine hidden cameras would be operating at once, capturing hundreds of hours of video of Dickson and Ashby as they rode in the car, sat in meetings, ate in restaurants, drank in bars and walked the city streets.

'Hello, Colin,' Dickson said as he slid into one of the seats behind the driver.

'Good afternoon, sir,' Colin said. 'Welcome to Washington.' He turned on the ignition and pulled away from the terminal.

A second car, which had been parked behind Colin's SUV, pulled from the kerb at the same time and followed the Tahoe into traffic. Inside that second car was Nic Dove, one of the Investigative Unit's video editors, and cameraman Craig Pennington, who'd been tasked with capturing car-to-car vision of the delegation's journey through the capital.

With Nic driving, Craig filmed discreetly through the windshield as Dickson and Ashby took an impromptu tour of the city. 'I'm in a country where you're allowed to own guns, so I'm pretty happy.' Dickson beamed as Colin turned towards the National Mall. 'What do they call that big thing in the middle there, that big spear?'

'The obelisk?' Colin said. 'That's the Washington Monument.'

Dickson and Ashby craned to take in the sights, snapping photos on their mobile phones, as Colin cruised around the Mall, finally pulling into the One Nation visitors' hotel driveway.

They had arrived. They were thrilled. And they were bursting to talk about what lay ahead for them in the US capital.

Rodger and Claudianna suggested that they all catch up at the hotel that evening, and the others agreed; with such a busy week in store, there was much to discuss.

Dickson and Ashby unloaded their bags from the car, thanked Colin for driving them from the airport, and walked briskly into the hotel lobby.

The first tranche of video of the One Nation visit was in the can.

* * *

Hours later, the four were back together.

'So, what do you really want to achieve this week?' Rodger asked Ashby as they sipped a beer at the hotel bar.

'If there are people here who are willing to back us with either ground support, if the NRA wants to rally their supporters within Australia, that's one start,' Ashby replied. 'Two, I'd love to get my hands on their software. And three, if they can help us with donations, super!'

Ashby declared his admiration for the NRA-friendly president who now occupied the White House, and he praised Trump's combative press secretary, Sarah Huckabee Sanders, who had been drubbed by mainstream news organisations for lying to journalists and for denigrating the press. Sanders had once told a gathering of journalists, for example, that 'countless' FBI officials had told her they were happy that President Trump had fired FBI chief James Comey.

That was a lie.[66]

She'd also told the media that Trump hadn't dictated the administration's response to news that his eldest son, Donald Jr, had met with a Russian operative in 2016.

That was also a lie.[67]

A year later, in late 2019, Sanders would say President Trump 'reads more than anybody I know'.[68]

Did she *seriously* believe that?

'I really like that young girl that Trump's got working for him that does his media,' Ashby said. 'I really like her. Young Sarah, I forget her last name. But I tell you what, she's been thrown in the deep end, and she's swum fucking hard to the point where she's making a name for herself because she's bloody good.' He added, 'That's what *we* do. We don't follow the press. I don't let them too close to me and I don't let them anywhere near [Pauline].'

'Oh, no, she needs some protection for sure,' Rodger said.

'Yeah, and see that's why they're all assholes,' Ashby said.

Thinking he was in the company of like-minded, press-averse comrades, Ashby relayed an anecdote about a recent approach to One Nation by Facebook.

'Don't tell people this, but I was [contacted] a couple of months ago by the head of Facebook in Australasia,' he said. 'Don't put that out publicly.'

'No, not at all,' Rodger assured him.

'They said, "We want to meet with you in Canberra,"' Ashby continued. 'They came to the office, and Pauline was in the office … and they sat down and they had this whole presentation for us. And they said, "Senator, your page is the most viewed Facebook page of any politician or any political party in this country."'

He looked around the group with a sense of pride.

'And they said, "[Ashby's] driving this … we can see what he does. We understand what he does. We just want to know why he does this because he's just hitting all the right buttons and we can't explain to other senators or any others because they just don't get it."' Ashby said Facebook then invited him to a meeting at their Australasia headquarters in Singapore, where he was shown 'what transpired there'.

I had earlier asked Claudianna to step away from their meeting to brief me if anything significant emerged.

She excused herself from their drinks, saying she had to confirm an upcoming appointment. She walked onto the street and phoned me. 'Ashby's just been talking about Facebook actively involving itself in Australia's politics,' she said. 'Looks like they've been advising senators on political messaging. Ashby said they asked for his guidance on how he manages his Facebook messages – I thought you should know.'

One Nation's secret meeting with Facebook struck me as astonishing. What was the social media platform trying to 'explain to other senators'? And what had it gleaned from monitoring Ashby's posts?

Claudianna returned to the bar, promising to let me know if anything further emerged on this subject.

Before Dickson and Ashby had landed in Washington, my team had reserved the table closest to the restaurant window on the ground floor of the two men's hotel. My team had chosen that spot to allow Craig, who was parked directly outside, to get a clear shot through his windshield of Ashby, Dickson, Rodger and Claude as they sat down to eat.

After their drinks at the bar, Rodger and Claudianna ushered them to the table. 'I just want a steak,' Dickson declared. 'I like it cooked, not burned and not bloody.'

Craig's camera rolled as they took their seats, with the conversation turning to how gun lobby donations could swing Parliament to One Nation's favour.

Their comments were staggering in their blatant calculations of how cash from the NRA or other pro-gun groups in America could 'buy' One Nation control over Australia's Parliament.

'If One Nation could get ten million dollars ...' Rodger began.

'... You'd pick up eight Senate seats,' said Ashby.

'Guarantees you the balance of power,' Dickson added. 'I mean, you'd have the whole government by the balls. If we could get that sort of money, imagine, we could change Australia.'

'And we would win potentially the balance of power if we took two seats in the Lower House,' Ashby continued. 'And you know what, I reckon we could do that with *two* million dollars. If you had *twenty*, you would own the Lower House and the Upper House.' He leaned forward and folded his arms, looking satisfied with what he'd just said.

His eyes glistening, Dickson allowed himself to fantasise about what *he* would do if ever he came by such large amounts of money. 'I'm going over to one of them drug-dealing mansions on the beach and hire it for a month. You know, the ones that are twenty-five rooms and the chef and everything? We'll drink and shoot the shit out of everything down the water – machine guns and everything, mate, that's my dream,' he said, beaming.

'Fifty cal'?' Rodger asked, referring to the 800-round-a-minute machine gun used widely by the US military in World War II.

'Well, we can protect ourselves just in case,' Dickson answered.

'I don't know, if the cartel or the narcos really come and have a crack, I don't think you'd have a chance,' Rodger said. 'Those guys are mental.'

'No, if they come, I'll shoot them,' Dickson said, looking suddenly serious.

'The stories that you hear about the narcos …' Rodger went on.

'… They're all stories,' Dickson interrupted. 'Mate, they all die the same.'

As the discussion turned to the need for self-defence, Ashby told a story of how he'd once lived in a house that was burgled – an event, he said, that 'frightened the living fuck out of me for at least six months afterwards'.

According to Ashby, the burglar had entered the Queensland house and attacked one of its residents who fought back, knocking the intruder to the ground. Ashby said the resident 'broke four or five toes on both feet' while kicking the burglar as he lay on the floor. 'He was kicking the fuck out of him,' Ashby said. 'In the end, we had this bloke subdued. And I said, "Don't get up." And he was grunting, almost like a feral animal noise. And he went to get up, and I grabbed one of the pool chairs off the back, and

I just smacked him across the head with it. And he fucking stayed down then.'

A brief silence fell over the dinner party.

'Ah, yeah,' Rodger said, reaching for his beer.

'He got brain damage from it,' Ashby said. 'When the cops came out … I just said, "It wasn't us … he fell over, and I saw he hit his head on the concrete … I can't explain how he got brain damage apart from that." We were never charged for it.' Ashby added, 'You know what? I would have *shot* that fucker. I really would have.'

Dickson nodded in agreement.

Ashby said he'd been pondering what to say when he delivered his speech to the Congressional Sportsmen's Foundation event later in the week. He said he thought he might include a warning about a threat to gun rights in Australia. 'We really do run the risk of some radical changes if Labor do hold government in their own right on a federal level,' he said. 'You know, you can see it right now – they will, during their term, have a chop at gun rights.'

'I can tell you now – guns will be over,' Dickson chimed in.

'It wouldn't surprise me one bit,' Ashby said. 'If that's what they went down the path of. And it would be with the Greens' support.'

'And that's where we can stop it,' said Dickson. 'The first handbrake we have is getting the balance of power in the Senate. They can't get anything through like that. Bang, stop it dead!'

A couple of drinks later, Ashby said he was worried about the contents of his speech leaking to the public. 'I'm aware that there might be, in 150 people, there might be a person with a recorder and it might get out.'

'No way in hell,' Dickson said, lifting a slice of Argentinian rib eye to his mouth.

'Well, if it gets out, it'll fucking rock the boat!' Ashby said. 'This shit goes through my head every single minute of my day.'

* * *

After dinner, the group returned to the bar for a nightcap. Macallan 18 Year Old single malts – at $26 a shot – were ordered all 'round.

When the bill was delivered for the evening's food and drink, Ashby offered to pay. 'Fuck!' he said.

The total was $470.

'I'm beginning to not like America as much,' Dickson said, looking over the details of what they'd been charged. He called out the numbers: twenty-seven dollars for the salmon, eighty-five for two rib-eye steaks ... 'Liquor, two hundred and six bucks! Beer – ninety-three! Fucking *hell*! *Can't* be that expensive,' Dickson said, shaking his head.

'It's America,' Rodger announced, flatly.

'No, no, no, no ...' Ashby said.

'Send it back!' Dickson said. 'We can't afford it!'

Ashby ran through the bill, line by line.

'I had two, um ... that's *ridiculous*! Steve, you had two bourbons, right?'

'Two,' Dickson replied, crisply.

Again, Ashby checked the food. 'Diana, you had one chicken ...'

'I don't think food's the problem,' Dickson suggested.

'One salmon,' Ashby continued. 'Two rib eyes ...'

'We're fucked,' Dickson said, as Ashby ploughed on, tallying each item out loud.

'Oh, hang on! *Hang on!* ... food sales a hundred and thirty-three. That's not correct!' Ashby said with an air of triumph. '*Huge* anomaly.'

'How much is the anomaly?' Dickson asked, suddenly cheering up.

'Oh, at least three hundred,' Ashby replied.

He started running through the sums again.

'Seven, seven, six, twenty-seven, eighteen ...'

Rodger and Claudianna glanced at each other, then looked away.

'Sixteen ...' Ashby stopped and looked up. 'They're *subtotals*! Jesus *Christ*!' He stared at the bill, ashen-faced. 'It's a hundred per cent right,' he said.

Rodger drained the last of his Scotch and gently placed the empty glass down in front of him.

'They were really good Scotches,' he said quietly.

'They were,' Dickson replied, casting a sideways glance at Ashby.

'What was that Scotch again?' Dickson asked. 'What was it called?'

Ashby paused for a moment, looking back at the bill, before he answered. 'Expensive,' he said.

He pulled out his credit card and handed it to the waitress.

Chapter 17

The Tahoe was waiting outside Dickson and Ashby's hotel the following morning, ready to transport them to their first meeting with the NRA.

'If we can make half of the stuff we spoke about happen here tonight, it'll be a revelation,' Dickson had said at dinner the previous evening. 'I mean, think about it. We're sitting in fucking Washington, DC, the centre of the free world, talking about how we want to change the future of the planet.'

Colin opened the car door, and the One Nation visitors climbed inside.

Though discussion about the future of the planet had been swept aside the night before by the shock of the dinner-and-drinks bill, Dickson was now back in form, regaling the car's passengers with a description of the damage that can be inflicted by a sniper's bullet. 'It's a piece of metal, like, that's flying through the air, and it's probably spinning all the time, and it hits you … so it hits you in the head and your head's gone,' he said.

'Red mist is basically what's left,' Rodger said, running with the story.

'If it hits you in the hand, it takes the whole arm off,' Dickson went on.

'It's similar to golf,' Rodger continued. 'Like every shot you've just got to set up a game and go through the routine, the muscle memory.'

'Kind of cool, though,' Dickson said.

'Cool,' Ashby added.

The car was travelling to the NRA headquarters in Fairfax, Virginia – the building that had given me the idea for my investigation into the US gun lobby almost three years earlier.

Dickson and Ashby were scheduled to meet there shortly with the NRA's Grassroots Division director Glen Caroline.

Before the meeting, though, they were keen to explore the building's museum, a series of galleries that housed three thousand guns and other weapons.

Ashby, Dickson and Rodger climbed out of the car and stepped eagerly into the building.

'That's when men were men,' Ashby said, peering at a glass cabinet displaying Daniel Boone's knife.

What they were seeing here seemed to energise the One Nation visitors – as if the items on display represented a better time, a long-lost era of decency and honour and courage when truth was spoken plainly, free of the weasel-word nonsense of dandy PC politics.

Ashby had brought a camera to the museum to shoot a video that he would post later that week on the One Nation website. He positioned Dickson in front of a display cabinet and signalled for him to start talking. '*Amazing*, I'm at the NRA museum in the United States,' Dickson said, grinning, as he walked towards the camera. 'There's stuff here from *Buffalo Bill*, there are *Geronimo's* weapons! You can go right through this museum, it is really, really *incredible*. We should be enticing young people to learn how to shoot, it's a *great* sport!'

And ... *cut!*

Ashby nodded, happy with the take.

The two walked with Rodger through to the building's gift shop where Ashby stopped at a display of NRA pins and badges. 'I should get one of these for Pauline to wear into the chamber one day,' he said, still buzzing from the thrill of the museum.

'Why not?' Rodger answered.

Ashby turned to Dickson.

'What do you reckon? Do you think Pauline would wear one of these into the chamber?'

'I don't think that's a good idea,' Dickson advised.

Ashby looked again at the pin.

'I'll do it for political purposes.'

Dickson suggested an alternative.

'You can get a set of gun earrings.'

The group purchased some mementos and moved on to the NRA cafeteria where they were joined by Glen Caroline and a member of his staff.

This meeting, eagerly anticipated by Ashby, was a chance for him to get information on the way the organisation was motivating its grassroots base to push its political agenda.

When the group settled around a table, Caroline shifted his chair to make sure he could see all four visitors.

'My tongue is still dragging on the ground,' Dickson said.

It took Caroline a moment to understand what he meant.

'Oh, from the *museum*,' he replied.

He managed a faint smile as he turned to the others in the group.

'So, what are you guys up to today?'

Rodger introduced his fellow Australians, opening the way for Ashby to deliver a profile of One Nation as a significant, gun-friendly political force in Australia.

'Glen, we hold the balance of power in the Senate in Australia in Federal Parliament,' Ashby said.

'And we also hold the balance of power in our Western Australian state government as well. We've also got a Member of Parliament in Queensland who's the only gun dealer in Australia that's been elected at present. We strongly believe that people should have the right to bear arms and have strong gun ownership laws.'

Dickson joined in, warning that a new round of gun confiscations would take place in Australia unless One Nation gained the numbers in Parliament to stop it.

'When you get Labor in power in our country, it means ... taking guns away from people,' he said.

'Labor and the Greens get into federal government and we're in deep shit.

'I think you guys need to know the truth. You're very fortunate to have the Second Amendment here, we don't. I grew up with guns above every door of our house. Laws changed, I think it was '96 or '98, and guns were taken off us. We could have semiautomatic weapons, now you can't.

This is where we're going as a country, and it will get a lot worse.'

On the subject of potential changes to Australia's gun laws, Dickson said, 'There are many, many rules that need to be tweaked. And if we get the balance of power, very simply that means that we have the testicles of the government in our hand at every given stage. We will be able to dictate, and make sure that we still have the freedom to be able to shoot.'

The message from One Nation could not have been clearer: gun owners in Australia were under threat, and the party was ready and willing to carry out a rescue mission.

But first, they needed to win more seats in Parliament.

They needed twenty-four seven access to the gonads of the government.

Dickson and Ashby let the message hang in the air for a beat or two as Glen Caroline pondered how One Nation might deal with the anti-gun activists in Australia. Then he said, 'It's probably an unrealistic goal to wipe out a national gun ban overnight. But if you can work around the *margins*, what it does is, it improves the lives of gun owners on a daily basis. It does demonstrate to them that if they get united and get involved, they can start making a difference. And you find that once people start having successes and victories, it builds momentum and more people want to get involved.'

Caroline suggested that One Nation test its push for gun law reform in a 'fair but challenging region' of Australia. 'So, you can gauge what you have success with and test it and massage it. And then you kind of tweak and refine what works well with the challenge, then you can expand and go on from there.'

Dickson was keen to show that he understood precisely what Caroline was saying. 'If we can get a herd of people delivering a message of, you know, do you want to protect your family, lady, wife ...' he said, playing on the self-defence argument he knew was one of the key planks of the NRA's good guy/bad guy message.

'Yeah, you have to kind of break down the narrative so that people's initial reaction to a gun isn't *negative*,' Caroline replied. 'The key is to get that to the right segment of the population who will take that message and turn it into activism.'

Ashby and Dickson sat upright, rapt, as Caroline spoke. Dickson: puppy-like, straining to show his appreciation for the advice he was receiving; Ashby: reptilic in his silent observation, saying little, watching keenly.

'We try to put together a profile of what somebody who *isn't* an NRA member would look like,' Caroline went on, describing the NRA's strategy for expanding a pro-gun agenda. 'We're looking for somebody who kind of fits the *profile* ... in the hopes that they'd be receptive to our message. We're trying to identify that sweet spot of what a Second Amendment voter would look like so we can deliver a Second Amendment message to them.

'This is not a shotgun approach,' he continued. 'Everything is rifle-shot precision. We cull lists based on a gazillion different data points to try to find that sweet-spot list that we think we're going to get the best return on that investment. It's almost like triage. I want to reach out first and foremost to the people that identify themselves as supporters and activists. And then, as I have higher time and resources, I'll expand that to ...'

'… ground troops,' Dickson jumped in, with a knowing nod.

'We have a lot of gang violence starting to occur in Australia now, particularly in Victoria,' Ashby added. 'And we have many immigrants coming in …'

'I think the issue that resonates, especially with *women*, is the issue of choice,' Caroline continued. 'Telling them that you don't *have* to own a firearm, just don't let the government tell you that you *can't* have a firearm. Leave the choice up to them. You may exercise the choice to do so, you may exercise the choice *not* to do so. But right now, you really don't have a choice. That's been legislated away from you.'

'Very, very powerful,' Dickson said.

'I'm most impressed with the fact that you guys reinstated a bit of hope in some of the practices that we've been doing,' Ashby added. 'We say it all the time: boots on the ground. And for you to say that just tells me we're on the money with that.'

* * *

Later that day, One Nation would meet with Brandi Graham. Before arranging this, Rodger had been keen to establish whether she'd fully let go of her doubts about his identity that had nearly blown the undercover assignment over lunch in Atlanta the year before. On 26 July 2018, a little more than a month before the One Nation visit to America, Rodger visited Graham at her Capitol Hill offices. The two walked to a nearby restaurant for a bite of lunch, and I settled at the bar next to their table and listened as they began to chat. It was clear that the paranoia Rodger had seen in Atlanta was still very much alive.

Against the backdrop of mounting anti-gun sentiment in America – thanks, in part, to the Parkland school protests, and to ongoing mass shootings that would claim another twenty-four lives across America that month alone – Graham gave Rodger a rare glimpse into the fear and sense of persecution that had taken hold in her office.

'[We] get people calling saying they're going to shoot us and kill us because they hate guns,' she said.

'And it's like, "No, *you're* the person that shouldn't have guns because *you're* insane."'

'It's ironic,' Rodger said.

'It's *crazy* talk,' Graham replied. 'So, we've got our own security guard out front. And I'll tell you this off the record, but we don't have arms in our office, so we all have random weapons in case the guy gets past our security guard. I even have a ladder to throw out my window. James at the end has got a hatchet, and one of the others has a golf club.'

Graham said she exercises extreme caution outside the office too. Recently, she said, she'd become suspicious when someone parked a trailer on the street outside her house. 'Why is this in front of my house?' she asked. 'Is there something *dangerous* in there? Is somebody trying to *hurt* me? Like, what's going *on?*'

And it wasn't just at home. Graham said that whenever she travelled, she was haunted by the possibility of being attacked. 'When I get on a plane, the first thing I do is pull down my tray, and I yank on it to see if I can get that little runner out, I might need it as a knife,' she said. 'I usually travel with a scarf whether it's summer or winter because I might need that to choke somebody.'

She held up her hand, as if holding a dagger. 'Get a *pen*,' she said. 'Like, I'm ready to roll everywhere I go!'

Rodger took a sip of his drink. 'Right,' he said.

'We're ready to protect ourselves,' Graham said, glancing sideways as a group entered the restaurant and sat at a table nearby. 'We're armed and we're ready to *roll!*'

Chapter 18

Brandi Graham welcomed James Ashby and Steve Dickson into her office with a cautious smile.

Rodger and Claudianna followed, positioning themselves at either end of the table to make sure their cameras took in everyone in the room.

Graham had tried to make up for her moment of 'craziness' over lunch with Rodger, and her commitment to meet the One Nation visitors that day was as much a gesture of goodwill to Rodger, their host, as it was a desire on her part to acquaint herself with a pro-gun political party from Australia.

'So nice to meet you,' Graham said to the One Nation visitors, 'going well so far?'

'Yeah, yeah, been really good,' Dickson said.

Though conversation would soon turn to their mutual love of guns, and to One Nation's need for money, the meeting found its footing in a common loathing for the extremes of the worthy PC left.

Dickson recounted a story he'd recently heard about upcoming changes to the children's TV program *Thomas the Tank Engine.* 'It's becoming politically correct,' he said, spitting the last two words. 'We're going to have *Indian* trains and *Chinese* trains, and the Fat Controller now is a *drag* queen!'

'Oh, no!' Graham said. 'Such a *bummer* this whole *PC* thing is.'

Ashby weighed in with his own story of PC madness. 'They don't want people to have dogs as companion animals because it's degrading to the dog.'

'*What?!*' Graham shrieked.

'That's the animal liberationists,' Ashby said. 'I'm just telling you this is where they're going. Every time they go there, they go past it. They keep going. They keep outdoing themselves. It's mental.'

'It's the tip of the iceberg,' Dickson intoned, crafting the words with a tinge of doom. 'If we don't change things, people are going to be looking at Australia and going, "Well, it was okay for them to go down the path of not having *guns*, it was okay for them to go down the *politically correct* path." I mean, it's like *poison*! It will poison us all unless we stop it.'

Graham took the cue. 'In the United States, a lot of times, they go, "Well, look at Australia, look at *Australia.*"'

'There's the *problem*!' Dickson said, as if driving a nail into a piece of wood with one mighty blow.

'And we have to fight that argument continually,' Graham went on, her voice trailing into a whine. 'They're continually attacking us. It's never-ending.'

'Well, we want to kill it now,' Dickson said, with an air of confidence. 'That's the plan. Guns in Australia is probably one of the most important things, and we'll lose those rights if we don't change the way our country's going.'

He sat straight in his chair, his voice rising.

'We're in a position at the moment where we're continuing to grow our popularity, and Senator Hanson's popularity is growing exponentially. I think we'll do very well at the next federal election. Our numbers are there for anybody to have a look at. If you're buying stocks, *we're* the people to buy.'

Graham looked from Dickson to Ashby and back again. 'Okay,' she said.

* * *

'This is beginning to look like One Nation coming to Washington with a begging bowl,' I told Phil Rees in a call from my office. Phil was now running Al Jazeera's global investigative operations from Doha, with Clayton Swisher on sabbatical leave to complete a PhD.

'And there seems to be an implication that if US gun lobby donations help them win the balance of power in Australia, that they'd be willing to alter Australia's gun legislation to bring it more into line with laws in America.'

The notion of a political party even hinting at a loosening of gun laws in Australia seemed extraordinary to me. The fact that those suggestions were being made as mass shootings dominated the news and to – of all groups – the NRA was absolutely explosive.

That Ashby had said he hoped the NRA might also 'help with donations' raised the troubling spectre of a potential quid pro quo.

'You're getting this on tape?' Phil asked.

'We're filming everything that moves,' I answered.

* * *

Brandi Graham had moved the conversation in her office on to the complications faced by the NRA with increasing gun violence in America. 'It's difficult sometimes, especially with all the mass shootings that we have,' she said. 'And we want to say, "Hey, we know what *crazy* is."'

Rodger shifted in his seat.

'The first hour after something like that happens, we start getting these phone calls – you know, "What *happened*?"' Graham went on. 'And we're quiet, and that frustrates people. But we have to wait because the media is always giving bad information. So, you have to wait until you know what the facts are.'

Even with their we–can't–comment–until–we–have–all–the–facts defence, the NRA knew that the Florida high school massacre – and the student protests that had grown from it – had pushed America's gun control argument into new territory.

Within days of the Florida high school shooting, car rental companies Enterprise Holdings, the Hertz Corporation and Avis Budget ended NRA member discount deals. The First National Bank of Omaha axed its NRA-branded credit card, while MetLife, an insurer, cut a program that had offered discounts to NRA members on car and home policies. TrueCar also weighed in, cancelling a deal for NRA members that had saved them an average of nearly $3400 off the retail price of new and used vehicles.[69]

Others were to follow.

North American and Allied Van Lines announced the termination of their affiliate relationship with the NRA. Home security company SimpliSafe declared, 'We have discontinued our existing relationship with the NRA.'

Cybersecurity firm Symantec also said that it was stopping an arrangement in which NRA members were eligible for discounts on LifeLock identity theft protection services and Norton anti-virus software.

On 24 February 2018, United Airlines joined in, announcing in a tweet that it had ended its relationship with the NRA. 'United is notifying the NRA that we will no longer offer a discounted rate to their annual meeting and we are asking that the NRA remove our information from their website,' it said.

The same day, Delta Airlines sent out a similar tweet.

'Delta is reaching out to the NRA to let them know we will be ending their contract for discounted rates through our group travel program,' it said. 'We will be requesting that the NRA remove our information from their website.'

The NRA struck back, accusing those companies of 'a shameful display of political and civil cowardice'.

'Let it be absolutely clear,' the organisation said in a statement on 24 February 2018, 'the loss of a discount will neither scare nor distract one single NRA member from our mission to stand and defend the individual freedoms that have always made America the greatest nation in the world.'[70]

In reference to the Parkland massacre, the NRA said: 'The law-abiding members of the NRA had nothing at all to do with the failure of that school's security preparedness, the failure of America's mental health system, the failure of the National Instant Check System or the cruel failures of both federal and local law enforcement.'

But the damage had been done.

And US voters – moving towards congressional elections that take place halfway through each president's four-year term – the mid-term elections – were taking notice.

Political scientist Dr Bob Spitzer credits the Parkland movement with the significant political achievement of elevating the issue of gun control as a key November 2018 mid-term election issue in the minds of US voters.

'Surveys around the election time showed that the gun issue was the third-most important issue among voters in the country. Health care was number one, the economy number two, and the gun issue was number three ... not number nine or twelve, number *three*.'

Brandi Graham seemed bitter that the Parkland protest movement had triggered such pushback.

'That felt different than any of the other shootings because they were kids who could voice their opinions,' she told the One Nation visitors. 'What was frustrating was that Hollywood and the gun groups just dumped all this money in. They took buses down and they were organising these kids and telling them what to say, what to do, who they could do interviews with and who they couldn't.'

She looked directly at Ashby and Dickson.

'So, it was all organised by these anti-gun organisations,' she said. 'It was not organic in any way. Hollywood and these gun groups, they *used up* these kids.'

Dickson nodded, as if her message made perfect sense.

'It was every day you had that David Hogg in the media and now they're getting bored of him, it's time to move on to something else,' Graham continued with a touch of pathos in her voice. 'And this kid, he's going to be a *mess*, I guarantee you, for the rest of his life, because all of a sudden these people are going to walk away from him and he's going to be, like, "I thought I was really *important.*"'

Graham seemed to savour her perceived demise of one of America's new gun control poster boys.

'Yeah,' Dickson said, nodding.

'Never mind that he wasn't actually *there* when the shooting took place,' Graham continued. 'He went home and came back. But the media, you know, that was uncovered, but then they decided, "Well, that doesn't really matter."'

'Don't let the facts stand in the way ...' Rodger said.

'That's it,' Ashby added.

Graham's comments reflected an attack on David Hogg's credibility fanned, in part, by comments on the right-wing, conspiracy-focused *Infowars* website which had accused the student of 'not remembering his lines' – a reference to allegations that he was not a student at Parkland at all, but an actor hired to play the role of a shooting survivor. *Infowars* had first raised the idea of 'child actors' pretending to have witnessed a mass shooting after the Sandy Hook massacre in 2012, posting claims that the elementary school shooting had never actually taken place.[71] Conspiracy theories claiming that Hogg and his fellow students were 'actors' gained such momentum that on 20 February 2018, less than a week after the Parkland massacre, more than a hundred and eleven thousand Facebook users had shared a post claiming Hogg and his classmates were performers.[72] Another fringe website, *The Gateway Pundit*, posted claims that Hogg and others in the Parkland protest movement were all members of the same drama club, and that they were 'being used as political tools by the far left to further anti-conservative rhetoric and an anti-gun agenda'.[73]

The wave of negativity being directed towards Hogg prompted him to appear on CNN on 21 February 2018, with his father, a former FBI agent, to declare that 'I'm not a crisis actor'.[74]

* * *

America's reaction to the Florida shooting was a distillation of hardline US politics; pro-Trump and anti-Trump camps, like the nation's pro-gun and anti-gun groups, viewed each other with profound contempt and suspicion. And, against a backdrop of a resurgent, teenage-driven gun-control movement, the media, already grappling with allegations that they were peddling 'fake news', was being drawn further into a quandary over how best to handle coverage of the President's relationship with the truth – not just in regard to his views on the NRA and firearms law reform, but on an expanding range of issues, nationally and internationally. When the media knew he wasn't telling the truth, should they simply call him a liar? Something about the revered standing of the president seemed to mitigate against such an accusation. Instead of using the word 'lie', some reporters said Trump and others had 'told an untruth'.

Readers of the *New York Times* rankled at the paper's coyness.

'Dear *NY Times*,' one wrote on 25 June 2018. 're: your use of the phrase "falsely claimed." In the future, please call a lie for what it is. A lie.'

'Why do your headlines not clearly state that Trump is lying?' another asked. 'It is not an opinion that he is lying, it is a fact. Please state that in your NEWS headlines, not just the op-eds.'

Dean Baquet, the executive editor of the *New York Times*, tried to address readers' disquiet by writing that 'most politicians obfuscate or exaggerate at times. But I wouldn't use the word "lie" in a news story in cases like that. I don't think we should use that word every day in the *New York Times*. The word "lie" is very powerful. For one thing, it assumes that someone knew the statement was false. Another reason to use the word judiciously is that our readers could end up focusing more on our use of the word than on what was said. Adding "lie" repeatedly could feed the mistaken notion that we're taking political sides. That's not our role.'[75]

The *Washington Post* chose to handle the matter by applying its 'Pinocchio Test' — a fact-checking system the paper had been using since 2007 to gauge the truthfulness of political rhetoric. The paper scrutinised comments made by Trump and others which, if found to be untrue, were classified as deserving one or more 'Pinocchios'.[76] The rankings were accompanied by images of Carlo Collodi's fictional wooden puppet wearing a blue hat covered in stars and a collar with red and white stripes, his long, thin nose lengthening with each lie he told.

'The purpose of this website … is to "truth squad" the statements of political figures regarding issues of great importance,' the *Washington Post* wrote.

A 'One Pinocchio' rating meant that the paper had determined 'some shading of the facts … but no outright falsehoods'. 'Two Pinocchios' referred to 'significant omissions and/or exaggerations' which might involve 'some factual error'. Statements that were determined by the *Post* to be 'mostly false' were awarded 'Three Pinocchios', while 'Four Pinocchios' were simply labelled as 'whoppers'. The paper would later introduce the 'Bottomless Pinocchio', which represented statements that had been awarded up to Four Pinocchios but which had been repeated twenty times or more.

By the end of 2019, the Post had determined that Donald Trump had qualified for the 'Bottomless Pinocchio' at least twenty times – having made, in the paper's estimation, up to twenty-two false or misleading claims every day that year. One year later, the paper calculated that Trump had made 16,241 false or misleading claims in his first three years in office.[77]

* * *

One Nation's meeting with Brandi Graham had been humming along for thirty minutes or so when Dickson went directly to the issue of One Nation's need for assistance. 'We lack *money*. And we lack people on the ground,' he said.

'So, I hope you can point us in the right direction with the people we need to talk to.'

Claudianna shifted her phone camera slightly on the desk to make sure she was capturing Graham's reactions.

'The Koch brothers,' Graham replied, 'are you familiar with the Koch brothers at all?'

'I thought it was Coca-*Cola*,' Dickson said.

Graham smiled.

The Kansas-based energy giant, Koch Industries, then run by brothers Charles and David Koch, would be rated by *Forbes* magazine the following year as the second-largest private company in America, with an annual revenue of US$110 billion. The company had grown from an engineering firm in the 1960s into a sprawling, multinational behemoth with a vast array of interests including chemicals, electronics, fertilisers, minerals and cattle. The Kochs had donated heavily to conservative causes over the years, raising a reported US$889 million to support the Republican Party in the lead-up to the 2016 elections.

'I mean, I don't know what sort of money they give to issues outside of the country,' Graham said, making it perfectly clear she understood that Dickson and Ashby were seeking political donations on their trip to America. 'But, clearly, I think if you could talk about the effect of your gun policy and some of the other issues that affect them … you never know, they might be able to help out in some way.'

The One Nation visitors were already aware of the Kochs as a possible source of political funding; Brandi Graham had suggested this to Rodger when he'd contacted her while setting up meetings in America on One Nation's behalf.

Dickson, intoxicated with the potential of a Koch-funded electoral boost, had said over dinner on the night he and Ashby arrived, 'they could buy the next election if they wanted to'.

'If we pull this thing off,' he'd said that night, 'we protect Australia from what could potentially happen with Labor and the Green alliance. If we could do that, that would change Australian politics.'

As the meeting with Graham was nearing the end, Dickson turned suddenly to a subject that would emerge repeatedly on his trip to Washington. 'I believe in God,' he said, looking directly at Graham. 'I'll throw that on the table. You may not, *I* do.'

He peered flatly at Graham through his neat, clear-rimmed glasses.

'Oh, I *do*,' Graham responded quickly.

'*I* do and I think things are destined to happen for a reason,' Dickson replied. 'If we don't all step up, we fail ourselves, we fail our country and we fail our future. So that's where we are,' he said, speaking with the air of a pastor at the pulpit.

The anti-gun, politically correct world was suffering from an 'infection', Dickson said, and he needed help from people in Washington to 'stop it spreading'.

'I'm *in*!' Graham said.

'And you believe in God, so you can't go wrong,' Dickson proclaimed, smiling, as if something in their mutual declaration of belief had bonded them there and then.

As Brandi Graham drew the meeting to a close, she promised to watch out for her new friends at an event they would all attend the next day. If she thought she'd just met with a couple of out-of-their-depth amateurs, she didn't let on. She stood, shook their hands and thanked them for coming to visit.

There was a sense of buoyancy, of mutual respect, as Dickson walked with Ashby from Graham's office back to the Tahoe, parked on First Street, with Colin sitting dutifully in the driver's seat.

Dickson appeared happy with the way things had gone so far today.

Though he couldn't be sure yet where they would take him, he seemed glad – almost giddy – as he took his next steps on his predestined journey into the capital of the free world.

Chapter 19

Brandi Graham had given One Nation some clues as to how the NRA acted to deflect criticism in the wake of a mass shooting.

But the real secrets for how to manage the news agenda – the dark arts of media control – were kept by members of the organisation's public relations team at NRA HQ in Fairfax, Virginia.

Dickson, Ashby, Rodger and Claudianna stepped into a private dining room there to meet two of these PR professionals: Catherine Mortensen, a bouncy, smiling brunette, and her grey-haired, bespectacled colleague, Lars Dalseide, were part of the NRA team that managed crises whenever a mass shooting took place.

The group took their seats around a large dining table. On the walls were a series of wooden-framed images of guns.

'Nice to officially meet you,' Ashby said.

Dickson leaned forward to shake their hands, then gave the reasons why he and Ashby had travelled to Washington from Australia. 'We're looking to get all the information that we humanly can from you guys,' he said. 'When I grew up ... we had guns at the door of every house in the land, basically, and then that has changed so dramatically. If [Australia's Labor and the Greens] get in, they will take every single weapon off every person in our country.'

Dickson cast a quick glance around the room as if to gauge the impact of what he'd just said.

'And it scares the living *hell* out of me,' he went on. 'So, I'm just letting you know: be afraid because we are the weather balloon and it's coming your way!'

Mortensen and Dalseide sat back, looking a little stunned by Dickson's prediction that America may somehow be forced down the same road as gun-averse Australia.

'We never say "weapons",' Dalseide said, flatly.

'So, what *do* you say?' Dickson asked.

'It's a gun or it's a firearm, it's a rifle,' Dalseide answered. 'Once you start saying "weapons" ...'

'... you're in trouble,' Dickson jumped in, finishing Dalseide's sentence for him.

Dalseide nodded.

'It's a *dangerous* thing.'

Dickson seemed to understand, going on to declare that instead of allowing people to own guns, a Labor/ Greens government would make sure that 'we all should be walking around patting butterflies, and [thinking] the world's a wonderful place ... but I want the right to bear arms if necessary'.

'Right, yeah,' Dalseide said.

Mortensen offered a strategy: stir your base into a state of anger. 'You want to get people *mad*,' she said. 'When you start talking about issues that get too complicated or make them think too hard, you've kind of lost them.'

'Yeah, absolutely,' Dickson said.

'The thing we find that has been really effective communicating,' Mortensen said, 'is the armed citizens stories. These are where our members write in, or they'll send us a new clip from their local TV station or where a citizen uses a firearm to protect themselves or someone else. They're *hugely* popular.'

'*Positive* stories,' Dickson chimed in – grasping the potential.

'Yeah, and they're short little snippets,' Mortensen continued. 'You know, Joe Blow, cashier at the local convenience store had his firearm with him, protecting himself. And they're good because they're short and they kind of get you outraged. They call it "outrage of the week", and, my gosh, they're easy to understand.'

Mortensen bared a row of dazzling teeth as she smiled to emphasise the point.

'We try to get stories mostly in regional newspapers and in some national press,' she went on. 'We work a lot with what we call "Second Amendment advocates and influencers", people who own guns and have a story to tell. And we have them all over the country. And we push those people out more than our *own* voices, actually. Because they're the most effective spokespeople, as you would imagine, right?'

Another toothy grin. Mortensen was delivering her message as if addressing a group with a limited understanding of the media. She glanced at her colleague, Dalseide, before turning back to her guests.

'We pitch surrogates, we pitch guest columns in the local papers,' she continued. 'A lot of the time, we write them for, like, a local sheriff in Wisconsin or whatever … because these people are busy, and this is our *job*. And they'll submit it with their name on it, so it looks like "organic",' she said, using air quotes. 'You know, that it's coming from the *community*. But we'll have a role behind the scenes.'

Dalseide picked up Mortensen's thread.

'Yeah, the word … you get it from somebody who's a local person, the single mom … getting those who support our side out there, talking.'

The core strategy of the media team at NRA HQ was precisely what Brandi Graham had accused 'Hollywood elites' of using to push their *anti*-gun agenda via the Parkland high school protest movement: using non-media professionals to generate a sense of authenticity – creating the illusion of public sentiment being 'organic'.

By engaging the public in this way, Lars Dalseide said, messages could be framed in Australia to support the idea that more guns lead to a safer society.

'How do you deal with the negative press when there's a [mass shooting] incident?' Claudianna asked.

'Well, if you go up to my office, you'll see there's this big hole in the wall, just about the size of my head,' Dalseide answered, smiling.

The room erupted into laughter.

Mortensen told her Australian visitors that, as a result of a hardening anti-gun campaign in America, the NRA –

through its advertising arm, Ackerman McQueen – had adopted a highly aggressive stance towards the news media.

'[It's] offence, offence, offence,' she said. 'And that's a very effective communication strategy and that's what the NRA does very well.'

The *New York Times*, written off by the NRA's Dana Loesch as an 'old, grey hag' and an 'untrustworthy, dishonest rag', was being portrayed in that communication strategy as symptomatic of a twisted society where gun control advocates 'use their media to assassinate real news'.

'The *only* way we stop this,' Loesch says in one NRA video, 'the *only* way we save our country and our freedom, is to fight this violence of lies with the clenched *fist* of *truth*!'

Loesch's video formed part of the organisation's trench-warfare approach to managing the Second Amendment message.

As Catherine Mortensen and Lars Dalseide were briefing their One Nation visitors on how to deal with uncomfortable questions from the media, NRATV was playing on monitors throughout the building. In the cafeteria next door, visitors – just in from the gun museum – feasted on burgers and quesadillas as screens around the room beamed messages praising the sanctity of America's Second Amendment and pushing the value of owning firearms for self-defence.

The TV channel was a vehicle for a wholly unbridled NRA take on the world – including a scorching attack on former President Barack Obama delivered by an American country music star, Charlie Daniels.

'You might have met our fresh-faced, flower-child president and his weak-kneed, Ivy-league friends,' Daniels said, talking directly to camera. 'But you haven't met *America*. You haven't met the steelworkers, the hard-rock miners or the swamp folks in Cajun country who can wrestle a full-grown gator out of the water.'

Dressed in an oversized cowboy hat and a buckskin jacket, with a guitar twanging in the background, Daniels seemed angry in the message he was delivering. 'No, you've never met America. And you ought to pray you never do!'

He squinted into the camera through his tinted spectacles.

'I'm the National Rifle Association of America,' he said. 'And I'm freedom's *safest* place.'

'We try very hard to promote that the NRA is made up of average Americans that look and sound like the *rest* of America,' Catherine Mortensen said to Ashby, Dickson, Rodger and Claudianna.

'We want to be *relatable*. That we're not some sort of outlier, you know.'

Dickson leaned forward on the dining-room table, his mouth slightly agape, soaking up Mortensen's words. Ashby sat back in his chair, his eyes roving across the others in the room.

'We want to speak directly to our members and supporters, and that's where social media allows you to go,' Mortensen went on. 'It's to get your message out there, unfiltered by the media.'

Charlie Daniels' anti-Obama rant, his talk about 'swamp folks' wrestling full-grown alligators, was something they thought was *relatable*? Something that 'looks and sounds like the *rest of America*'? And those clever enough to have graduated from Ivy League universities were 'weak-kneed' –

a group whose high level of education meant that they were now considered *not* to be part of America?

In my many years living in and travelling around the United States, I believe I'd met a member of the 'swamp folk' community only once before – at around 3.40 a.m. in a bar on Manhattan's Christopher Street in the mid-1980s. To the best of my recollection, there wasn't a single alligator in sight, though a number of very friendly men were there in cowboy hats and buckskin jackets; some of whom, I am certain, held Ivy League qualifications ...

James Ashby added to Mortensen's comments about media messaging, complaining about a trend in Australia that had led to left-wing activists managing to have 'press releases' published as 'news'. 'So, it's not *filtered*,' he said. 'It's bad ... the content is full of shit. And that's exactly what the public are buying. They're buying *bullshit* on databases.'

Though Ashby's comments were awkwardly at odds with Mortensen's comments that the NRA wanted its material to be *unfiltered* by the media, he carried on, declaring that the public now seemed to lack the will to engage with the written word. 'The other element that we find is that people are becoming lazier and lazier and lazier, and they don't actually want to read.'

'Well, one thing we say here that would probably translate there is that we say, "The right to protect and defend yourself is a God-given right,"' Mortensen said. 'It doesn't come from the Constitution. The constitution *guarantees* us, but it comes from God.'

'I like it,' Dickson said. 'I think it's a good angle ... I mean, I'm a Christian.'

He and Ashby complained that options for self-defence in Australia were very much restricted by the nation's gun control laws.

'Well, maybe *that's* the angle you have to deal with!' Dalseide declared. 'That's a story for you to put out and say, "If this person had the right to defend themselves ..."'

Dickson ran with the idea. 'We have African gangs now that have been imported to Australia,' he said. 'They're coming into houses with baseball bats to steal your car.'

Claudianna leaned forward a little. She was beginning to enjoy the role of capturing additional secret vision. She turned her water bottle to make sure the camera inside was taking in the conversation.

Lars Dalseide sat up. 'So, every time there's a story about the African gangs coming in with baseball bats,' he said, 'a little thing that you put out there ... like, "not allowed to defend their home, not allowed to defend their home. If only the *government* recognised our rights!"'

Dalseide suggested comparing gun deaths to other ways people can die, a strategy that could be used to show that – when put into context – guns don't really pose that much of a danger, after all. 'When you look at assault rifles, what they *classify* as assault rifles, you know more people drown in *pools*,' he said.

Catching on, Dickson said, 'More people get killed with *trucks* in Australia. You know, people run a lot of people over on the street. That's what happens in Australia these days.'

To get such guns-aren't-*so*-dangerous messages to the people of Australia, One Nation would need help from the media, Dalseide said.

He offered strategies for how to make that happen. 'You have somebody who maybe leans to your side that worked at a newspaper or maybe covering city hall, or a crime reporter. And you say, "We want to print up stories about people who were robbed at their homes and beaten or whatever it might be, that could have been helped had they had a *gun*." And that's going to be the angle of their stories, and that's what he's got to write. He's got to put out five of those a week.'

Dickson said, 'That might be something that we put out as, like, "This is *ridiculous*, there's no reason why this person shouldn't have been allowed to defend their home."' There is a time for such comments, the PR team said, but there are also moments when silence is more effective – when the media calls for comment on a gun violence incident, for example.

'We will not comment because we don't want our name in that story,' Mortensen said.

'They want to *drag* our name into it. If it's a bad story, like a child gets hurt or shot with a gun, they want to call the NRA first of all. I'm like, "Why are you calling *us*? What did *we* have to do with this?"'

The NRA team offered a suggestion to the One Nation representatives on what their party might say to Australian critics in the event of another Port Arthur–type mass shooting. 'How *dare* you stand on the graves of those children to put forth your political agenda?' Dalseide said. 'Like, if your policy isn't good enough to stand on its own, how *dare* you use their deaths to push that forward?'

There was a brief silence in the room as the Australian visitors took in the power of Dalseide's strategy.

'Mm,' Ashby said. 'That's really good, it's very strong.'

***

'When you look at gun violence in America, it really is a health crisis we are facing.'

Dr Joseph Sakran, a trauma surgeon, was talking to me after completing his morning's work in the operating theatre at the Johns Hopkins medical centre in Baltimore. I had gone to visit him – a man on the medical front lines of the mass-shooting crisis – to ask for his perspective on gun violence in America.

'I mean, the fact that we are having one mass shooting after another is just horrible,' he said. 'This is not a Democratic issue, it's not a Republican issue. This is an American issue. This is a uniquely American problem.'

Dr Sakran was himself a victim of gun violence – he had been shot in the throat as a teenager. He said that at his hospital alone, he was seeing an average of one victim of gun violence every day of the week. It was taking a toll on doctors and nurses, he said, as well as the obviously devastating impact on gunshot victims and their families.

'When I'm going out to talk to the families of these loved ones that have been killed, sometimes I'll just sit there and stare at them in the waiting room, knowing that what I'm about to do is going to completely change their lives,' he said. 'I'm about to tell them that their loved one is never coming back. And I will tell you, looking at the faces of those mothers, sisters, brothers, fathers ... those faces are chiselled into my memory. When you have time to reflect, you know, sitting on the couch and letting what's happened through the day or the night kind of revolve around in your mind. Sometimes, all of a sudden, you're in tears.'

When Dr Sakran and other trauma surgeons called for sweeping changes to reduce gun violence, the National Rifle Association struck back at them, tweeting on 7 November 2018: 'Someone should tell self-important anti-gun doctors to stay in their lane'.[78]

In response, Dr Sakran launched the Twitter campaign #thisisourlane in which surgeons from around the United States posted photographs of their bloodied scrubs, gore-splashed operating-room floors and other graphic displays of what they were experiencing – *their* truth – as a result of gun violence in America.

One doctor, Stephanie Bonne, posted a photograph of an empty chair in a waiting room. She wrote, 'Wanna see my lane? Here's the chair I sit in when I tell parents their kids are dead.'

In another photo, bloodstains had been trodden into an operating-room floor as surgeons crowded around a patient. The caption read, 'She didn't make it.'

Judy Melinek MD tweeted: 'Do you have any idea how many bullets I pull out of corpses weekly? This isn't just my lane. It's my fucking highway.'

In an open letter to the NRA, doctors wrote: 'We cut open chests and hold hearts in our hands in the hopes of bringing them back to life. We do our best to repair the damage from bullets on pulverized organs and splintered bones. We hold the hands of gunshot victims taking their final breaths.'

Dr Sakran told me, 'We have the responsibility to do the right thing here. I mean, people are dying, this is not some abstract number, right? People are *dying*. People are being injured and they're being paralysed. This is a real issue that is facing Americans in a uniquely disproportionate way.'

Chapter 20

'I believe we have some guests from Down Under,' the master of ceremonies said, peering across a sea of tables to Steve Dickson, James Ashby, Rodger Muller and Claudianna Blanco. 'They're from One Nation and Gun Rights Australia.'

Dickson and Ashby stood to a roar of applause and nodded to guests around the room.

'That's good, I like that!' the MC said as the visitors from Australia settled back into their chairs.

They were at the Congressional Sportsmen's Foundation's annual gathering, a $1500-a-head event that had drawn together gun lobbyists, firearms manufacturers, members of Congress, hunting club members and assorted pro-gun collectives from around the United States. It was Washington, DC's most significant gathering of the year for Second Amendment advocates, and the most promising place for Dickson and Ashby to make friends – and find potential political donors. It was also where Ashby was to make his speech, the one that would 'fucking rock the boat' if the details were ever disclosed to the public.

The guests had gathered in a vast downstairs conference space at an upmarket city hotel just a few minutes' walk from the Capitol Building. Dressed in suits and ties, some with cowboy hats and pointy-toed, Cuban-heeled boots, the hundred or so attendees found their places at starched linen–covered dining tables as their expectant murmuring filled the room.

After prayers and a declaration of America's Pledge of Allegiance – an expression of fidelity to the American flag and the republic – the US Secretary of Agriculture Sonny Perdue was called to the podium as the keynote speaker. As he stepped to the microphone, secret service agents emerged from the back of the room and wandered through the crowd. The agents, with their telltale earpieces and dark glasses, were there to watch over Secretary Perdue, a former governor of Georgia now presiding over a department with an annual budget of US$151 billion. Though he was very much among friends at this gun-friendly gathering, the agents were taking no chances.

Two of them stopped at the edge of the One Nation/GRA table.

Rodger and Claudianna sat stiffly in their chairs.

Holy *shit*!

Claudianna looked quickly at Rodger, who stared straight ahead.

Please don't tell me these agents carry gear that can detect hidden recording devices, she thought.

'My lovely wife, she got a little worried about me a couple of years ago,' Secretary Perdue said, winding his way into a hunting gag. 'And she said, "Sonny, do you like turkey hunting or me the most?" And I hesitated – that was my first mistake.' Laughter swirled through the room.

Getting hidden cameras into the event had been complex enough. I'd visited the hotel the previous evening to try to find out whether metal detectors were likely to be used to scan guests. There had been no signs that security of that nature was planned. I had also taken note of the position of security cameras in the meeting rooms and had identified escape routes for Rodger and Claudianna if, for whatever reason, they had to leave quickly. Though the conference room seemed free of anything that might detect our concealed equipment, I had instructed Rodger and Claudianna to enter in the morning *without* any cameras – just to be sure.

Once they'd confirmed that no metal scanners had been put in place that morning, they were to make their way to a hotel room upstairs where I had installed Craig Pennington, who would fit them with the miniature cameras that would record the day's proceedings. Fully rigged up, they would then return to the event, where they were to connect with Ashby and Dickson.

Seemed like a fair plan. But none of us had expected the secret service to turn up when the speeches began.

'And I thought for a second,' Perdue said, still working on his joke. 'And I said, "Spring or fall?"'

Laughter turned to cheers.

One of the agents moved slightly closer to Claudianna. She sat with a fixed grin, nodding along to Perdue's words but not really taking in what he was saying. All she could think was, *Are the agents' earpieces feeding them information that somebody in the crowd is secretly recording this event?*

'You know what it's like,' Perdue said, very much at ease in front of the crowd.

The agent closest to Claudianna scanned the table, then looked away.

'Having grown up on a farm … I got a great start,' the secretary said.

'Last Saturday was the opening of duck season in Georgia. And if you've seen those little boys and girls that were just out there, it was so much fun!'

At this point Sonny Perdue had demonstrated that he was not only capable of talking under wet cement, but also that he was capable of talking *until the end of time* under wet cement … or so it seemed to Rodger and Claudianna.

The agent looked back again, then joined his partner and stepped towards the back of the room.

Claudianna and Rodger tried not to show the heaviness of their breathing.

Come on, Perdue! For fuck's sake!

'And [the dog] was going out after the birds that I shot, and some were not quite dead,' Perdue went on, smiling. 'And that's truly what it's all about … It's all about being able to protect the great things that we love. And I'm committed to do that as long as the Lord allows me to stay here.'

It looked briefly as though he had ended his speech at last, but the secretary sputtered on with another line.

'My dad, he was a farmer all of his life and he told us very clearly, "You take care of the land and it'll take care of you."' Perdue stepped off the stage.

One by one, guests who were scheduled to address the gathering were called to the microphone, their speeches cheering America's right to keep and bear arms. As each speech ran over its allocated time, Ashby's chances of making it to the podium were draining away.

The speech before his went on. And on – a droning endorsement of the powerful group hosting the gala.

When it ended, the MC made the call: no more speeches – the day's events were already too far behind schedule.

Ashby's chance to appeal to the very heart of America's pro-gun community had been snatched away, and the details of what he'd been planning to say would never be revealed.

Claudianna leaned across the table. 'I'm sorry you didn't get to speak.'

Ashby was stoic in his response. 'It's okay.'

But there were still opportunities to get One Nation's message to the room: one-on-one encounters with the Second Amendment advocates assembled here. With the speeches now over, and lunch out of the way, Dickson and Ashby stood to mingle with guests.

They had plenty of time to work the room; after-lunch drinks would be followed later that day by afternoon cocktails, a dinner, and more drinks into the night. Dickson was in his element: part tourist, part gun enthusiast, part you-can't-get-the-country-out-of-the-boy politician, he shook hands with as many people as he could, singing the praises of One Nation, decrying the gun-loathing PC left, and making it clear to all he met why he and Ashby had come to America.

'The bottom line where we are is we've got all the political grunt to make happen what we need to happen,' he said to one guest. 'It's the cash. We don't have the cash. We get the cash, we change the world.'

Rodger and Claudianna followed the One Nation visitors around the room, their cameras rolling as the conversations flowed. When Ashby and Dickson separated, Rodger stuck with one and Claudianna with the other, making sure that nothing either of the One Nation guests said was missed.

Dickson grabbed the hand of one man, shaking it hard, as he leaned in, shouting against the din. Australia's experience with guns and political correctness, he boomed, was a sign of things to come in the United States. 'It's coming your way next,' he said. 'We'll *all* be dead. We're going to stop it. We have to stop it. We don't have a choice.'

The man nodded and took a sip of his Scotch. 'You're not going to stop it, buddy. You're going to *reverse* it.'

'We are!' Dickson replied.

'We're here to make friends,' he added, as he moved to another of the guests. 'And we want to make sure that we continue to be friends and we need your help.'

The man seemed to understand. 'We need each *other*,' he replied. 'We need as many people pulling in the right direction.'

'Well, if you think about it, when it becomes less of us, we're easy to kill,' Dickson said. '*That's* the problem.' He paused for a beat to let the message sink in. 'I've got God on my side, so I'm going alright.'

'We can hang together or we can hang separately,' the man responded.

'We're not going to hang at all,' Dickson responded. 'We're going to kill *them*. That's the plan.' He grinned slightly, looking pleased with what he'd just said. He told another man, 'We're not even allowed to own *guns* in Australia for self-protection for women. It's insane! We've been importing all these Muslims into Australia. We have 230,000 people coming in a year. Our population's only twenty-five million. Some *really* dangerous people.'

A small crowd had gathered around Dickson. He turned, as an actor might on a stage, while he continued his tale of a darkness engulfing his homeland. 'And they're just breaking into people's homes with baseball bats and killing people,' he said, making a bashing movement with his hands. 'Basically, stealing everything they own. Gangs. Our country's going into chaos.'

As if to endear themselves to their Australian visitors, many at the gathering were quick to share hunting stories, boasting of the number of species they'd killed.

'I'm only six species shy of having harvested the entire African super-slam,' one man told Dickson with a sense of pride.

'I do buffalo with my bolt-action,' said another.

'You know how many ducks I killed last year?' another man asked in a Texan drawl. 'Probably four hundred.'

Some wanted detail of what it felt like to have experienced the banning of firearms. 'Is there much resentment from the population towards the gun confiscations?' asked Congressman Ted Budd – an NRA-endorsed politician from North Carolina who 'strongly opposes gun control', according to an October 2018 NRA newsletter.[79]

'Yes,' Dickson replied. 'A *huge* amount of pushback.'

His claim was gobbled up by an audience eager to hear that gun control measures were dividing Australia. But Dickson's comments were a clear misrepresentation of the facts. Polling in 2016 by Essential Research in Australia found that 44 per cent of Australians believed the nation's gun laws were 'not strong enough', while 45 per cent said they believed the laws were 'about right'. Only 6 per cent of respondents said they thought the laws were 'too strong'.[80]

With Claudianna by his side, Steve Dickson pushed his way further into the crowd, encountering a woman who told him, 'Somebody comes into my house, they're getting shot. I carry every day. Usually in my purse.'

The woman fished her phone from her handbag and trawled through photographs of her gun collection. 'I have gun porn on my phone. There's my SIG. Oh, and that's my favourite.' She held an image on her phone for Dickson to view.

'You're shitting me!' he said. 'Semiautomatic or auto?'

'Semi.'

The would-be Queensland senator was entranced by a story the woman told of how a burglar once broke into her home. Dickson then found Ashby in the hotel foyer and proposed that a recounting of her experience would be a sure-fire way for One Nation to replicate the outrage-of-the-week-type stories suggested earlier by the NRA's PR team. 'I reckon it would be a smasher,' Dickson said to Ashby. 'Like, she got a home invasion, a guy came into her house. She was robbed, she's got a little girl of eight, and she was terrified, thought she was going to be *murdered*.

'And from that point in time,' he continued, 'she learned to shoot and do everything that she can to protect the family. It's just a *great* story to tell the Australian people!'

Ashby nodded. 'It is,' he said.

After a midafternoon break, the crowd reconvened for pre-dinner cocktails and were then ushered to their tables to eat. Steaks, declared by Rodger to be 'as tough as buggery', were delivered to all but Claudianna, who took the opportunity to head upstairs to Craig's room. While one camera lens had been threaded into her dress, the actual recording device – 'the brain', as Craig called it – was taped to her thigh, and after a full day of recording it was beginning to overheat. The device was so hot, in fact, that her dash to the room upstairs was a matter of urgency; her leg was starting to burn. Claudianna pounded on Craig's door and made her way into the bathroom, where she pulled the recorder away from her leg and pressed a cool towel against a throbbing welt.

Craig took the device and held it in front of a fan until it cooled. Twenty minutes later, the recorder was back against Claudianna's thigh as she returned to the table in time to catch dessert.

* * *

At dinner and during conversations that flowed as guests stood and mingled afterwards, there could be no mistake in the room that the One Nation representatives were openly hunting for cash.

Some assured the visitors that money – *big* money – was tantalisingly close to them.

'No shit, go to *that* one,' a gun maker said when he learned One Nation was scheduled to meet with Koch Industries later in the week. 'Get *lots* of money! They have more money than God and Jesus and Mohammed all put together.'

Ashby looked pleased. 'I like the sound of that.'

But with an election looming in Australia, things needed to happen in a hurry. Ashby pulled Claudianna aside and made it clear to her that he needed her help driving home a message to key gun lobby contacts. 'We don't have time to muck around,' he said. 'Not being rude or too blunt, but that's the message that needs to come across. With all due respect, time is not our friend.'

Dickson walked to the edge of the room to fondle guns that were up for auction that night. He held a rifle to his shoulder and peered through the sights at a wall. His finger hovered near the trigger. He put the gun down and, using the language of a mobster, reminded Rodger how important it was for One Nation to capture more seats in Parliament. 'The thing you need to understand about the balance of power,' he said, 'is the headlock and the 9mm to the back of the head. That's where it sits. Once you say, "We want something," we will get it. Without it, they don't get any legislation through.'

Dickson was talking about the possibility of One Nation gaining enough seats in Parliament that the party could control the flow of legislation – blocking laws they didn't want, and using their numbers to pressure politicians to support their legislative agenda.

Rodger used the moment to raise the possibility that potential donors – including Koch Industries – might want political favours from One Nation in return for their investments. 'You've got to think about what you can do,' he said.

'We can do just about *anything*,' Dickson replied. With a slight shrug, he added, 'What do you *need* done?'

The crowds were beginning to thin, but Dickson still had work to do. He walked to the bar where he found a tall Texan in a black cowboy hat. 'I'm actually here to get donations,' Dickson told him.

The Texan took a sip of his drink. 'I'll donate to you.'

'We need about ten million dollars,' Dickson responded.

'Well, it ain't going to be ten fucking *million*, I'll tell you that.' The man leaned towards Dickson. 'I'll give you a hundred bucks,' he said. 'I'll give you a hundred bucks right now, no shit.'

'You know what, I prefer you spread the word,' Dickson said, looking slightly dejected. 'It's about the principle of what we put into it.'

Like so many others in the room, the man in the cowboy hat was appalled by Australia's gun buy-back program and wanted to know how he could help Dickson to change the law. 'How do we make sure that you never have to melt down another firearm?' he asked Dickson. 'I never want you to melt down another shotgun. I never want you to *ever* have to walk over and hand it to somebody and they go, "I'm going to literally throw this in the furnace."'

'My fucking guns got burned in their fire!' Dickson said. 'I'm still angry about it. It was *criminal* … It's wrong.'

The man nodded. 'Y'all have been fucked for multiple years.'

He suggested how Dickson might lead a charge to peel back restrictions on gun ownership in Australia: seek financial help from gun makers in America. 'Here's what you need to do, and I'm not joking about this at all,' he said. 'Have you ever walked up to, I don't know, American Armor, someone who manufactures firearms in Texas?'

'This doesn't go anywhere except us,' Dickson said, moving closer.

'Have you ever gone to those guys?' the man asked again. 'You know why? Because you need to sit down with those guys right now [and say] "the last thirty years, you sold twenty-two or fifty thousand dollars' worth of arms to Australia … if you did away with how all of us are getting screwed, next year you're going to send, literally, twenty-eight thousand dollars' worth of product to Australia, in, literally, the first two months." They will!'

'It will be a *gold*mine!' Dickson exclaimed.

'And when you do that,' the man went on, 'every one of those guys will go, "You know what? You're right, I'm going to give you ten grand, I'm going to give you twenty grand", whatever.'

Along with those political donations, the man suggested a degree of deception: give gun reform laws a more politically palatable name. 'And at that point, you've going to have a two-million-dollar campaign to get "hunting and fishing rights". Not gun rights! You're *never* going to put gun rights, *never* put gun rights on the ballot.'

Dickson glanced around the room. 'You're right, you're *right*!'

'And all of these people are going to give you fifteen, twenty grand,' the Texan continued. 'And you're going to pass it, and you're going to go, "How can I hunt without a *gun*?"'

'I love you, mate,' Dickson shouted over the roar of the bar crowd. 'And what you just said tonight is *amazing*! Seriously, you're a good man. God will make you do whatever you want to do. I can guarantee that. Absolutely guarantee it!'

Before they left the gathering that night, Claudianna suggested that Ashby, Dickson and Rodger pose for a photograph in front of a stuffed lion that had been placed as a decoration in the room where the remaining guests were mingling.

The three assembled around the lion, peering into Claudianna's phone camera lens.

She took a shot. 'C'mon, guys, one more,' she said. 'A silly one, this time. A *silly* one!'

Ashby and Rodger leaned towards the camera, held up their hands and curled their fingers like claws.

Click!

'Thanks, guys.' Claudianna slipped her phone back into her handbag and walked out of the room.

Chapter 21

Steve Dickson and James Ashby were on a high. The Congressional Sportsmen's event two nights earlier had opened important doors, connecting them directly with highly influential lobbyists, gun makers, firearms retailers and sitting members of the US Congress.

Now, after a day to themselves, they were being transported by Colin to the Washington offices of Koch Industries – to a potential game-changing fortune in political funding. It didn't get much better than this.

With the temperature outside sitting at thirty-three degrees Celsius, and with humidity at more than 50 per cent, Washington felt like a tropical swamp. From the car, Dickson and Ashby could see people on the street wearing shorts, sandals and T-shirts. Dickson, dressed in a jacket and tie, was concerned about how he'd look when he made his all-important pitch for money. 'I reckon we get there early,' he said. 'I don't want to be a sweaty shithole when I get there.'

He turned towards Ashby, Rodger and Claudianna, sitting behind him, and delivered an animated briefing on the fortunes they might soon be tapping into. 'Between them, I think [the Koch brothers] have got $245 billion *each*,' he said. 'They donated $887 million towards Trump's campaign. In 2015, they put $500 million towards another campaign. That's fucking *serious* money!'

Rodger asked whether Dickson and Ashby had considered how much cash they would ask for if the meeting led to offers of a political donation to One Nation.

'I'm thinking ten,' Dickson said.

'No, I was thinking twenty,' Ashby added, smiling, as he peered through the car window onto the steamy streets outside.

* * *

The visitors were ushered into a large, light-filled meeting room at the Kochs' grand offices on 14th Street, just a few minutes' walk from the White House.

As they sat at a conference table and waited for the Koch representatives to arrive, Dickson raised the idea that listening devices may have been installed in the room to record their conversation. 'Anything you say or anything you write, be prepared to read it on the front page of the paper,' he warned.

'That's exactly how I'd put it,' Ashby added.

Perplexed as to what might have prompted those comments, Rodger and Claudianna nodded in agreement but said nothing. Instinctively, Rodger double-checked that his camera was still rolling.

As they waited for the Koch representatives to enter the room, conversation meandered from praise for Colin

('He's a nice bloke and he doesn't slack off,' Dickson said), to a recounting of a scene from the sitcom *Seinfeld*, leading Dickson to opine on the similarities between the TV program and the global push to combat climate change. '[*Seinfeld*] made multimillions of dollars out of that and it was about nothing,' he said. 'He sold nothing to the world. It's like climate change, they've sold nothing to the world except misery and debt.'

A woman stepped into the room accompanied by a male colleague. There were warm smiles and handshakes all round.

A former NRA employee, Catherine Haggett was Koch Industries' director of federal affairs. With a regal air she sat down, her colleague taking the chair to her right, and she gestured for the meeting to begin.

Though no date had yet been set for Australia's federal elections, Ashby started the meeting with his prediction of a schedule. 'It's pretty likely that we're going to be on an election front door within the next few months.' This positioned him to take a shot at Australia's Labor Party and the Greens. 'Just overnight, [the Greens] have banned the nursery rhyme "Three Little Pigs" because there's inequality in the brick house that Aborigines can't afford,' he said. 'So, they are slowly but surely shifting the way in which we teach kids today. It's scary, it's bloody scary.'

Ashby looked from Haggett to her colleague and back again, as they took in his message.

Sitting to Ashby's left, his hands clasped in front of him, Dickson let loose with his own volley of complaints about left-wing politics, moving him to the focal point of the day's meeting. 'It's going to get down to *money* at the end of the day,' he said. 'I don't know what you can do to help us.'

He tilted his body forward, pressing his palms together.

'We can change the voting system in our country, the way people operate, if we have got the money to do it. The ingredients are there, we just don't have the petrol to put in the engine. I could talk for a day about why you should help us.'

'Things can change with money,' Ashby added, arguing that Australia – at risk of being moved 'more left than left' under Labor – needed a seismic political shift to correct its wayward path.

Haggett leaned on the conference desk. 'I'm not familiar with your election financing rule, regulations, you know,' she said. 'I'm not familiar with … what sort of money you're allowed to take. Just help me understand that better.'

'There are no set limits on donations,' Ashby answered flatly.

Haggett turned in her chair and glanced at her colleague. 'That's one of the reasons I wanted to sit down and have this conversation,' she said, looking back to Ashby and Dickson. 'To learn more about what was going on, because we're not naïve to the importance of the policies that Australia has and how they relate here in the US. Particularly when you've got our western coastal states that are probably more heavily influenced by Australian politics.'

Specifically referencing One Nation's request for cash, Haggett said, 'I will inquire and potentially, you know, if there is interest, have you kind of visit with some other folks.'

She seemed businesslike in her delivery, but twenty million US dollars was not being offered on the spot.

'I do think it would be beneficial to connect you with some of our partners who we work with on these various policies,' she went on. 'We all understand that international influence is very real.'

'We're turning socialist,' Ashby said, as the meeting drew to a close.

'We are, too!' Haggett exclaimed. She looked from Dickson to Ashby and back again. 'It's terrifying.'

***

Dickson hurried to the front door of the Kochs' building, on fire with excitement over what he'd sensed Catherine Haggett had just signalled to him.

'She fucking gets it really quick,' he said to Rodger. 'What she's doing is *great*! She's pure. This is dark-magic shit.'

'Dark magic?' Rodger asked.

'It is dark-*magic* shit,' Dickson repeated, as they made their way onto the street where Colin sat waiting for them at the wheel of his air-conditioned Tahoe.

It was midafternoon – beer o'clock. Rodger guided them to a nearby pub where they settled into a booth on a side wall, opposite the bar. It was part-saloon, part-diner, with wood-panelled ceilings and a gallery of framed posters along the booth-side wall, featuring beer advertisements and sports stars. 'No shoes, no kilt, no service', one of the signs said.

As they perused the drinks menu, Dickson enthused about the progress he and Ashby were making on their Washington visit – boiling One Nation's needs down to a solitary issue. 'It's money,' he said. 'Everything is money.'

In an echo of his first conversations with Rodger back in Queensland, in which he'd suggested that the NRA spend a million dollars 'punching shit in' to social media on One Nation's behalf, Dickson said, 'Mate, I don't even mind if we don't *see* the money, and then they sell the message for us. It's the vehicle. And I think we've already lit the fuse here for that thing to happen.'

But he wouldn't turn down a cash handout, he suggested. 'I mean, if we *get* the money for the resources to direct us to where we're going at the moment, with the power we have behind us, I mean it's just like a *tsunami*. You know, it's already hit, the shockwave has gone off.'

Dickson waved his hands in excitement as he spoke.

'We just need the money to get that message out there.'

Outside, Washington's stifling humidity had broken into a thunderstorm. 'It's monsoonal!' Rodger said, as lightning strafed the street and rain hissed against the pub's windows.

Rodger and Claudianna each ordered beer, and Dickson called for a bourbon and Coke.

Ashby, feeling unwell, ordered a Fireball cinnamon whisky. He took a sip and rejected the drink, switching to a glass of water. 'I've been a bit chesty all day,' he said.

'It's because you're around us, we're sexy,' Dickson joked.

Ashby didn't smile.

Claudianna asked whether Pauline Hanson had been briefed on the progress of the trip.

Ashby's response hinted that he wanted details of the visit to be kept quiet. 'I've just said "meetings have gone well" – that's all,' he answered, his face devoid of emotion. 'We keep everything out of writing. If something of that nature was to be said it needs to be said in person.'

Claudianna leaned a little closer.

'I always have a private email and a work email,' Ashby continued, explaining his method for keeping sensitive messages secret. 'Because work emails are never private. They can be subpoenaed like that,' he said, clicking his fingers. 'As Steve [Dickson] said, monitor everything you write, and write it as though the whole world will read it.'

Claudianna nodded. 'Got it.'

Ashby stood to leave, and Claudianna phoned Colin. 'Can you come and get James, please? He needs a lift back to the hotel.' The others chose to linger with their drinks, waiting for the storm to pass.

'I don't think we've embarrassed ourselves in any way,' Dickson said, pulling a handful of business cards from his pocket and shuffling through them. 'This guy is supposed to be super rich,' he said, squinting at the writing on one of them. 'And there's this guy, the executive chairman, so he probably runs the place.' He peeled off more. 'Executive director ... deputy chief ... he's a senator ... strategic adviser ... I don't even know who these bloody people *are*.

Dickson glanced through the pub's front window. 'Still raining sideways,' he said. 'I think something may still come of the Koch brothers with a bit of luck,' he added, slipping the cards into his pocket.

He turned to Rodger and Claudianna. 'You've done everything you've said you're going to do.'

The time they'd spent together in Washington so far had been a marvellous bonding exercise – at least, Dickson seemed to think so. He was grateful that Rodger and Claudianna had spent so much time helping him and Ashby with meetings and social events, and here, in the cosiness of the pub, he wanted to make clear his appreciation. 'You haven't failed in any way or form, and both of you together have worked extremely hard.'

More than that, it felt like a genuine friendship was beginning to form – particularly between Dickson and Rodger. Dickson downed his drink and ordered another, asking the waiter to bring Rodger another beer while he was at it.

Dickson said he'd like to focus on arranging a visit to Australia for some of the key contacts One Nation had developed in Washington. 'We could organise, like, a banquet dinner in the state Parliament,' he said. 'Get Pauline to come along. It's beautiful and everything's silverware. And you can drink there and do all that shit.'

But a visit to Australia wouldn't be complete without his guests being given the chance to shoot animals there.

'Take them out shooting pigs and deer,' Dickson said, smiling. 'You've got to excite them, make them *horny*, go shooting! Mate, that's what we've got to do next.'

The new round of drinks arrived at the table. Dickson reached for his bourbon and Coke and took a gulp.

'I'll organise the shit that needs to happen,' he said. 'We've just got to get the money out of them.'

Rodger and Claudianna nodded.

Dickson took the conversation back to his life in Queensland, reminiscing about the way his wife treated his pet dog.

'The fucking dog gets better treated than me,' he said. 'I'm jealous of that dog. I love him to death, but he had a three thousand dollar operation. I shit you not! I would have given him a fucking bullet in the head.'

He leaned back and smiled, as if he'd just figured out a way to solve all the problems of the world. 'Everything's a game of chess. Chess and mathematics.'

He picked up his phone and held it in front of him, his fingers searching for the camera button. 'I should take a photo for posterity's sake,' he said, grinning.

He snapped a shot of the bar. 'Mate, they'll make a movie about this sometime in the future.'

Rodger and Claudianna sipped their drinks in silence.

A clap of thunder shook the room, and the rain suddenly stopped – as if someone up above had just turned off a tap. Claudianna stepped from the table to take a phone call. Dickson watched her walk away, then leaned in to Rodger and lowered his voice. 'Mate, let's go find some strippers.'

Chapter 22

'**F**ill me in.'

Phil Rees was on the phone from Doha. His calls were coming daily now, as the material we were gathering looked more and more like the makings of a major Australian political scandal.

While we were still interested in the NRA's internal deliberations, our focus had turned to Ashby and Dickson.

I gave Phil a briefing on the meetings and conversations that had taken place since we last spoke, and I described the hidden camera footage I'd reviewed that showed Dickson declaring contempt for Australia's gun control laws – and his declaration that he would 'reverse them'.

I also pointed out that One Nation was trying to source money in America while legislation designed to outlaw foreign political donations was awaiting a vote in Australia's Parliament.

(Just ten weeks later, on 15 November, Pauline Hanson would stand in the Senate claiming that she wanted nothing to do with foreign political donations, although she'd known her delegates were in Washington, and Ashby had told her that 'meetings have gone well'. 'I think that overseas money should not have an influence in our political scene,' she would say in Parliament. 'So, I believe foreign donations should be stopped totally. There's no big organisations that donate to One Nation, I can assure you of that. It's been the hard work of having the fish and chip meetings, or we actually have sausage sizzles.')[81]

But everything we'd seen in Washington pointed to Hanson's men manoeuvring to grab what they could – *while* they could.

'And there's no hint that anyone's onto us?' Phil asked me.

'Our camouflage is solid,' I said.

Less than an hour later, a panicked call from Claudianna would cause me to question that.

* * *

We'd arranged for Colin to drive Ashby and Dickson to a spot within sight of the US Capitol Building, and for him to then leave the Tahoe, ostensibly to get coffee for his passengers. The idea was to give Rodger and Claudianna time alone in the car with Dickson and Ashby without 'the chauffeur' potentially causing the One Nation visitors to restrain their comments. This was an opportunity for totally uninhibited talk – and Dickson and Ashby made full use of it.

An earlier discussion with a representative of America's gun makers was still fresh in the minds of those in the car. In describing the fight against anti-gun political correctness, the gun-manufacturing rep had said to One Nation, 'It's smash-mouth, grind-it-out, in-the-trenches every day. You can't give an inch because you will never get it back.'

'We have to kill them,' Dickson had said, adding that he was 'still crying' after his guns had been confiscated by the Australian government. 'Not *physically* kill them, but stop their ideas,' Dickson went on. 'By killing it in our country, we'll kill it in your country – it's like inoculating against a *disease!*'

He'd glanced around at those who were part of the discussion. 'If I said that to the public, I'd probably lose everything I've ever worked for in my whole life.'

Now, in the confines of the car, Dickson followed on from the mood of that gathering. He warned that if One Nation failed to secure the balance of power in the upcoming election, gun sales in Australia would grind to a halt. 'That's where it's going,' he said to Rodger. 'That's what the outcome will be … there will be *no* sales, *none!*'

But if One Nation was serious about changing Australia's gun laws, they were likely to encounter strong resistance in Parliament, Rodger suggested. 'It's not going to be an easy law to get through.'

'Well, what's so tough?' Dickson snapped back.

'Well, [the gun control law] basically needs to be ripped up and started again,' Rodger replied.

'Well, Rodger, that's the thing,' Dickson said. 'Do you want to go for the end of the journey or go for the start of the journey?'

Ashby joined in. 'Do you want the loaf or the half-loaf?' he asked Rodger. 'The half-loaf, or none of it?'

'And none of it is not an option,' Dickson added.

'We start with a slice, we take what we can get,' Rodger replied.

'We need to make it so we can get a piece of bread and know we can get it and it's safe,' Dickson said. 'And we can do something with it. And then we can get another piece of bread and end up with the whole loaf.'

The whole loaf of bread. New firearms laws. More guns in Australia. And an end – at last – to the upside-down world of PC lunacy. This, it seemed, was what Dickson meant by his reference to 'the end of the journey'.

Then Dickson made an extraordinary suggestion to Rodger. 'Why don't you knock up a policy for us on guns that we can run through One Nation?' he said.

Dickson looked at Ashby. 'What do you think of that?' he asked.

'Yeah,' Ashby replied.

So, Rodger – an undercover operator working for Al Jazeera and *pretending* to want a revision of Australia's rigid gun control laws – was now being asked to help write One Nation's gun policy. That was *never* going to happen.

When Rodger reported Dickson's request to me, I told him that he could *tell* them he was willing to help, but he could never actually write a word on their behalf of proposed ways to water down firearms laws. What if – somehow – a hidden-camera-wearing pet-food manufacturer I'd employed to join my Investigative Unit actually penned a pro-gun document for One Nation that went on to influence Australian firearms laws? And what if new laws led to more guns, and more guns led – God forbid – to another mass shooting in Australia?

Dickson turned and looked through the car window to the shimmering dome of the US Capitol Building. 'I think we'll break through on the Koch brothers,' he said. 'We *need* that financial assistance.'

* * *

The conversation was being recorded by cameras in Rodger's sports coat, hat and phone, as well as by cameras in Claudianna's dress, phone, water bottle and handbag.

Also rolling was a camera that Colin had secreted in the driver's sun visor, and another one that Colin had built into a tissue box between the driver's seat and the front passenger seat.

Craig had parked his follow-car nearby and stood behind a grove of trees on the grassy National Mall, filming the Tahoe as it sat on the street, the passengers visible through the windows while their 'loaf of bread' discussion was taking place.

Colin was still out of the car 'getting coffee' when Ashby reached down to the tissue box and tugged at it. The box tore away from its velcro base.

Claudianna saw the camera's tiny lens glint in the light and she was certain Ashby had seen it too. *Shit!*

Ashby placed the box back on its base, opened the door and stepped quickly out of the car.

* * *

'Pete, we've got a situation.' Claudianna sounded shaken. 'I'm pretty sure Ashby just saw the camera in the tissue box.'

She'd got out of the car just after Ashby and had walked across the road to call me.

As she was speaking, Colin returned to the Tahoe carrying ice creams for Ashby, Dickson, Rodger and Claudianna. 'The coffee place was selling these, so I thought I'd pick some up,' he said cheerily. 'You know, it's pretty hot out here ... it's an ice cream kinda day!'

Ashby, who appeared to be trying to make a phone call, took his ice cream from Colin, nodded thanks, and walked back towards the car.

When Colin turned towards Claudianna, he could see immediately that something was wrong.

'*What?!*' he mouthed, with his back to Ashby.

'Um, Colin's here now,' Claudianna said to me.

'Tell him to de-rig the car,' I told her.

'Got it,' she replied and hung up.

The two of them walked back to the Tahoe together. 'Bloody warm outside,' Claudianna said, as she tugged open the door and sat down.

Ashby sat beside her.

She licked her ice cream.

The tissue box was still in place.

* * *

Colin dropped Ashby and Dickson back at their hotel, then returned to Al Jazeera's studios to strip the car of its hidden cameras.

If Ashby had seen anything, he hadn't let on – but then, he was a man who rarely gave much away.

'There are some people that have got hyperactive emotions,' he once told Rodger and Claudianna. 'And there are others, like me, that don't have any.'

Maybe the man with no emotions was waiting for a chance to inspect the tissue box more thoroughly with nobody else in the car? Or maybe he simply hadn't seen the wires? We would never know.

From that moment on, cameras weren't hidden in the car. Rodger and Claudianna caught every word on the devices they were carrying. From a total of nine hidden cameras, we were down to seven. After the stress of near-discovery, that was okay with me.

* * *

While Colin was tending to his Tahoe, Rodger and Claudianna sat with Ashby and Dickson at their hotel.

Dickson laid out a horror scenario in which a woman, alone at home with her children, would need to defend herself against an intruder. 'I can guarantee you a guy who comes in with a gun and puts it to your wife's head and says, "Take all your gear off", and *rapes* her,' he said, looking around the group. 'You know, he's only going to go to jail for a couple of years. *If* he gets caught! If he doesn't shoot her with the gun afterwards.'

As if the gunshot itself had just been heard, the group hushed.

'Is there anything you *don't* want me to broach – like, "don't go there"?' Rodger asked quietly, referring to his new task of writing One Nation's firearms policy.

Once more, Ashby warned against committing pro-gun messages to writing. 'Just keep those sorts of discussions over the phone,' he advised.

On guiding Rodger towards the parameters of his policy, Dickson said, 'you've got to be able to sell the message without scaring [people] off'.

'Would you guys then be comfortable with open carry in Australia, like they do in Texas?' Rodger asked.

'It's not something I'd lead with tomorrow,' Dickson replied.

'No, I wouldn't do that tomorrow,' Ashby said.

'Concealed carry?' Rodger asked.

'You could not come out and say that tomorrow,' Dickson advised. 'I'd like to have it *all*,' he went on. 'But I know it's like trying to introduce nuclear energy to the Australian people at the moment. They're not ready.'

'You have to put in progressive steps,' Ashby said. 'You need to soften people back up again. It's like Vegemite. You don't put a bucket, a bundle of the shit, on the toast. A light smear at first. Get 'em used to the flavour.'

There was something chilling in Ashby's analogy. Just a little change to the gun laws, at first. You just have to wait until people can no longer taste the bitterness.

Chapter 23

One Nation's visit to Washington, DC, was coming to a close, and Ashby and Dickson were keen to squeeze in some shopping before they left.

Colin was called to drive them to Tysons Corner Center, a sprawling complex of designer stores some twenty kilometres across the Potomac River from the city. Rodger and Claudianna came along for the ride.

Ashby had his eye on clothing sales. 'I just want cheap shit, mate,' he said to Colin as they drove north along the George Washington Memorial Parkway.

But Dickson had a different idea. 'Let's go to a gun shop,' he said.

'That's *Steve's* idea of shopping,' Ashby said, with a wry smile.

'Yeah, I'll go there every day,' Dickson replied. 'Crawl in on my *knees* if I got to.'

Colin pulled off the Parkway into a strip mall near the Virginia–DC border. He stopped in front of a firearms store, and Dickson hurried inside.

'I lost all my guns,' he told a bearded salesman standing in front of a wall stacked with rifles and pistols.

'Really?' the salesman asked. 'They took *all* of them.'

'No, no, I'll start to cry.' Dickson feigned grief as he recounted Australia's strict gun control program. 'I'll lie on the floor and do bad shit that I don't want to do.'

'Fair enough!' the salesman said, laughing.

'It was terrible,' Dickson went on. 'That was a bad time for us. It was like hell on earth.'

While the One Nation visitors roamed the store, handling pistols and rifles, Claudianna asked the salesman, 'Do you sell to many ladies?'

The man answered by saying that he's seen his business change since Donald Trump came to power. 'What we've seen with Trump getting elected into office is there has been a rise of nutjobs,' he said. 'Like, there's a lot more scary people out there, like burning-cross kind of people that think, whether it's true or not, that they feel like they're in a much more friendly political climate.'

'Really?' Claudianna asked. Behind her, Dickson had lifted a semiautomatic off one of the racks and was feeling its weight in his hands.

'So, we're getting a lot more left-leaning people buying guns for the first time – female buyers, minority buyers,' the shopkeeper said. 'After the [Pulse nightclub massacre] in Orlando, we got a lot more of the LGBTQ community coming out. So, as people are recognising or feeling that they're in more danger, they're protecting themselves.' He adjusted his baseball cap. 'We've seen a huge shift just in the last few years that I've been selling firearms from being more of a right-wing, centrist-oriented thing to *way* more across-the-board.'

The so-called Trump Slump may have dented sales in other parts of the country – dropping sales by 6.1 per cent in 2018.[82] But trade in this shop, at least, showed that the core NRA strategy of keeping people angry and afraid, of arguing that guns are necessary to keep people safe from *other* people with guns, appeared to be holding firm.

If that strategy was designed to stop America's mass shootings, though, there was little evidence that it was working. Just days before One Nation's gun shop visit, the Gun Violence Archive recorded an incident in Cincinnati, Ohio, in which 'a gunman entered a loading dock at the Fifth Third Center skyscraper and opened fire before entering the lobby. Four people were killed.'

Other shootings that month included an incident in Silver Spring, Maryland, in which 'a father shot and killed his wife and two children ... before committing suicide', and one in Bakersfield, California, in which 'a gunman killed two women and three men before carjacking a woman and child and committing suicide when police approached'.

'I wish it was under better circumstances, but everybody's coming into the fold,' the shopkeeper said to Claudianna.

Dickson stopped at what looked like a sawn-off shotgun mounted on the wall. 'Mate, this is very cool.'

'Yeah, this one doesn't even require any special paperwork,' the salesman said.

'So, I could buy this and go?!' Dickson asked, astonished.

'Yeah, you can buy and walk out the door with it.'

'You're *shitting* me!' Dickson swivelled back to stare more closely at the gun.

'Because it's designed specifically to skirt around the laws,' the salesman explained. 'It's an 870 receiver, but it's never had a shoulder stock on.'

'How many rounds?' Dickson asked.

'Five plus one.'

'*Fuck*, yeah!' Ashby said.

'So, because it's never had a shoulder stock, it's never been designed to fire from the shoulder, so it's *not* a shotgun because a shotgun is designed to fire from the shoulder,' the salesman said. 'So, it's a twelve-gauge, *pistol-grip* firearm – not a shotgun. And because it's more than twenty-six inches long, it's not *any other weapon*. So, it flows right between the two narrowly defined rulings. It was designed to literally tiptoe around all of the laws and get through.'

Dickson listened, slack-jawed. The intricacies of America's firearms laws, and the genius of the methods being used to skirt them seemed to mesmerise him.

'So, how long are you guys in the country for?' the salesman asked.

It took Dickson no time to reply, 'Not long enough!'

* * *

At Tysons Corner Center later that day, Dickson and Ashby walked with Rodger and Claudianna into a ground-floor restaurant. Their shopping was now complete, and it was time for a quick bite before the drive back to Washington. The four were at ease; a great deal had been achieved in the six days since the One Nation delegates' arrival, and the Australians would have seemed, to any outside observers, to have been – at the very least – good friends.

Rodger suggested they take the table by the window.

Outside, from his van with blackened windows, Craig filmed as Dickson and Ashby were ushered to their seats. The restaurant and the seating arrangements had all been worked out in advance to give Rodger, Claudianna and Craig the best opportunity to capture their lunch conversation with as many camera angles as possible. Ashby and Dickson simply needed to be guided to the right spot, and they were happy to follow Rodger and Claudianna's lead.

Settled at the table, Ashby, Rodger and Claudianna placed orders for pasta, chicken and pizza. After a brief struggle with the menu ('What are *scallions*? ... What's a *tortilla*?'), Dickson settled on a plate of spaghetti bolognese.

As they ate, Dickson and Ashby started a discussion about how they weren't convinced that New York's Twin Towers had collapsed as a result of being hit by aircraft in the 9/11 attacks. Dickson said he thought elements of the incident were 'all very strange'. 'Think about how the building fell *down*,' he said.

'Sometimes I sit back and I think to myself, you know, the tinfoil-hatters come out and make a song and dance about it,' Ashby added. 'And then you actually read some of the evidence that they've put forward as to how those buildings fell, and you think, *Fuck, there is something dodgy there*.'

Rodger pushed back, saying that if the buildings had been demolished by explosives, surely clearly visible wires and detonators would have given the game away as people entered the building that morning.

'They don't need to wire them,' Dickson answered. 'There'd be one [explosive] here, one over there on that pillar. Electronics.'

Soon, talk turned back to political funding, with Dickson informing the table that he'd read of the elaborate methods used by the Koch brothers to dispense cash to political allies. 'The truth of the matter is that when you're dealing with the Koch brothers, mate, they do this shit all the time,' Dickson said. 'In countries all over the world. This ain't the first time. It's impossible to track where the money's coming from. Because it's like spaghetti. It all goes there, there, here and bounces off this and up this.' He waved his hands in the air to demonstrate the complexity of the way the money is moved. '*Boof, boof, boof!*' he said. 'And, like this, and it ends up in your glass. And you drink it.' Dickson looked at Rodger in silence for a second or two. 'But it's *money* we're talking about,' he added, perhaps thinking that his analogy of 'drinking spaghetti that had ended up in your glass' might have needed clarification.

Though it may have been obscure, Dickson's spaghetti reference was close to the mark. The Koch empire has pioneered a method of dispensing money to influence politics through a complex conglomeration of groups set up to avoid having to reveal the source of funding. Viveca Novak, the editorial and communications director at Washington's Center for Responsive Politics, said the Koch's Byzantine system of channelling money for political influence has been described as 'a daisy chain' – with money being passed from one group to another in a scheme that allows the Kochs to observe 'the letter of the law, not the spirit of the law'.

* * *

Before lunch Rodger and Claudianna had announced that they would remain in Washington for a few days before returning to Australia. Now, as they were eating, the One Nation visitors asked them to maintain contact with the people they'd met on the visit, including Koch's Catherine Haggett; her 'dark-magic shit' might still deliver after all, Dickson suggested.

'I think every single person that we got a card from, shoot them an email,' Dickson said to Claudianna. 'So, "great meeting you" … "fantastic" … "keep in touch",' he said, suggesting ways for her to phrase her communication.

But Ashby urged caution. 'A really important thing we need to be mindful of is that anything in writing can always be tracked and traced and used against you,' he said. 'So just be mindful of any wording that's used, especially if it's being CC'd to us. Sometimes, it's not worth putting some things in writing.' He said he wanted details of his meetings in America to be kept from the media. 'People will be like, "What the *fuck* is he doing over there? What are they doing? There's a contingent of One Nation people in the *United States!*"'

But one Australian journalist was already aware of the trip, he said. Though he didn't name the reporter and wasn't clear on how she'd found out, he said she had quizzed him on what he was up to. 'She said, "Can I ask who you met with?" And I said, "If I told you, you wouldn't believe me, anyway." I just left it at that,' he said, with a 'gotcha!' grin.

Dickson returned to the proposal he'd made earlier that Rodger help One Nation draft the party's proposed firearms legislation.

He wanted to confirm that Ashby was onboard with the idea. 'James, are you happy with what I spoke to Rodger about as far as assisting in knocking up some policy for us?'

'Yeah, I think that's a really wise decision,' Ashby replied. 'We need something that we can put forward to the federal government to supersede all state legislation.'

A little later, the idea of gun lobby money flowing to One Nation via Rodger's Gun Rights Australia group was raised.

Dickson shot it down. 'If he gets money and he starts donating to us,' he said to Ashby, 'they're just going to jump on you. The Electoral Commission will just come at you going, "We're doing a full audit, where's the money coming from?" It will take them five seconds, mate, to find out it's coming from the NRA.'

As the group finished lunch, Craig eased his camera from its mounting, slipped into the front seat of his van outside the restaurant, and waited to follow Colin's Tahoe back to the capital. He continued to film when the group, clutching their shopping bags, stepped into the foyer of Ashby and Dickson's hotel.

Chapter 24

The strip club came into focus through a rain-streaked cab window, lights beckoning from a forlorn leg of Washington's M Street.

Dickson dashed out of the taxi through a downpour to the safety of the building's awning, where a tattooed doorman gestured for him to enter.

Rodger stepped in after him.

In a murky room, the two men made their way to a bench seat at a table near the foot of a pole-dancing stage.

At eleven dollars a beer, this wasn't Rodger's kind of establishment, but — on his last night in Washington — Dickson had pushed hard for the outing. 'He wants me to take him to see strippers,' Rodger had told me in a call earlier that evening. 'He keeps pestering me to go.'

'What about Claudianna?' I'd asked.

'Dickson didn't invite her.'

'Well, go ahead and take him to a strip club, then,' I'd said. 'Just make sure you have your cameras rolling when you do.'

As they settled at their table, Dickson nodded at one of the waitresses.

'Little tits, nothing there,' he said to Rodger. 'Now, *that* young lady has got a wonderful set of kahoonas,' he said, pointing to another woman. 'I reckon we watch this bitch dance, hey?'

'She's hot.'

Music pounded from speakers mounted in the ceilings, and Dickson, enlivened by everything around him, started to sing along to a rock song.

A dancer settled onto Dickson's lap. He poked a dollar bill into her bra, taking the opportunity to fondle her breasts while he was at it.

He slipped another note in, then another, groping her more openly each time. 'You need to slide your hand on my cock now,' he said to her.

'Right now?' she asked.

'Yeah, absolutely.'

'I can't do that, sorry.' She looked over her shoulder. 'They'll probably notice.'

Dickson shifted his attention to the woman's groin, slipping cash into her garter, as he moved his mouth to her ear, whispering to her.

The woman left to fetch more drinks, and Dickson turned to Rodger.

'She said she wants to come home and suck my dick,' he said. 'I'm going to give her my address. Mate, she said she'd come over and fuck me.'

Dickson stood and made his way to the edge of the pole-dancing stage, holding a wad of dollar bills. A dancer lifted one of her legs and rested it on his shoulder; she leaned back, gyrating, as Dickson pushed a dollar note into the elastic of her garter, his fingers lingering at her crotch.

The woman Dickson claimed had offered him sex brought a new round of drinks to the table, passing a comment to Rodger about Dickson's behaviour.

'He's so *demanding*. He said, "You haven't touched my cock!"'

Dickson returned to the table and took a sip of his drink. 'I think white women fuck a whole lot better,' he said. 'They know what they're doing. Asian chicks don't. I've done more Asian than I know what to do with.'

The music swelled as more men crowded into the room.

'Mate, I've never been to one of these before for a long time,' Dickson said. 'The last time would have been in the Philippines. That's actually better because they dance on top of the bars and then take everything off.'

'So, you couldn't do this in Australia?' Rodger asked.

The One Nation Senate candidate and proud Christian paused for a moment. 'Ah, probably not a good idea.'

He pulled out another dollar note and leaned down, reaching again for the waitress's crotch.

***

Al Jazeera's investigation into the NRA and One Nation was nearing its conclusion. By mid-September, I'd gathered hundreds of hours of video on the association alone; One Nation's late arrival had added a vast amount of new material, and I was now in the midst of trying to work out how, exactly, I would turn what had been recorded into a TV documentary.

Transcribers had been hard at work viewing everything we'd filmed and providing me with a written record. Rows of ringbinders holding those documents lined the walls of my office in the Investigative Unit's bunker, spanning the length of the room and spilling across my desk.

I was also working my way through our video to confirm that transcriptions were accurate, and to take my own notes on how this story might be told.

It was obvious to me that the material we'd gathered would horrify the people of Australia. That Pauline Hanson's delegates had gone to a foreign country in search of funding and political support from a rabidly pro-gun lobby group and other entities seemed, at the very least, to be a catastrophic political misstep.

In his role as the leader of Gun Rights Australia, Rodger Muller had made no secret of his desire to wind back Australia's gun laws. And yet One Nation had not only enlisted him to help set up meetings for them in America, they had also invited him to help fashion their new gun policy. With the vast majority of Australians still very much in favour of the post–Port Arthur firearms laws, it seemed clear to me that One Nation's behaviour in Washington was something Aussies wouldn't swallow – no matter how light the smear of Ashby's Vegemite.

'Do we have a film?' Phil Rees had asked in his latest call.

'We do.'

'An hour?'

'I think it's more like two,' I'd answered. 'But it's not quite over yet.'

* * *

Colin stepped onto the pavement and helped Dickson and Ashby lift their suitcases into the back of his car as the One Nation delegates readied for their ride back to the airport on 9 September 2018. From their perspective, friendships had been forged here, opportunities had been created. Brisbane — and a reunion with Pauline Hanson — was now just a day's travel away.

'It's been really good,' Dickson said to Rodger and Claudianna, who stood by the car. They were tantalisingly close to the end of this leg of their undercover assignment, and both were counting the minutes until Colin drove the One Nation visitors away — finally, a chance for them to strip themselves of their hidden cameras and relax.

'Mate, I didn't know that this was all going to happen,' Dickson said, as if to suggest he'd once doubted Rodger's ability to deliver the meetings he and Ashby had requested. 'I've heard a lot of people tell me shit in my lifetime and most of it *didn't* happen.'

If Dickson was feeling fatigued from his late-night strip club frolic, he showed no sign of it. There was no discussion of the pleasures he had sought in the club's dimly lit rooms, nor of his behaviour at his hotel bar afterwards, where drinking and pawing at women had continued into the early morning — all of it captured on film by Rodger.

There was also no mention of the money Dickson and Rodger had spent at the club – by Rodger's count, close to five hundred US dollars on food and drink, in addition to the many US dollar notes wedged against the breasts and vulvas of waitresses and dancers, as Dickson had set about to single-handedly demolish the narrative – driven so hard on this trip – that he was a man of piety, integrity and fidelity working to make Australia a safer place for women.

Was that fake news? Or an alternative truth?

Dickson had been clear, on this trip, that he believed a guiding hand was steering his journey in life. 'I'll tell you something I haven't told anybody,' he'd said at one gathering. 'About a year and a half ago … I walked out to my front yard and looked up to the sky, and I saw a cloud and it was shaped like a hand. And the next thing, the finger grew out of it, and came down at me and it touched me. And my whole life changed. *Everything* changed. And that's why I'm doing exactly what I'm doing right now.'

* * *

Dickson and Ashby's drive to the airport took them past some of the key venues they'd visited on their trip.

Colin went along 14th Street, past the Koch offices that still held promise as a potential source of funding.

The car crossed the Potomac, moving away from the strip mall where Dickson had marvelled at a gun built to avoid all regulations, and away from Tyson's Corner where, over lunch, discussions had advanced Rodger's mission to write One Nation's new firearms policy. The Tahoe pulled into Reagan Airport where, just a week ago, Dickson and Ashby had arrived in Washington, flushed with excitement.

One Nation's delegates gave warm thanks to Rodger and Claudianna for their help.

'We'll do a barbecue over at [Pauline Hanson's] house,' Dickson offered. 'And you might want to shoot some hares while you're there.'

Just before they parted, Ashby had a final word of advice for Rodger and Claudianna: be very careful, indeed, in dealing with the media.

'You can't be mates with a journalist,' he warned. 'It's like owning a viper. It will bite you eventually.'

Chapter 25

Rodger and Claudianna flew back to Australia after Ashby and Dickson had departed and set about confirming the barbecue invitation at Pauline Hanson's house.

It would be one last undercover filming opportunity, and a chance to hear from the party leader herself about what she thought of her delegates' achievements in Washington, DC.

Dates were set, then reset, until the idea of a barbecue was changed to a December 2018 dinner with Hanson and Ashby at a restaurant in the town of Yeppoon on the central coast of Queensland, following a One Nation fish and chip event with supporters there. Such gatherings had become commonplace as a way for the senator to connect with One Nation members – a nod to her days running a fish and chip shop in Ipswich before entering politics.

Rodger and Claudianna travelled to Yeppoon a day ahead of the dinner to conduct a reconnaissance of the restaurant, and Craig flew in from Washington to help with the filming operations. The team was joined by video editor

Adrian Billing – aka 'Neil', the 'wedding photographer' – who made his way up from Brisbane.

Apart from a brief encounter with Pauline Hanson at the Penrith Panthers club earlier in the year, Rodger had spent no time with the One Nation leader. Now he would have a chance to bond with her, as he had done with those who'd visited Washington on behalf of the party she led. As the Yeppoon event got underway, a tropical storm howled into town, lashing the beach club where the One Nation faithful had gathered in a meeting room. About fifty supporters – men in shorts and thongs, women in summery dresses – sat on white fold-out chairs as Hanson stood at the end of the room holding a microphone in one hand, her other pressed against her hip. Curtains were drawn against floor-to-ceiling windows, blocking views of the Capricorn Coast.

Hanson, wearing a black knee-length dress with a floral print, her flame-red hair neatly coiffed, fashioned her remarks, in part, to address the foul weather. 'The whole climate change issue has been an absolute *scam*,' she told the crowd. 'And, yes, it's raining today. Yes, it's a cyclone. It's not the first one and it won't be the last one that we've ever had.'

A number of people in the audience nodded.

'A lot of these scientists now have got jobs that they've never had. And the science that they put forward hasn't been investigated by others. We've been taken for *fools*, and I don't go along with it. I want to see the *true* science.'

Hanson's voice was quivering with anger.

'The whole fact is that they're brainwashing the kids through the educational system, and people think it's all coming to an end, like the icecaps are melting. Well, they are in the northern hemisphere, but they're actually growing in the southern hemisphere so there's not much difference whatsoever.'

Rodger and Claudianna sat among the crowd, their hidden cameras taking in the scene, as they nibbled on fish and chips.

'I've worked too bloody hard,' Hanson went on. 'I haven't stood here all these years and put up with all the crap that I've been dished out to not want to achieve something for the people that I believe in for this country.'

It was a familiar refrain: the educated 'elites' are out of control, duping the rest of the country – the honest, hardworking people – with outrageous distortions of reality.

The 'science' used by those warning of climate change was not *true* science.

You are being lied to by frauds.

What you are being told is 'true' is really 'false'.

I will show you the difference between the two.

Hanson's supporters applauded, and she stepped into the crowd, shaking hands and thanking people for making their way to the event through the storm.

She spotted Rodger and moved towards him. 'I'll see you tonight,' she said, smiling.

From the edge of the crowd, James Ashby watched as Rodger stood, nodded yes to Hanson, and sat down again.

* * *

Rodger had arranged to interview Hanson on camera just after the fish and chip event, telling her it was for his

Gun Rights Australia website, just as he'd done with Steve Dickson ahead of their visit to America. Video editor Adrian Billing remembered, this time, to use his alias 'Neil' when he introduced himself.

Rodger started the interview with an effort at flattery. 'Pauline, from your politics, we know you're a straight shooter,' he said. 'And from your Facebook videos we know you're a good shot. What is your message to Gun Rights Australia supporters who are thinking about who to support in the upcoming elections?'

Hanson's response was pure NRA. 'I think it's about the right to bear arms,' she said. 'Firearms have always been part of the Australian culture and way of life.'

Playing to what she believed to be a staunchly pro-gun audience, while echoing Dickson's multiple references in Washington to the failure of Australia's gun control laws, Hanson went on. 'I oppose what John Howard did. He took legitimate firearms and antique firearms off people. They were in the families for a long time. All they're doing is taking it out of the hands of legitimate people. And they're actually allowing criminals to actually have the firearms.'

In what sounded like a paraphrasing of the Second Amendment's reference to a 'militia being necessary to the security of a free state', Hanson added, 'I believe that everyone, male and female, should have some knowledge of how to handle a firearm, how to protect themselves, because I don't trust our governments to be able to do it for us.'

* * *

Some hours later, Craig and Adrian were ready to video from a van positioned directly in front of a window into the restaurant where Rodger and Claudianna, wearing their hidden cameras, were due to dine with Hanson and Ashby.

Under the unlikely restaurant logo of a goat smoking a joint, the group assembled at a large table. Fairy lights adorned the walls around them.

'So, all in all, you were happy with the boys, they did a good job in the States?' Rodger asked Hanson as he sipped a beer.

'Of course they did, *yes*,' she replied, appearing slightly offended that he may have suggested otherwise. 'They wanted me to go over there, and I said, "No." I've got to tell you how I go on my gut feelings. And it's really to do with the gun issue and tied up with the American issue at the moment, it's not going to be good for me in the first place.'

She took a sip of white wine.

'Okay ...' Rodger said, leaving the senator to continue.

'I have to actually take it in baby steps,' Hanson went on. 'I have to actually get more people elected to Parliament, which I will do after this next federal election. And then these are things that can be looked at. At the moment, they will use everything they possibly can, because they see me as the biggest threat against them. That's why I didn't go. Because I thought it's not a politically smart move for me to do.'

Hanson appeared to contradict her suggestion, made to Rodger earlier that day, that women in Australia should be given access to guns for self-protection. 'I'm in fear of people carrying, especially women, carrying guns,' she said as they cut into barramundi and steak fillets. 'You have idiots out there who will attack them, take the gun from them, you've got to have *more* handguns.'

Hanson's apparent change of heart on her earlier statement that all Australians should have 'the right to bear arms' led Rodger to try to clarify where she stood on the issue.

'Do I want to see *females* carrying guns for protection?' Hanson said to him. 'No … I don't. You won't get it in Australia, I'm telling you,' she added sharply, as if a blazing anger was stirring within her. 'If I actually went out there saying that, it would be political *suicide* for me. With massacres happening in America, it's going to take a lot to shift people's way of thinking.'

What she said next stunned Rodger and Claudianna, as the conversation turned to Australia's most infamous mass shooting, the Port Arthur massacre.

'An MP said it would actually take a massacre in Tasmania to change the gun laws in Australia.' Hanson nodded as she spoke. 'Haven't you heard of that?'

She looked directly at Rodger.

'I hadn't heard *that* one,' Rodger answered, taken aback.

'Have a look at it,' Hanson said, with a knowing look.

'It was said on the floor of Parliament. Those shots, they were *precision* shots. Check the number out. I've read a lot and I've read the book on it … on Port Arthur.' She looked at Rodger, nodding again. 'A lot of questions there.'

If what we'd seen of One Nation's behaviour in Washington was the party's pro-gun face, it seemed we were now being exposed to its raw and pimply bottom: a leader prone to conspiracy theories – and not so keen on guns for self-protection after all. Or at least not so keen on guns for the vulnerable women Dickson and Ashby had spoken about so passionately in their week of meetings in Washington – women who Dickson had suggested might feature as part of an NRA-inspired media campaign to push for more firearms in Australia.

As the Yeppoon dinner progressed, One Nation made it clear that it planned to maintain its relationship with the cashed-up US gun association.

'We're going over there … in January,' Rodger said, referring to Gun Rights Australia's plan to meet with a group in Texas that donates heavily to international pro-gun organisations.

Ashby, sitting at his leader's side like a mole-rat sniffing the semi-darkness for political opportunity, said he and Hanson would come too.

'Wait till the federal election is over and we're there,' he said. 'After the federal election, we're laughing. We'll go.'

* * *

Undercover filming for the investigation that had begun in 2015 was now complete.

The dinner with Hanson and Ashby was the final concealed video sequence we needed, and it was time to finish piecing together a structure for how the two-part documentary would flow.

The 570 hours of video was sent to Adrian in Brisbane, who began the process of viewing and categorising elements of the film in preparation for his edit.

I packed my research files, transcripts and field notes — along with enough clothes to last for several months away — and flew from Washington to Sydney, where I would spend the remainder of December scripting the documentary in a hotel room.

With a two-month edit scheduled to commence in the first week of January, the film would be ready for broadcast, at the very earliest, in March 2019.

I now had to stand my undercover team down.

I phoned Claudianna and Rodger together with news that their hidden-camera operation was finally complete.

'You've both done a brilliant job,' I said.

'Hey, there were some close calls, but we got through this without being detected, which is an extraordinary achievement given the length and complexity of the project. Thank you so much.'

Claudianna said, 'So no more hidden cameras? Okay. It's been an amazing experience. But what about the Gun Rights Australia website — should we leave it up and running?'

'Keep it going for now,' I answered.

Rodger's response to the news that undercover filming was finished left me stunned. 'But, mate, there's no *story* here,' he said, a touch of anxiety in his voice. 'These guys haven't done anything that's worth putting to air. And, besides, the people we've been filming are *good people*.'

I realised then that I had a major problem on my hands.

Chapter 26

This wasn't meant to happen. Rodger was solid. Rodger was one of ours.

But 'the founder and president of Gun Rights Australia' had been filming people within the National Rifle Association and other gun lobby groups not just for months – he'd been at it for *years*. The relationships he'd forged there went far beyond a businesslike meet and greet. He had grown to *like* some of these people. And he knew that some had grown to like him too.

Now he was showing strong signs of what looked like Stockholm syndrome, a condition in which bonds develop between captives and captors: he either couldn't see the significance of what he'd helped procure for Al Jazeera's Investigative Unit, or he didn't want the people he'd been spying on to be hurt.

He called me several times, urging me to hold off on going to air to give him 'more time to find more material'. 'There's nothing we've filmed that's of any use,' he said in one call.

'*I'll* make those judgements,' I told him.

I was, of course, aware of the sacrifices Rodger had made on Al Jazeera's behalf in his transformation into a gun nut. The physical abuse he'd suffered at the hands of enraged Australians who didn't want changes to gun laws had been difficult for him and painful for his family. I later learned that he had taken himself to see a psychologist as he wrestled with his dual personalities. Hiding the reality of what he was doing for me had strained him profoundly.

In the first days of the project, Rodger later told me, he would return to his hotel room and strip the place, searching for cameras that Al Jazeera may have hidden to film *him*. Such were the mind games tormenting the man who was secretly videoing hundreds of hours of unguarded comments – sometimes deeply private remarks – from people who saw him as a friend and an ally.

Were hidden cameras recording *all of us*, he wondered at one point?

As for his family and close friends, Rodger told me they saw his sudden interest in guns as 'Rodger being Rodger' – just another example of a man with eclectic, sometimes hard-to-understand interests. But some friends drifted away from him, disturbed by his newfound fascination with firearms and his emerging public profile as somebody who was uncomfortable with Australia's gun control laws. Others – the gun-lovers – embraced him as a comrade.

I understood Rodger's concern for the many people he knew were about to learn that their comments to a 'friend' had been covertly recorded in meeting after meeting, year after year. I thought, *It's only human to feel for those who will soon suffer as a result of what he's been doing, right?* But the decision on whether to move forward with the documentary – and how the film would look – wasn't Rodger's to make. That call rested with Phil Rees and me, along with a team of lawyers we'd assembled around the world to give guidance on what could be shown in the film.

Rodger and I arranged to meet in Sydney in December 2018, to talk the matter through. Over lunch, then beers, then dinner, we discussed what it would mean for him to return to the life he'd led before I called him in late 2015, asking him to join the NRA investigation. Though, with typical bravado, Rodger expressed no fear of reprisals from people he'd been secretly recording, I told him that Al Jazeera would put him in an overseas safe house when the film came out – just in case. Claudianna would also be protected.

Soon, I said, your inside-out world will right itself – as much as it can. Soon, you can remove your gun-lover mask, at last. And when you do, you will be seen as a hero by some, and as a traitor by others. Enemies will target you, I said – they will target everyone who worked on this project, claiming that we tricked them, deceived them, entrapped them, misrepresented them, misquoted them. They will muster their allies to harm us however they can. But that's a price we pay for exposing the truth.

* * *

'For three years, Al Jazeera has been investigating the pro-gun lobby ...'

I scanned my laptop screen, reviewing the first lines of the documentary script.

'... filming with hidden cameras inside America's National Rifle Association ...'

I had moved to a Brisbane hotel in preparation for the edit, which was about to take place at a secure location nearby.

The first draft of the script was complete, and I was now working through the film, line by line, finessing sentences as I went.

'... And tracking a political party from Australia, as they seek millions of dollars from the US gun lobby.'

From my hotel-room desk, I could see – just across the Brisbane River – the very building that housed Dickson's and Ashby's offices, which Rodger had visited with his hidden cameras to discuss One Nation's much-anticipated introduction to the NRA.

'If they threw ten million dollars at us, we could fucking win a heap of seats, plus a shitload of seats in the Senate,' Dickson had said to Rodger at the time.

I imagined Ashby and Dickson inside those offices now, peering over the city as the summer heat pressed onto the streets below.

'In secretly recorded meetings, the One Nation political party promises to reverse Australia's gun control laws ...'

What on earth would they think when the film I was now working on went to air? And how would they feel when they learned I'd been sitting just across the river from them – almost close enough to see people through the windows of their office tower – as I worked on the film that would soon engulf them in a political firestorm?

I turned back to the script.

'One Nation learns from the US gun lobby how to sell the message that more guns are good ...'

* * *

I'd brought Claudianna to Brisbane with me to help with the edit. Her firsthand recollections of our undercover filming within the groups we'd infiltrated – including One Nation – would be an invaluable cross-reference as the story took shape. Soon, a second video editor, Leo Sofogiannis, would fly in from the Investigative Unit's Doha headquarters to work with Adrian Billing as the documentary was being assembled, and Phil Rees would visit to oversee final production of the project.

Over the next ten weeks, key decisions would be made among our group about the tone and phrasing of the film: Have we portrayed One Nation's Washington visit accurately? Are the interview 'grabs' we've selected truly representative of what was said by the infiltrated groups? Should we use *this* vision or *that* vision? Is it fair to couple these pictures with these words?

And what about that damning video of Steve Dickson in the strip club? Should that be included? Dickson had behaved inappropriately, sure. What he'd said and done ran counter to his public image as a family man, a Christian committed to the safety and wellbeing of women. But the film was about a grab for foreign gun lobby cash. It was about the suggestion from One Nation to potential donors in gun-mad America that the party was open to lessening some of the restrictions that came with Australian laws – legislation that Dickson said 'still made him angry'. The Senate candidate's behaviour with strippers was clearly in the public interest, but I didn't believe it advanced the editorial thrust of our film. Indeed, it was likely to be a distraction.

After lengthy discussions on the pros and cons of bringing the strip club event to light, we agreed that the vision would not go to air.

* * *

With the team in Brisbane rushing to meet the March broadcast deadline, Rodger was now back at work at his dog food business, knowing that soon the NRA and One Nation would become aware of his real identity. Since our discussions, he'd come to accept the release of the film, and his concerns that 'there was nothing there' had eased after he'd read the script and viewed a rough cut of the edit.

He could see, now, the damning recordings in context; One Nation's interactions with America's gun lobby would not be well received by Australians who were *glad* to have strict gun control laws in place. And the video he and Claudianna had filmed had shown that the party was eager to secure funding from American donors just as Australia's Parliament was moving to make such activities illegal.

'Jail time if you get done,' Ashby had told Rodger over dinner in Yeppoon, in reference to the anti-foreign donation laws that came into effect just ten weeks after he and Dickson had been seeking cash in Washington.

Rodger's true role in the project would be disclosed the moment those we'd covertly filmed received their 'right of reply' notifications: emails and hard-copy letters sent by Al Jazeera to the main figures in the film, outlining the content of the upcoming documentary and inviting the recipients to respond.

I was aware of the alarm those letters would cause when they were opened by Pauline Hanson, Steve Dickson, James Ashby and others. The comments we'd caught on hidden camera were laid out to them in stark and shocking terms.

Hanson's right of reply letter said, in part:

Al Jazeera's Investigative Unit is in the final stages of preparing two documentaries concerning the pro-gun lobby in the United States and its interactions with Pauline Hanson's One Nation party in Australia.

As part of our research for these programs, an undercover investigator infiltrated parts of the U.S. gun lobby and, over a three-year period, observed evidence of their activities.

Undercover investigators also observed the activities of Pauline Hanson's One Nation party in Australia as members of the party prepared for meetings with members of the U.S. gun lobby, and also as representatives of your political party visited the United States and attended a series of meetings with members of the U.S. gun lobby in Washington, DC and in Fairfax, Virginia.

It is our intention to broadcast details of these activities, including comments made by you and members of your political party, in our two scheduled programs in March 2019.

Among other questions, the senator was asked to confirm:

That you were aware that James Ashby and Steve Dickson had travelled to the United States in an effort to secure up to US$20 million in political donations from the U.S. gun lobby?

That you were aware that James Ashby and Steve Dickson had discussed with members of the U.S. gun lobby their intentions to change Australia's gun control laws?

Whether you believe the Port Arthur massacre was an event that had been pre-planned and orchestrated specifically to create a climate in which the government would be justified in removing guns from Australian citizens?

Steve Dickson was told:

The Al Jazeera documentaries will include references to you expressing the following views:

That you wish to seek political donations of up to US$20 million from the National Rifle Association (the NRA).

That you would like the NRA to establish 'a political wing in Australia'.

That political funding from the NRA would guarantee Pauline Hanson's One Nation party 'a heap of seats, plus a shitload of seats in the senate'.

That in meetings aimed at securing funding for Pauline Hanson's One Nation party, you have informed members of the U.S. gun lobby that you intend to roll back Australia's National Firearms Agreements (the NFA).

That, if sufficient funding is secured in the United States, you would obtain the balance of power in the Australian Parliament and that you would 'have the (Australian) government by the balls'.

That if Australia doesn't change its gun control laws, 'people are going to look at Australia and go "well, it's okay for them to go down that path of not having guns, it's okay for them to go down that politically correct path"' and it's 'like a poison. It will poison us all unless we stop it.'

That by 'killing' anti-gun sentiment in Australia, 'it's like inoculating against a disease'.

That you asked Rodger Muller, the founder and president of the pro-gun group Gun Rights Australia, to help write a new firearms policy for Pauline Hanson's One Nation party.'

That if Rodger Muller can provide you with contacts at the NRA who might be able to provide millions of dollars of funding to One Nation, you will, 'make sure you open any fucking door you need open'.

James Ashby was told that he'd been observed saying, 'that, in order for pro-gun advocates to prepare the Australian electorate for a softening of the nation's gun laws, they need to introduce the idea of change "like Vegemite, you don't put a bundle on toast at once. Just a smear, at first. Get them used to the flavour.'"

And that he had said, '"you need to soften people back up again" in order to prepare them to accept less stringent gun laws in Australia and that part of that process will involve implementing women's shooting range programs and self-defence programs.'

Once the right of reply letters had been approved by our lawyers and signed off by Phil Rees, I loaded them into Al Jazeera's right of reply email portal, double-checked that they were all in order, and hit send.

* * *

A week later, I sat at my hotel desk and glanced again across the Brisbane River to the building housing One Nation's offices. There was still no response to the right of reply letters.

I opened my computer to check once again.

Nothing.

I stood to leave for the edit suite when I glimpsed a breaking news headline on my hotel TV screen: 'Gunman opens fire in Christchurch mosque'.

An Australian citizen – unable to buy an assault rifle at home because of Australia's gun control laws – had travelled to New Zealand to purchase an AR-15 and other firearms.

While livestreaming to the internet, he'd walked into a mosque, gunning down worshippers as he went.

He killed fifty-one people and wounded forty-nine.

The 15 March 2019 attack had given grisly context to the revelations of our soon-to-be-released film, and to the discussions Dickson and Ashby had held with the gun lobby in America. It had set the scene for a re-run of the NRA's talking points on how to behave in the wake of such events.

Sensing a groundswell of anti-gun sentiment in New Zealand, the NRA reached first for its good-guy-with-a-gun argument, with the organisation's Dana Loesch retweeting claims on the day of the attack, that someone had fired shots at the Christchurch shooter, scaring him off.[83]

That was incorrect.

But the core narrative of One Nation, reflecting what Dickson had told pro-gun advocates on his visit to America, had been drawn into the open by the mosque atrocity.

'Does anyone still dispute the link between Muslim immigration and violence?' former One Nation senator Fraser Anning tweeted hours after the shooting. The massacre, he said, 'highlights the growing fear within our community, both in Australia and New Zealand, of the increasing Muslim presence'.[84]

Even by the standards of a hard-bitten Islamophobe, Anning's take on the slaughter in a mosque was staggering.

His remarks had attracted such odium that when a seventeen-year-old boy smashed a raw egg into Anning's head on 16 March, causing the former One Nation senator to punch him in the face in reprisal, video of the incident went viral — earning the boy brief global fame as 'eggboy', with praise for his actions flooding his Instagram account.[85]

New Zealand's Prime Minister, Jacinda Ardern, meanwhile, pressed on with plans for Australian-like gun control laws.

'Today I am announcing that New Zealand will ban all military-style semiautomatic weapons,' she said on 20 March – five days after the mosque attack.

'We will also ban all assault rifles,' Ardern added. 'We will ban all high-capacity magazines, we will ban all parts with the ability to convert semiautomatic or any type of firearm into a military-style semiautomatic weapon.'[86]

The NRA reverted to driving anger through its ranks – its outrage-of-the-week strategy – with claims that the New Zealand gun laws represented 'tyranny' and amounted to the work of 'a dictatorship'.[87]

'Gun confiscation, not "common-sense reform," is the ultimate goal of gun control advocates,' the NRA wrote in a newsletter on 22 March. 'This goal existed long before the Christchurch attack. The recent stateside reaction to the New Zealand government's actions has only served to further reveal this long-held but oft-concealed position.'[88]

It was a classic use of the strategy suggested to Dickson and Ashby by the NRA media team during their Washington visit as a way to claim political high ground after a mass shooting. 'How *dare* you stand on the graves of those children to put forth your political agenda?' Lars Dalseide had proposed as a form of words for One Nation to use against gun control advocates. 'Like, if your policy isn't good enough to stand on its own,' he'd added, 'how *dare* you use their deaths to push that forward?'

Three weeks after the Christchurch shooting, the Senate would vote to censure Fraser Anning for his remarks linking the attack to Muslim immigration.

Pauline Hanson abstained.

Chapter 27

My phone rang at 5 a.m.

It was Washington on the line. I was told to get ready for a live appearance to discuss my story. It was 26 March and I was back in Sydney. Al Jazeera had just released *How to Sell a Massacre* internationally, and part one of the story would be aired around Australia on ABC TV that evening. The ABC's editorial policy manager, Mark Maley, had earlier viewed the program and, based on its strong public interest, had green-lit its national broadcast.

My phone rang again: Radio National, ABC Radio, ABC *News Breakfast*, Radio 3AW and triple j wanted me on air.

This was going to be a crazy day.

I took a cab to the ABC Ultimo studios and was ushered upstairs to the radio department. Presenter Fran Kelly greeted me in the Radio National waiting room.

'Well,' she said, 'haven't *you* stirred up a hornets' nest?'

As she was interviewing me on air a few minutes later, news emerged of reactions around the country to the documentary. Attorney-General Christian Porter expressed concern about One Nation's US visit, saying, 'I think there's a real question that needs to be answered here.' Meanwhile, One Nation announced that it had referred Al Jazeera to Australia's intelligence agency, ASIO, and the Australian Federal Police, accusing the network of acting as foreign agents for the government of Qatar.

Fran Kelly asked for my reaction.

'[Al Jazeera] is indeed foreign-owned,' I replied, 'as the ABC is owned by the government of Australia. And it could be argued that Australian ABC correspondents operating overseas may also be representing the interests of *their* government, which is clearly preposterous.'

Fran asked me whether Al Jazeera would be prepared to release the full context of what had been recorded. I said I was happy to do so, but that there may be some conversations recorded by Rodger and Claudianna that One Nation wouldn't want disclosed.

Had Dickson revealed to Pauline Hanson that he had groped women in a Washington strip club, I wondered? Had Ashby told her that a man had received brain damage after Ashby had smashed a chair across his head, and that Ashby had then told police 'the man fell over and hit his head'?

Whether Hanson knew these details or not, there were things on Al Jazeera's tapes that One Nation surely would not want brought to light.

Interviews followed on the ABC News 24 channel, on triple j's *Hack* program, on ABC Radio's *PM*, and with Associated Press, Reuters and multiple other radio programs around Australia and New Zealand as requests flooded in for appearances on channels Seven, Nine and Ten.

In Canberra, politicians lined up to address the cameras in what ABC reporter Melissa Clarke described as 'a cavalcade of MPs condemning and asking for explanations of One Nation'. She said, 'The prospect of an American gun lobby group influencing politics in Australia has clearly been repellent to the broad Australian politic.'

Prime Minister Scott Morrison weighed in, telling reporters that 'no law should be up to the highest bidder as some part of foreign interference'. He added, 'And it's our government that has actually put in place the laws that would make that impossible. If you're ever wondering why you shouldn't be voting One Nation, there's a pretty good reason.'

All this before the documentary had even gone to air on the ABC.

Then news broke that Steve Dickson and James Ashby had called a media conference to give *their* side of the story.

* * *

That afternoon, the two men at the centre of the storm shuffled onto a lawn in Brisbane in front of journalists, explaining that Pauline Hanson would not be joining them. She was very unwell, Ashby told reporters. Only later would it emerge that she'd been bitten by a tick.

A *tick*?!

So, Ashby and Dickson went it alone.

Looking dumbstruck, Dickson kicked off. 'It's the first time I've ever seen anything like this in my life,' he said.

'Not only was it the first time I'd gone to America, but to see that somebody had gone to the trouble from a Middle Eastern country, and Al Jazeera paying a spy to come to Australia to set up Gun Rights Australia, I mean this is the stuff you see in James Bond magazines. I would never, ever suspect that you would see this for real in the *real* world.'

Dickson described the process he and Ashby had gone through, after receiving their right of reply letters, as they'd tried to identify who at their meetings had been secretly recording them. After eliminating everyone they'd met with, they had reached the stunning conclusion that it was none other than the affable Rodger Muller, someone Dickson now said 'seemed like a very reasonable guy' who 'wore the Akubra hat'.

I wondered, when he said that, whether Dickson was aware yet that Rodger's disarming headpiece had housed a camera.

'I never, ever, *ever* suspected in my wildest dreams that this guy was employed by a Middle Eastern country, by Al Jazeera, as an Australian spy to interfere in Australian politics,' Dickson said.

Ashby spoke next. With a frown creasing his forehead, he tried to explain why he and Dickson had travelled to America in the first place. 'This was *not* about sourcing money from the NRA,' he said sternly. 'This was about sourcing technology, sourcing an understanding about how they operate, but never was it about seeking twenty million dollars from the NRA. The conversations that have been recorded where there is a talk of ten or twenty million dollars, I'll be the first to admit, we'd arrived in America, we'd got on the sauce, we'd had a few drinks, and that's where those discussions took place.'

So, they'd been drunk?

Yes, they'd consumed alcohol in Washington on their first night in town (Dickson confirmed, as Ashby was tallying the restaurant and bar bill, that he'd had 'two bourbons').

But there was no evidence of the booze talking when, in One Nation's Brisbane office, Dickson had said to Rodger: 'This is the thing I want to get through your head: if [the NRA] threw ten million dollars at us, we could fucking win a heap of seats, plus a shitload of seats in the Senate.'

Nor was liquor involved when, en route to their meeting with Koch Industries in Washington, Dickson had said, 'I'm thinking ten [million]', and Ashby had added, 'No, I was thinking twenty', when Rodger had asked them how much they were hoping to secure if the Koch representatives 'started talking figures'.

'There were many, many things that were videoed, and I believe a lot of those things were taken out of sequence,' Dickson told reporters at the media conference. 'I put it on Facebook. I showed the world we were there,' he said, talking about his visit to the NRA headquarters. 'Everybody in this country knew we were there ... the *world* knew we were over there. We never hid a thing.'

Indeed, Dickson had published his enthusiastic review of the National Rifle Association firearms museum, but he hadn't referenced meetings with NRA officials that took place immediately after the museum visit. Nor had he published anything about his meeting with NRA lobbyist Brandi Graham, or the discussions in which the NRA media team had offered advice on how to drive fear into society in order to justify 'the right to bear arms' in Australia.

'This next election is fast approaching,' Ashby declared to the media throng. 'This was a deliberate set-up by the Qatari government under Al Jazeera. This is skulduggery at its worst. This is the very first time Australia has witnessed political interference from a foreign government. Nothing could be more damaging to a political party like One Nation than what we've seen today.'

As the two men drew the news conference to a close, Dickson offered one last comment to reporters. 'I'm sorry about sweating,' he said. 'But it's hot.'

* * *

The fever pitch that had driven media interest in the film throughout the day was about to crank up to eleven. While part one was being broadcast on the ABC that evening, more interview requests came in, as news of the documentary – and its impact in Australia – spread around the world.

Claudianna and Adrian, who were with me in Sydney to help manage the frenzy of media interest, arranged my schedule for the following day: there would be more radio, more TV, more comment to the press and to wire services.

By then, stories on *How to Sell a Massacre* were being carried in every major Australian hard-copy and online newspaper, they were leading TV and radio news bulletins around the nation and they were trending on Twitter.

The story was on fire.

By midafternoon the day after part one went to air, news of *How to Sell a Massacre* was in mainstream media all over the world – in outlets from the *New York Times* and the *Washington Post* to the *China Daily* and Zimbabwe's *Mail & Guardian*.

The overwhelming majority of stories pointed to the behaviour of One Nation in America and the audacity of the undercover operation to infiltrate the NRA. But there were also accusations that Rodger Muller had 'entrapped' One Nation by tempting the party into meetings with the NRA.

It was my strong view that 'entrapment' would have involved efforts on our part to lure One Nation, against their better judgement, into actions that they would otherwise not have wished to have taken, knowing they were illegal or inappropriate. Nothing of the sort had occurred. In fact, James Ashby had shown a willingness from the start to connect with the NRA, having told Rodger at their first meeting that 'I should really go to America to meet them', and asking for Rodger to connect with Steve Dickson and to share with One Nation the contacts he'd developed within the US gun community.

Other journalists questioned our construction of a fake gun rights organisation as a way to penetrate the fortress of the National Rifle Association. *The Conversation* was one of the first to address this issue, publishing an article on 25 March with the headline, 'Did Al Jazeera's Undercover Investigation into One Nation Overstep the Mark?'[89]

Andrew Dodd, director of the Centre for Advancing Journalism at the University of Melbourne, wrote that, 'from where I stand, it looks like Al Jazeera's motivation was to get to the heart of something fundamentally important that would otherwise remain opaque ... the public has a clear right to know what One Nation is up to'.

Dodd concluded that the Investigative Unit had been justified in using concealed cameras.

'For me, the use of hidden cameras can clearly be defended when a publicly funded Australian political party, that knows what it's doing is dodgy, is making connections to "change Australia" by gaining the balance of power in the Parliament and "working hand in glove with the United States".'

From the other side, a former Al Jazeera reporter emerged as a critic of our report. Peter Greste, who had spent more than a year in prison in Cairo on politicised charges, said he believed we'd 'crossed a line' by introducing One Nation to the NRA and others in America.

While stressing that he considered it 'perfectly understandable and acceptable to have undercover investigations', Greste said he believed that 'journalists should never be actively involved in creating a story'.

'And what Al Jazeera did here is ... they became intermediaries between the NRA in the United States and One Nation,' he told the ABC. 'And they in fact brokered some meetings. And I think in brokering those meetings they crossed a line from simply being reporters of what was happening, reporters of a relationship that had been unfolding and observers to that relationship, into participants who were actively engaged in brokering and setting up those meetings which they then filmed. And I think that is the point at which they crossed the line.'

I consider Peter a friend, and I have deep respect for the courage and dignity he showed during and after his ordeal in Egypt. I believe he is a fine journalist. But I disagree with his views on our story. Having spent two and a half years secretly filming meetings inside the NRA – time that gave us extraordinary insights into the thinking and operation of that organisation and its executives – would we seriously just walk away when a pro-gun Australian political party indicated an eagerness to connect with the US association, hoping they might extract tens of millions of dollars from it to help their party succeed in an upcoming election?

And would we forgo an unprecedented opportunity to monitor, in real time, private meetings in which we could see how the NRA sought to export its ideology as it interacted with a foreign political party from the very country with gun laws it was so keen to have changed?

No way.

Chapter 28

Part two of the film was broadcast two nights later. In it, Dickson and Ashby were shown being coached by the NRA media team on how to manipulate the media to push the message that more guns would make Australia safer. They were seen receiving advice on how to use mass killings to smear proponents of gun control.

Dickson was seen telling a man at the Congressional Sportsmen's Foundation dinner that 'I'm actually here to get donations' and 'We need about a million', before taking in advice on how to persuade American gun makers to donate to One Nation on the understanding that gun control laws would be softened and that firearms sales in Australia would increase as a result.

Then there were Pauline Hanson's astonishing comments on Port Arthur.

Conservative commentators who had, just the day before, risen to One Nation's defence were now struggling to explain away what Australia had just seen go to air.

'Pauline Hanson, who killed the twenty-five victims of the Port Arthur massacre?' newspaper columnist and TV presenter Andrew Bolt asked on *The Bolt Report* that evening.[90]

'Martin Bryant,' Hanson answered quickly – as if she were in a rush to extinguish the dumpster fire she now realised she had ignited with her comments in Yeppoon. 'And I have no doubt about that whatsoever,' she added.

Bolt asked why she'd told Rodger Muller about 'precision shots' and how there were 'lots of questions' concerning the mass shooting. 'Precision shots?' Bolt declared. 'There were *no* precision shots. Martin Bryant walked up to people lying there and shot them in the head – that's not a precision shot.'

'There was a couple of photos in the book of him holding the gun,' Hanson answered, looking shaken. 'He wasn't up close to all these people.'

There was a brief pause in which Bolt seemed to be struggling to process what Hanson had just said. 'The book I take it you're referring to is *The Port Arthur Massacre Conspiracy* by Joe Vialls ... that's the one?' Bolt asked.

'I can't, um, it was a blue, it was a blue book,' Hanson replied.

Another pause.

'It wasn't real thick,' she said.

I'd heard of Vialls' conspiracy theory that the Port Arthur massacre had not been conducted by Martin Bryant at all, but was really the work of American and Israeli special forces who wanted guns confiscated in Australia so that its citizens would not be able to defend themselves.[91] I'd written the theory off as utter nonsense.

The One Nation leader's efforts to rein in the damage of her Port Arthur comments flowed into the following day, when she appeared on the Nine Network's *Today* program.[92]

In the tradition of the NRA's 'offence, offence, offence' strategy, she had decided, by then, to place the blame entirely with Al Jazeera, accusing the network of dubbing words into the interview to misrepresent what she'd said.

'They've cut-and-pasted the questions and the answers that we've actually given,' Hanson told presenter Deborah Knight. With the swagger of somebody who believed they'd just cracked a code, Hanson went on to say, 'I don't even see [Rodger Muller's] *face*, I don't see his *lips* moving. And I feel like it's been dubbed out and it has been cut and pasted so many times.'

It was apparent that Hanson hadn't grasped the fact that Rodger had been *wearing* the camera and couldn't possibly have filmed his own face during their conversation.

'But Pauline, we see *your* face,' Knight said. 'We see the words coming out of your mouth. It's on *tape*. You can't deny that those are the words that you said.'

Hanson stared back, blankly.

I could almost hear the hissing and popping of the fire as the dumpster glowed red, its metal walls buckling in the inferno.

***

The day after the broadcast of the second and final episode of the film, Pauline Hanson made another public appearance –

this time flanked by the two men she said had been the victims of 'a hit piece'.[93]

'I am here to inform you today that James Ashby *will* remain as my chief of staff,' she said in a steely voice. 'And Steve Dickson *will* remain on the Senate ticket in Queensland. These are two very good men who want nothing but the best for this country and the people of Australia.'

The three One Nation members stood side by side: Ashby showed no emotion at all, Hanson seemed to struggle to contain her rage, and Dickson was stony-faced, staring ahead, as if he could sense the gallows beckoning from somewhere not far away.

Ashby had made 'some stupid remarks, as we *all* have', Hanson declared, lifting her voice above the flutter of press cameras. 'But I've worked so closely with this man for years to know that his integrity is unquestionable, and he will not be given a trial by media in an effort to have him sacked.'

Hanson went on, 'When I first saw Steve Dickson's comments, I was *disgusted*.'

Dickson flinched.

'But having watched my own comments, knowing how out of context they were portrayed to the Australian people, I knew he was stitched up.'

The One Nation leader may have at least felt some relief that Al Jazeera's two-part documentary was out of the way.

But there was worse to come.

Chapter 29

'It's less than three weeks until election day,' Channel Nine's Tracy Grimshaw intoned from the set of the network's *A Current Affair* on 29 April 2019. 'But one senior politician has given his leader a huge headache by being filmed in a strip club.'[94]

Channel Nine had been running promotional clips of the story all day, without revealing the identity of the man at its centre.

Behind Grimshaw, as she introduced the 'exclusive', a large, purple question mark hung over the words 'Striptease Shocker'.

'The secret video shows the happily married politician groping dancers and asking them to come home with him,' Grimshaw continued. 'It's a bad look, and it's very bad judgement from a man who campaigns on family values. This is uncomfortable to watch, but we've blurred the worst vision and bleeped the worst language.'

The vision Rodger had filmed of Steve Dickson in the Washington strip club in September 2018 – the very vision

284

we had decided would not go to air – had been leaked to another network. Now, everything that Dickson had said and done that night was about to be revealed to the world.

'It's the striptease that will stop a nation,' reporter Dan Nolan's voice-over said. 'And shred this married politician's credibility at the worst possible time.'

I'd already called Phil Rees, now back in Doha, to warn him that a story featuring our video had been heavily promoted by Channel Nine throughout the day.

'But we gave *no* permission for the vision to be used,' he snapped. Phil would later quiz all Al Jazeera employees who had access to the strip club vision to try to identify the source of the leak. He would conclude that no network employee had passed the footage on, and that it must have been given to Channel Nine by one of the many contractors who had access to Al Jazeera's files in the lead-up to our edit.

Phil issued a statement condemning the unauthorised use of the images, saying they had 'been published without Al Jazeera's consent'. But it had been too late to stop what was now going live to air.

Grainy vision from Rodger's camera showed the Senate candidate standing at the pole-dancing stage, pushing dollar bills into the elastic of a dancer's garter as she leaned back, thrusting her hips at him.

A Current Affair picked out Dickson's voice from the din of the strip scene, beaming his words in bold red subtitles to its 1,116,000 viewers.

'Little tits, well, I feel for her,' Dickson said, craning to see one woman walking past.

'And soon enough, this former state government minister is going a lot further than just *looking*,' Nolan went on, over images of Dickson pawing a waitress. 'We'll keep a count on just how many times Steve Dickson gropes this exotic dancer over the course of the night.'

Split-screen images showed Dickson's hand reaching for the breasts and groin of one woman over and over.

And over again.

'All up, he does this *twelve* times,' Nolan declared.

'Slide your hand on my cock now,' one subtitle showed Dickson saying to the woman.

Another showed him announcing to Rodger – in an oddly matter-of-fact way – that the waitress had agreed to 'come over and fuck me'.

Steve Dickson's senatorial ambitions had been on life support since Pauline Hanson's post–*How to Sell a Massacre* press conference in which she'd said she believed he was 'a good man' who had been 'stitched up' by Al Jazeera. By the time *A Current Affair*'s eight-minute-and-ten-second report had ended, Dickson's political future no longer had a pulse.

* * *

'I am both shocked and disappointed at the vision I forced myself to watch,' Pauline Hanson said in a live-to-air media announcement early the following morning. 'I have always spoken very highly of Steve Dickson, but the footage I saw last night cannot be ignored or condoned. Steve's language and behaviour was unacceptable and does not meet my expectations, nor the greater public's expectations of a person who is standing for public office.

'Steve Dickson yesterday offered his resignation from all positions within the party, which I have accepted.'

As reporters questioned her, Hanson stormed away from the cameras and climbed into a waiting car.

* * *

Steve Dickson's public statement announcing his departure from One Nation started on a note of contrition. 'I would like to sincerely apologise for my behaviour,' it said.

The statement contained an unfortunate – perhaps Freudian – typo. 'As I will no longer be of pubic [sic] interest, I ask that you please respect my family's privacy.'

Dickson's own 'pubic interest' had proven to be more destructive, in the end, than his interactions with the gun lobby in Washington, DC – a point noted by Channel Seven reporter Chris Uhlmann.

'Well, if this tawdry affair wasn't damaging to One Nation, then Steve Dickson wouldn't have resigned,' Uhlmann said on air the evening of April 29. 'People can spot a fraud and this man was a politician who was selling himself as a family man. But it's telling that the party didn't believe his role in helping to trade Australia's tough gun laws for American gun lobby donations was as serious as misbehaving with a stripper.

'The second is idiocy. The first, [Independent Australian Senator] Derryn Hinch rightly describes as equivalent to treason.'

* * *

'As we go to air tonight, Pauline Hanson's One Nation Party is in damage control,' Tracy Grimshaw said on *A Current Affair*.

She had persuaded Hanson to talk about the crises that had consumed One Nation since the broadcast of *How to Sell a Massacre* four weeks earlier – leading to the Steve Dickson strip club exposé the previous night.

'I just feel I keep getting kicked in the *guts* time and time again!' Hanson said, sitting in her home near Brisbane. 'I'm *sick* of them going on about that we actually asked the NRA for *donations*. We never even *spoke* to the NRA about donations!' Her voice was a whipper snipper hacking into wet grass. 'I don't *care* what these two guys said,' she went on, rage building in her voice. '*I'm* the leader of this party, not *them*! And I'll make the final decisions, as I always have done. I'm *furious* about this!'

Soon, the One Nation leader was in tears.

'And I cop all this shit all the time, and I'm *sick* of it! Absolutely sick of it!'

The shocking images from the previous evening had transformed into an anguished howl from One Nation's leader that night – wounded, but loyal, still, to the men who had led her to this dreadful moment.

'Why are you still in it?' Grimshaw asked. '*Look* at you! Why don't you *walk*? Look at what it's *doing* to you!'

Hanson dabbed at another tear.

As the interview was nearing its end, she looked at Grimshaw and narrowed her eyes a little.

'Don't write me off,' she said. '[Don't] underestimate me.'
She stood and walked away, not bothering to say goodbye.

* * *

Australia's media feasted upon the interview like crazed animals.

'"Sick of it": Pauline Hanson breaks down in tears on *A Current Affair*,' the *Sydney Morning Herald* said in a headline, while on News.com.au it was, 'All Pauline's men: Hanson's bitter tears at string of betrayals.'

A restrained ABC limited its headline to: 'One Nation unfairly targeted in federal election campaign following Steve Dickson strip club scandal, Pauline Hanson says.'

The 'vipers' that Ashby had warned Rodger and Claudianna about as he'd left Washington were a writhing mass, energised by the party's very public pain.

As the media storm swirled around reaction to our film, I phoned Rodger, now back in Australia from his overseas safe house, to ask how he was holding up. 'All good, mate,' he said.

Days later, in the NSW Southern Highlands, a man spotted Rodger at a service station. He leaned out of his car window, pointed his finger like a gun, and cocked his thumb as if pulling the trigger.

Rodger winced as if he'd been shot, then opened his window and called out, 'Flesh wound!'

He then smiled and drove away.

Chapter 30

My plane touched down at Washington's Reagan airport on a warm evening in April 2019. I had been away from home for 116 days.

What reaction might I receive in America from the NRA, I wondered? They knew my name, address and phone number; I had joined the organisation at the beginning of our investigation and had been receiving regular newsletters and promotional emails from them ever since.

And, though they never responded to them, the NRA had received lengthy right of reply letters from my team, detailing everything we'd filmed undercover during our infiltration of their organisation.

Would there be a welcoming party of some kind when I returned to my house? The building was now empty; I had moved my family back to Australia just before the documentary went to air and planned to keep them there until I was sure it was safe for them to return.

I heaved my suitcase into the boot of a cab and directed the driver to my neighbourhood, asking him to take me past my home once, then drive me around the block before bringing me back and dropping me on the street.

As we approached my address I could see two black Chevy Suburban SUVs with blacked-out windows parked directly in front of my house.

Hmmm … That was unusual.

We went around the block and came back.

They were still there.

I asked the driver to pull up behind them. I took note of their licence plate numbers, asked the cabbie not to leave until I'd entered my house, then wheeled my bag along the street, through my front gate and up the stoop to my front door.

I turned to look at the Suburbans. A passenger in one of them cracked his window and looked back at me.

I opened my door and stepped inside. As I turned back to lock the security grille, I saw him close his window as both cars drove off.

A random event, unrelated to our infiltration of the gun lobby? Probably.

But I was aware that Donald Trump's mantra that the media are 'the enemy of the people' had taken hold among his supporters. And the December 2016 'pizzagate' mass shooting by an anti-Hillary zealot had taken place just twenty minutes' drive from my home.

Could a deranged gunman come to my address too, outraged at the contents of the documentary? Possibly.

I secured the grille, double-bolted the front door and locked a second door behind that. I checked the locks on the back gate and back door of my house, and carried my bag to the bedroom upstairs.

* * *

In the time I'd been away from America, a further nineteen mass shootings had occurred there, leaving at least forty-five people dead and 319 wounded, according to the Gun Violence Archive. The plague of firearms violence – and the stream of disinformation that painted gun reform as an assault on 'freedom' – had rolled on, unchecked.

But big changes were in the air, and they were happening in the most unexpected places: in April, open warfare had erupted within the NRA between CEO Wayne LaPierre and the newly installed president, Oliver North. In an effort to oust LaPierre, North had warned that unless the CEO stepped down, 'a devastating account of our financial status, sexual harassment charges against a staff member, accusations of wardrobe expenses and excessive staff travel expenses' would be released by a key NRA contractor.[95]

LaPierre saw North's warning as 'an extortion attempt', and the bare-knuckled conflict that followed led to the departure of North as president, along with a string of high-level employees, including its chief lobbyist, Chris Cox.

Though LaPierre would survive the power struggle, receiving a unanimous vote of support from the NRA board, the organisation's turmoil prompted Donald Trump to tweet on 29 April that it 'must get its act together quickly, stop the internal fighting, & get back to GREATNESS – FAST!'

The NRA and the US president had been bonded, after all, in a blood-brother-like oath of unity at the 2016 NRA convention, when the gun rights group had endorsed the then presidential candidate, throwing its weight – and thirty million US dollars – behind his campaign. Trump had come good with his promises to 'never let the NRA down', having reportedly assured LaPierre that he wouldn't press for the introduction of universal background checks for people wanting to purchase guns in America, in spite of once indicating he was open to doing so.

The *Washington Post* reported that Trump's assurance to LaPierre on the background check issue had taken place after a meeting between the two men in which the NRA chief made clear his view that such checks should not be allowed to go ahead: 'The president's conversation with LaPierre ... further reduced hopes that major new gun-safety measures will be enacted after the latest round of mass shootings.'[96]

Senator Chuck Schumer declared that 'the effectiveness of gun safety measures will be severely compromised' as a result of Trump's capitulation to the gun lobby.

Schumer's remarks were dismissed by the Senate majority whip as nothing more than an effort to 'score political points'. The NRA's continuing grip on Congress was plain to see.

Trump had also thrown the power of the presidency behind the NRA when the newly elected Democratic governor of the state of Virginia proposed the introduction of modest gun control laws there.

In addition to reviving the background check debate, the governor called for authorities to be allowed to take firearms from people deemed dangerous to themselves or others, and for people in Virginia to be limited to the purchase of *one gun per month*.

The gun lobby went nuts. Protesters rose up, sparking what the *New York Times* called 'a backlash across the state' of

Virginia. 'Dozens of municipalities have declared themselves "Second Amendment sanctuaries," where local officials have vowed to oppose any new gun control measures,' the newspaper reported on 15 January.[97]

A pro-gun rally was organised, with people urged to come – with their guns – to Virginia's capital, Richmond, to condemn the governor's proposed firearm reforms.

Donald Trump was right behind the uprising. On 20 January, Trump tweeted: 'The Democrat Party in the Great Commonwealth of Virginia are working hard to take away your 2nd Amendment rights. This is just the beginning. Don't let it happen.'

'A sense of crisis enveloped the capital of Virginia,' the *New York Times* said. 'Police [are] on heightened alert and Richmond is bracing for possible violence ahead of a gun rally ... that is expected to draw white supremacists and other anti-government extremists.'[98]

The FBI was alerted to plans by one pro-gun group to shoot 'unsuspecting civilians and police officers' at the rally, and alleged members of a white supremacist outfit were arrested. But the rally went ahead anyway, drawing an estimated twenty-two thousand people.

'The sheer number of firearms was astounding,' the *Dallas Morning News* reported in an article published on 26 January. 'Almost every protester was carrying one, either a handgun or a rifle or both. Many others brought shotguns, sniper rifles, even tomahawks. Militia groups from across the country, clad in camouflage fatigues, some wearing body armour, marched down the street in formation, to the tune of a fife and drum.'[99]

What *Rolling Stone* described as 'Trump's backers and apologists [putting] both their white privilege and white fragility fully on parade' was playing out as an extraordinary show of the enduring power of the US gun lobby – the NRA's recent turmoil notwithstanding.[100]

In spite of the Parkland student protest movement, in spite of rising public anger over continued massacres in America, the gun lobby seemed bullet-proof – its members armed, angry, and spoiling for a fight.

Over images of the crowds massing around the Virginia State Capitol Building, I could hear the core messages of the NRA's media team. 'You want to get people *mad*,' Catherine Mortensen had told the One Nation delegates. 'When you start talking about issues that get too complicated or make them think too hard, you've kind of lost them.'

From among the crowd in Richmond, a common grievance emerged: many of the protesters believed Virginia's proposed gun control measures were the thin edge of the wedge, part of a grand plan to take *all* guns from Americans, just the way Australia's government had taken guns from its citizens.

Steve Dickson had predicted this in his meetings in Washington, warning his American hosts to 'be afraid, because we are the weather balloon and it's coming your way!'

'What's going on here, if not stopped, will spread to other states,' one Virginia protester, carrying a Smith & Wesson rifle and a .40 calibre handgun, told Reuters. 'They will come for our guns in other states if we don't stop them in Virginia.'

Another of the US president's tweets about the rally showed the protesters that he had their backs: 'I will NEVER allow our great Second Amendment to go unprotected, not even a little bit.'

There was never a suggestion, in the Virginia governor's gun reform proposals, that the Second Amendment would 'go unprotected'. But facts are not part of the 'post-truth' equation. Nor is the ticking tally of gun deaths across the nation, some so routine – so banal – that they hadn't even rated a passing reference in the national news:

22 December 2019, Chicago, Illinois: 'Thirteen people were shot at a party that was held to memorialize a victim of an earlier shooting.'

1 January 2020, Trujillo Alto, Puerto Rico: 'A family of four, including nine-year-old twin boys, were shot and killed at their home after celebrating New Year's Eve.'

8 January 2020, Bay St. Louis, Mississippi: 'Two people were killed and two injured in a random ambush style shooting. The perpetrator was arrested after arriving at his mother's house covered in blood.'

19 January 2020, Kansas City, Missouri: 'Two people (including the perpetrator) were killed and fifteen others were injured during a shooting at a nightclub.'

25 January 2020, Vanceboro, North Carolina: 'A man shot and killed his wife and three children, aged between eight months and four years old along with the family dog. He then killed himself.'

26 January 2020, Hartsville, South Carolina: 'Three people were fatally shot and four others were injured in a bar.'

27 January 2020, Lisle, Illinois: 'A woman killed one person and injured two others before killing herself at a cigar lounge.'

3 February 2020, Grapevine, California: 'One person was killed and five others were injured from a shooting on a Greyhound bus heading from Los Angeles to San Francisco.'

***

Steve Dickson had been silent for more than seven months following the release of his strip club footage. Then a video was posted to YouTube outlining *his* version of events in Washington.

The 42-minute-long, two-part film, titled *How to Massacre a Democracy*, was a seething-with-resentment bid to condemn Al Jazeera as the devil child of Qatar, an 'America-hating, Israel-hating' supporter of Islamic terrorism, hell-bent on warping the minds of America's youth.

'Why, you might ask, would the government of a Middle Eastern country care about influencing young Americans?' the anonymous voice-over asks. 'The answer is this: anything that weakens the US is a victory for *them* and their radical form of Islam. If they can convince young Americans that the US is a bad place, young Americans are less likely to defend it, and less likely to support its efforts to fight Islamic terror. And if *America* is bad, then anyone it supports must also be bad.'

The video claims that Al Jazeera is 'so contentious in many countries they have had to completely rebrand to the more friendly sounding "AJ+".'

Whoever wrote Dickson's documentary was obviously unaware that 'AJ+' is, in fact, an online news and current affairs strand of Al Jazeera, working as an adjunct to television broadcasts from the still-very-much-alive and un-rebranded Al Jazeera English and Arabic channels.

But *How to Massacre a Democracy* is more than just a stab at the network that exposed One Nation's Washington visit; the film is also a platform for Dickson to atone for groping strippers, and a chance for the public to hear – for the first time – from his wife, Deb.

Part two of the documentary introduces her clipping flowers in her Queensland garden while, over a tinkling piano, we hear her talk about the Al Jazeera report.

'There's no consideration for what really *happened*,' she says. 'It felt like it became a blood-sport.'

The video shows Deb entering the house and taking a seat at the family dining table. Steve Dickson walks into the room and sits beside her. 'There you go, darling,' he says, handing her a drink.

'Awesome, thank you,' she replies.

Dickson leans in, smiling. 'You're very welcome.'

Speaking to the camera, Deb says that, though the images of her husband groping women came as a 'total shock' to her, she blames Rodger for the way the strip club outing had been portrayed.

'I'm thinking, *Okay my husband's been to a strip club, yes, Rodger's manipulated it to look a certain way, he's asked certain questions at certain times.* It was all orchestrated from Rodger's point of view.'

Deb's biggest concern, she says, is her husband's welfare – pointing out that Dickson took to bed, lying in the foetal position, and at least eight weeks passed before he was able to leave the house.

'If I had not been here ... anything could have happened,' she says.

'I was absolutely devastated,' Dickson adds. 'I felt destroyed. I felt like I'd had my life taken away from me. I couldn't sleep ... every time I closed my eyes, I felt like I was in a *nightmare*. And I tell you what, I think it almost drove me to the point of suicide.'

Dickson explains that he misbehaved at the Washington strip club because, once again, he was drunk.

'I went out on the grog,' he says. '[I was] with a bloke that I thought was just a normal bloke but he ended up being an undercover agent from a Middle Eastern country who supports terrorism. I wasn't aware! I mean, I'd advise anybody out there: be careful who you go out with, get on the grog, because you might be going out with a Middle Eastern agent who's trying to infiltrate Australian *politics*.'

He shrugs. 'Who knows?'

When this documentary first aired, it ended by inviting viewers to comment on what they'd seen.

'It just shows how corrupt the media is with these lies they knew it was not true but kept running with the story,' one viewer wrote.

Another described Al Jazeera as 'thugs of journalism'.

And one left a message directed to Steve Dickson. 'You don't need to apologise for anything mate,' it said. 'You a true blue Aussie this country is rotten to the core we need to march on Parliament and hang these bastards from there [sic] necks.'

* * *

The week I returned to Washington, I walked past the White House on my way to the office. At the edge of Lafayette Park, a lone protester stood in the sun. He looked across to the executive mansion and lifted a sign.

An AR-15 had been drawn onto cardboard with a large 'X' scribbled across it. Along the top, he'd written a message to the president: '*NO MORE GUNS!*'

From the gates of the White House, security guards glanced over to him, then turned away.

The protester walked to a bench, sat down and laid his placard on the seat beside him. He lit a cigarette as a breeze lifted his sign and sent it tumbling across the lawn. He moved to pick it up, but it was too far gone. He sat down again and watched as the wind lifted the sign and carried it away.

The image of the AR-15 flashed in the sun as the cardboard flipped, then disappeared above the trees.

I turned from the White House, walked up 16th Street to M Street, and headed for the office.

Inside the bunker, Colin McIntyre was sitting next to a new undercover recruit on a couch outside my office.

Another assignment was about to begin.

In his hands, Colin held a shirt with a new button freshly sewn into place.

He held it to the light and squinted.

The lens was impossible to see.

Epilogue

Since the documentary *How to Sell a Massacre* was broadcast in March, 2019, there have been at least another 503 mass shootings in America, leaving 2472 people dead or wounded. During that time, the total number of gun-related deaths in the US, including homicides, suicides and accidental shootings, was at least 52,875.

The mass shootings included an incident on 3 August 2019 in which a 21-year-old man killed twenty-three people and wounded another twenty-three in and around the Walmart Supercenter in Cielo Vista Mall in El Paso, Texas.

In an anti-immigrant manifesto posted before the shooting, the killer said he believed an 'Hispanic invasion' was underway and said that he'd targeted Latinos in the massacre because they were contributing to 'cultural and ethnic replacement' in America.

With Democrats in America now describing gun violence there as 'a public health epidemic', access to firearms is likely to feature as a key issue in the 2020 presidential elections.

Donald Trump has already signalled his continued allegiance to pro-gun groups.

During the COVID-19 lockdown in the US, the gun lobby secured federal government support to ensure that gun shops in the majority of US states were allowed to stay open, their businesses officially designated as 'essential services'. Soon, armed protesters, encouraged by gun-rights provocateurs, were calling for an end to the lockdown.

* * *

The two-part documentary *How to Sell a Massacre* was awarded a Walkley award in 2019 for 'Scoop of the Year' and a Kennedy award for 'Best Investigative Report' in Australia; an Association for International Broadcasting award for excellence in the coverage of international affairs in the UK; and a Gold World Medal at the New York Festivals TV & Film Awards.

Though Australian senator Pauline Hanson called for an investigation into the documentary by the Federal Police and the Australian Security Intelligence Organisation, neither group had made contact with Al Jazeera at the time of publication of this book.

Endnotes

1   Brad Freed, *Raw Story*, 15 May, 2019

2   *American Rifleman*: www.americanrifleman.org/articles/2016/6/16/ gateway-to-fun-scenes-from-the-2016-nra-annual-meetings-in-louisville/

3   James Parker, 'Live-Streaming the Apocalypse With NRATV', *The Atlantic,* June 2018 issue.

4   Nick O'Malley, 'John Howard rejects US gun lobby's criticism of Australian gun laws', *The Sydney Morning Herald*, 31 July, 2019.

5   'NRA: full statement by Wayne LaPeirre in response to the Newtown shootings', *The Guardian*, 21 December, 2012.

6   Jonathan Weisman, 'Senate Blocks Drive for Gun Control,' *New York Times*, 17 April, 2013.

7   Amber Phillips, 'The NRA-ification of the Republican Party, *Washington Post*, 14 August, 2015.

8   *YouTube*: www.youtube.com/watch?v=5ju4Gla2odw

9   Callum Borchers, 'How the NRA came to demonize the media', *Washington Post*, 24 February, 2018.

10   Hugh Hewitt, 'Senator Ted Cruz On His Eligibility, The Triad, And Boxing Analogies, *HughHewitt.com*, 12 January, 2016.

11   Michelle Ye Hee Lee, 'Ted Cruz's claim that sexual assaults rate "went up significantly" after Australian gun control laws,' *Washington Post*, 25 January, 2016

12   Nick Evershed, 'Strict firearms laws reduce gun deaths: here's the evidence', *The Guardian*, 19 March, 2019

13   David Hemenway and Mary Vriniotis, 'The Australian Gun Buyback', *Harvard Injury Control Research Center*, Spring 2011 (issue 4).

14   Philip Alpers and Michael Picard, 'Australia – Gun Facts, Figures and the Law', *University of Sydney*, 29 January, 2020.

15   Mike Wendling, 'The (almost) complete history of "fake news"', *BBC*, 22 January, 2018.

16   Veronika Bondarenko, 'Trump keeps saying "enemy of the people" – but the phrase has a very ugly history,' *Business Insider*, 27 February, 2017.

17   Sam Frizell, 'Donald Trump Faces Backlash for Tweets About Orlando Shooting', *Time*, 12 June, 2016.

18   Heidi Taksdal Skjeseth, 'All the president's lies: Media coverage of lies in the US and France', *Reuter's Institute*, University of Oxford, 2017.

19   Alan Yuhas, 'How does Donald Trump lie? A fact checker's final guide', *The Guardian*, 7 November, 2016.

20   Jon Swaine and Ciara McCarthy, 'Young black men again faced highest rate of US police killings in 2016', *The Guardian*, 8 January, 2017.

21   Ohio Gun Laws, *NRA-ILA*, 13 April, 2017.

22   'NRA's Chris Cox Calls on Americans to Support Trump', *NRA Political Victory Fund*, 19 July, 2016.

23   Patrick Healy and Jonathan Martin, 'His Tone Dark, Donald Trump Takes G.O.P. Mantle', *New York Times*, 21 July, 2016.

24   Transcript of Donald Trump's Immigration Speech, *New York Times*, 1 September, 2016.

25   Robert Farley, 'Is Illegal Immigration Linked to More or Less Crime?', *FactCheck.org*, 27 June, 2018.

26   Court transcript, *The Queen v. Martin Bryant*, 19 November, 1996

27   Martin Bryant complete interview, *Wikileaks*.

28   'Martin Bryant Unseen police interview footage of Australia's worse mass murderer', *Sunday Night*, 23 April, 2019.

29   'Rally told guns rights must be bought back "with blood"', *Irish Times*, 17 May, 2016.

30 Simon Chapman, *Over Our Dead Bodies: Port Arthur and Australia's fight for gun control*, Sydney University Press, 2013.

31 Michael Gorden, 'John Howard on leadership: "People would say I can't stand you but I know what you stand for"', *Sydney Morning Herald*, 22 January, 2018.

32 David A. Farenthold, 'Trump recorded having extremely lewd conversation about women in 2005', *Washington Post*, 8 October, 2016.

33 Eliza Relman, 'The 25 women who have accused Trump of sexual misconduct', *Business Insider Australia*, 22 December, 2017.

34 Daniella Diaz, '3 Times Trump defended his "locker room" talk', *CNN*, 9 October, 2016.

35 Gary Langer, Gregory Holyk and Chad Kiewiet De Jonge, 'Clinton Vaults to a Double-Digit Lead, Boosted by Broad Disapproval of Trump (POLL)', *ABC News*, 23 October, 2016.

36 Amanda Robb, 'Anatomy of a Fake News Scandal', *Rolling Stone*, 16 November, 2017.

37 Burt Helm, 'Pizzagate Nearly Destroyed My Restaurant. Then My Customers Helped Me Fight Back', *Inc. Magazine*, July/August 2017 issue.

38 Fake News analysis, *factba.se*

39 John Gramlich and Katherine Schaeffer, '7 facts about guns in the U.S.', *Pew Research Center*, 22 October, 2019.

40 LVMPD Criminal Investigative Report of the 1 October Mass Casualty Shooting, LVMP Event Number 171001-3519, 3 August, 2018.

41 Jenna Johnson and Ashley Parker, 'Trump on Las Vegas shooter: "A very sick man. He was a very demented person"', *Washington Post*, 4 October, 2017.

42 'Gun lobby funding One Nation candidates', *Sunshine Coast Daily*, 17 November, 2017.

43 'Pauline Hanson's 1996 maiden speech to parliament: Full transcript', *Sydney Morning Herald*, 15 September, 2016.

44 'Pauline Hanson jailed for electoral fraud', *The Guardian*, 20 August, 2003.

45 Tom McIlroy, 'Pauline Hanson blames Tony Abbott and John Howard for prison sentence in new documentary', *Sydney Morning Herald*, 19 July, 2016.

46 Linda Silmalis and Richard Clune, 'James Ashby's abuse conviction for making threatening phonecalls', *Daily Telegraph*, 22 April, 2012.

47 'Strawberry saboteur strikes again', *Brisbane Times*, 20 May, 2011.

48 'Ashby v Slipper', *Federal Court of Australia*, 3 May, 2013.

49 Katherine Murphy, 'Pauline Hanson calls for immigration ban: "Go back to where you came from"', *The Guardian*, 14 September, 2016.

50 Richard Di Natale, 'When we walked out on Pauline Hanson, we reached out to decent Australians', *The Guardian*, 16 September, 2016.

51 Claire Bickers, '"Make my day": Pauline Hanson hits shooting range for One Nation', *News.com.au*, 22 September, 2017.

52 Pauline Hanson's One Nation firearms policy: www.onenation.org.au/policies/firearms-gun-control/

53 John Gramlich and Katherine Schaeffer, '7 facts about guns in the U.S.', *Pew Research Center*, 22 October, 2019.

54 Jugal K. Patel, 'After Sandy Hook, More Than 400 People Have Been Shot in Over 200 School Shootings', *New York Times*, 15 February, 2018.

55 Therese Apel, '"Nikolas Cruz" YouTube comment brings FBI to bail bondsman's door', *USA Today*, 15 February, 2018.

56 Michelle Mark, 'Local authorities and the FBI got multiple warnings that the suspected Florida shooter was dangerous – but no one followed up', *Business Insider*, 23 February, 2018.

57 Bart Jansen, 'Florida shooting suspect bought gun legally, authorities say,' *USA Today*, 15 February, 2018.

58 Mark Berman and David Weigel, 'NRA goes on the offensive after Parkland shooting, assailing media and calling for more armed school security', *Washington Post*, 22 February, 2018.

59 A.M. Joy, 'Parkland shooting survivor David Hogg demands gun control', *MSNBC*, 24 February, 2018.

60 Adam Edelman, 'Trump says he would have run into Florida school without a weapon', *NBC*, 26 February, 2018.

61 *Boston Globe*, 'Read a transcript of the listening session at the White House after the Parkland school shooting', 21 February, 2018.

62 Brandon Carter and Alexander Bolton, 'Trump to GOP senator: "You're afraid of the NRA"', *The Hill*, 28 February, 2018.

63 Editorial Board, 'Who's afraid of the NRA? Trump', *Washington Post*, 12 March, 2018

64 Paul Karp, 'Queensland MP Steve Dickson defects from LNP to join One Nation', *The Guardian*, 12 January, 2017.

65 Mike McIntire, 'Charity Takes Gun Lobby Closer to Its Quarry', *New York Times*, 6 March, 2013.

66 Erik Wemple, 'The Mueller report nails Sarah Sanders on an extravagant fabrication', *Washington Post*, 18 April, 2019.

67 Jeremy Diamond, 'Sarah Sanders refuses to explain false statement on Trump Tower meeting', *CNN*, 5 June, 2018.

68 William Cummings, '"He reads more than anybody I know": Sarah Sanders disputes "absurd" claim Trump doesn't read briefings', *USA Today*, 25 November, 2019.

69 Jack Moore, 'NRA boycott: Full list of companies that cut ties with gun lobby over Florida shooting', *Newsweek*, 24 February, 2018.

70 Josh Delk, 'NRA rips corporate sponsors that cut ties: Shameful display of cowardice', *The Hill*, 24 February, 2018.

71 Dave Collins, 'More families of Sandy Hook victims, FBI agent sue Infowars' Alex Jones', *Chicago Tribune*, 23 May, 2018.

72 Daniel Arkin and Ben Popken, 'How the internet's conspiracy theorists turned Parkland students into "crisis actors"', *NBC News*, 21 February, 2018.

73 Doug Stanglin and Christal Hayes, 'Conspiracy theorists find Florida student activists too good to be true', *USA Today*, 21 February, 2018.

74 Nicole Chavez, 'School shooting survivor knocks down "crisis actor" claim', *CNN*, 21 February, 2018.

75 Bulletin Board, 'Lies? False Claims? When Trump's Statements Aren't True', *New York Times*, 25 June, 2018.

76 Glenn Kessler, 'About the Fact Checker', *Washington Post,* 1 January, 2017.

77 Glenn Kessler, Salvador Rizzo, Meg Kelly, 'President Trump made 16,241 false or misleading claims in his first three years', *Washington Post*, 20 January, 2020.

78 Matthew Haag, 'Doctors Revolt After NRA Tells Them to "Stay in Their Lane" on Gun Policy', *New York Times*, 13 November, 2018.

79 'NRA Launches Ad Campaign for Ted Budd in North Carolina', *NRA-ILA newsletter*, 23 October, 2018.

80 Nick O'Malley and Sean Nicholls, 'The killer quirk hiding in Australia's gun laws', *Sydney Morning Herald*, 7 October, 2017.

81   Hansard, *Parliament of Australia*, November 15, 2018.
82   'US gun sales down 6.1 percent in 2018, extending "Trump slump", *CNBC*, 30 January, 2019.
83   Cydney Hargis, 'NRA and conservative media run with inaccurate report to try to make pro-gun point about the New Zealand mosque shootings', *Media Matters for America*, 15 March, 2019.
84   'Fury as Australian senator blames Christchurch attack on Muslim immigration', *The Guardian*, 15 March, 2019.
85   Michael Blackmon, 'A 17-Year-Old Has Gone Viral For Egging A Politician Who Blamed Muslims For The Christchurch Attack', *Buzzfeed*, 16 March, 2019.
86   Kate Lyons, 'Jacinda Ardern bans all military-style semiautomatic guns and assault rifles – as it happened', *The Guardian*, 21 March, 2019.
87   'NRATV's Grant Stinchfield: New Zealand is "the equivalent of a dictatorship" and "what tyranny looks like" after proposed assault weapons ban', *Media Matters for America*, 25 March, 2019.
88   'US Politicians Cheer New Zealand Gun Confiscation', *NRA-ILA*, 22 March, 2019.
89   'Did Al Jazeera's undercover investigation into One Nation overstep the mark?' *The Conversation*, 25 March, 2019.
90   '"I saw some pictures": Pauline Hanson tries to explain Port Arthur "conspiracy theory"', *Yahoo News*, 28 March, 2019.
91   Lee Zachariah, 'Why Does Anyone Believe the Port Arthur Massacre Was a Conspiracy?', *Vice*, 27 April, 2016.
92   Gavin Fernando, 'Pauline Hanson has revealed why she made those Port Arthur "truther" claims', *News.com.au*, 29 March, 2019.
93   'Pauline Hanson stands by staff caught up in Al Jazeera documentary', *ABC News*, 28 March, 2019.
94   'One Nation candidate Steve Dickson touches dancer in US strip club in leaked footage', *ABC News*, 29 April, 2019.
95   Michael Brice-Saddler, 'NRA ousts president Oliver North after alleged extortion scheme against chief executive', *Washington Post*, 27 April, 2019.
96   Tim Hamburger and Josh Dawsey, 'Trump tells NRA chief that universal background checks are off the table', *Washington Post*, 20 August, 2019.

97 Timothy Williams and Sarah Mervosh, 'Virginia Governor Declares State of Emergency Ahead of Gun Rally', *New York Times*, 15 January, 2020.

98 Timothy Williams, Adam Goldman and Neil MacFarquhar, 'Virginia Capital on Edge as F.B.I. Arrests Suspected Neo-Nazis Before Gun Rally', *New York Times*, 16 January, 2020.

99 Mark Satter, 'I went to the pro-gun rally in Virginia. It was now what I expected', *Dallas Morning News*, 26 January, 2020.

100 Jamil Smith, 'Trump, Guns, and White Fragility', *Rolling Stone*, 23 January, 2020.